ADVANCE PRAISE FOR *SOCIALISTS DON'T SLEEP*

"Cheryl Chumley's book, *Socialists Don't Sleep: Christians Must Rise or America Will Fall*, is a masterpiece. Unlike most politicians and academicians, she keenly understands the true greatness of America, and unequivocally sounds an alarm of caution if our nation continues down its current path of blindness toward our founding principles and values. There are few books that I believe should be read by everyone, this is one of them. The message Chumley lays forth is clear, profound, disturbing, and hopeful. It's time for America to have a reality check, a deep, soul-searching reality check. This is a great place to start."

—Representative Jody B. Hice, R-GA

"What is it about the founding principles of America that the secular progressive left would make better? The answer is: Nothing. In her new book, Cheryl Chumley reminds us of those principles and calls on those who still believe in them to engage the failed policies and ideology of socialism and atheism and to fight back."

—Cal Thomas, Nationally-Syndicated Conservative Columnist

"If you think socialism will inevitably lose at the polls, think again! As Cheryl shows in *Socialists Don't Sleep*, the far left—in both political parties—has been eroding our freedoms for decades. The long-term solution must come from the Judeo-Christian community. If the churches don't rise, America is sunk."

—Sam and Kevin Sorbo, Writer-Producer-Director Team
for *Let There Be Light*

"*Socialists Don't Sleep* is one of those timely books that just points out the roots of what's gone wrong in America, how we can get our country back on track to what founders envisioned, and the Judeo-Christian community that holds the key to America's long-term successes."

—Gov. Mike Huckabee

"Bernie Sanders, Alexandria Ocasio-Cortez—when it comes to socialism in America, these two aren't the problem. Per se. They're simply symptoms of the real problems that usher in socialism: a dysfunctional entitlement-minded society, a propaganda-pushing school system, a decayed culture, a sieve-like border. As Cheryl Chumley points out in *Socialists Don't Sleep*, we can't root out socialism unless we first address the real problems."

—Michael Savage, *New York Times* Bestselling Author

"An important book that shows just how close our country is to losing its freedoms—and why the younger generations need to learn truthful history about capitalism, freedom, and socialism."

—Will Witt, PragerU Personality

"*Socialists Don't Sleep* exposes the flawed thinking of the socialist left."

—Phil Robertson, *New York Times* Bestselling Author
and Star of Duck Dynasty

SOCIALISTS DON'T SLEEP

SOCIALISTS DON'T SLEEP

CHRISTIANS MUST RISE OR AMERICA WILL FALL

CHERYL K. CHUMLEY

Humanix Books
www.humanixbooks.com

Humanix Books

Socialists Don't Sleep
Copyright © 2021 by Humanix Books
All rights reserved

Humanix Books, P.O. Box 20989, West Palm Beach, FL 33416, USA
www.humanixbooks.com | info@humanixbooks.com

Humanix Books is a division of Humanix Publishing, LLC. Its trademark, consisting of the words "Humanix Books," is registered in the
Patent and Trademark Office and in other countries.

ISBN: 978-1-63006-147-0 (Hardcover)
ISBN: 978-1-63006-158-7 (E-book)

Printed in the United States of America
10 9 8 7 6 5 4 3 2

To Jesus, the hope of humanity.

To Savanna, Keith, Colvin, and Chloe, the hope of this nation.

And to Doug, my love.

Contents

Prologue

Socialism is not the same as big government.

But the left has taken the word socialism and reshaped, redefined, and reworked it to suit its needs, so that it's nearly impossible to reach consensus on what's socialist, what's not— what's democratic socialism versus social democracy versus social justice versus progressivism versus communism versus all the rest. This confusion is not without its benefits for the left. After all, what better way for a socialist to disguise socialist intent than by pretending not to be a socialist?

By loosest definition, socialism means force—a forced government taking, a forced government redistribution, a forced government takeover of the means of production. That's different from big government—from a government that grows big on the entitlement-minded wings of entitlement-minded politicians and people. But big government and socialism are linked. Big government can oh-so-easily tip into socialism. And America's actually been tip, tip, tipping that way for some time now.

Today's socialists are yesterday's progressives are last week's Democrats are last month's democratic socialists are last year's communists—are last decade's socialists. It's a constant morphing, a constant redefining, a constant convoluting, and conflating of policies, platforms, and politics, designed to constantly change so as to avoid detection. But let's not get caught in the weeds. Here's the real enemy: collectivism.

Let's not get hung up on the ever-changing definitions, and in so doing, play right into the left's hands. Instead, let's keep it simple.

- There's freedom—and there's not.
- There's sovereignty—and there's globalism.
- There's the Constitution—and there's unconstitutional.
- There's the notion of God-given rights—and there's a government that treads on those rights.

Socialism may be the latest attention grabber for today's youth. Socialism may be perceived as today's biggest threat in America, and to America's system of capitalism and free market and freedom.

But really, it's the seeds of socialism we need to beware. It's the change of mindset that comes from a nation of people who are taught in public schools that America is not exceptional; who are told by politicians that hard work means nothing and that if you live, if you breathe, you are owed; who are trained to believe that absolutes are the chains that enslave and that boys can be girls, and girls, boys, simply by trading clothing; who are brainwashed into scorning once-admired traits like self-rule, self-governance, and self-sufficiency; and who are raised without God, or with a god that can be whatever is wished at the time—so that courteous culture crashes, polite society falters, and voilà, government whisks into the picture to instill control.

Want an up-front and close encounter with seeds of socialism as they grow and spread? Look at the video of Black Lives Matter riots in the streets at the police killing of black suspect George Floyd, right around the summer of 2020. Scour the YouTubes of

Antifa thugs as they smashed windows, burned up cars, destroyed and defaced monuments and memorials and statues of America's history—all sparked by the death of George Floyd. Watch the news feeds of the militants and anarchists who took over the city streets of Seattle, Washington, and set up a Capitol Hill "Autonomous Zone," or CHAZ area, barricaded and patrolled by armed guards who kept out police, shook down residents and businesses for cash and protection money, and facilitated the distribution of a myriad of demands to local and state political leaders—all due to the horrible white officers' handling of George Floyd.

Among CHAZ "warlord" demands? A total dismantling of local law enforcement departments. The firing of Seattle's mayor. The providing of free—i.e., tax-paid—health care to all local citizens. The freeing of all prisoners serving time for marijuana-related offenses. The abolition of jails for youth. And more—much more. It was complete chaos in the streets, made all the worse by a Democrat mayor and governor who wanted it believed the insurrection was simply a peaceful protest, conducted by peaceful protesters exercising, peaceably, their First Amendment rights. It was also a sign of the cracking of America; a harbinger of the socialism that's already seeped. The thuggery was driven by ignorance —by youth long-taught, long-trained to believe America, at root, is inherently racist and therefore, from the beginning, inherently evil. The violence was fueled by victimhood mentalities and entitlement natures; by the lies of leftists who've successfully convinced segments of America's populations they're nothing without government assistance and that they can't achieve because they haven't been given the right government tools. The anger was kept alive by exploitative members of the media and Democrat Party who saw in Black Lives Matter and the Antifa anarchists a way to jab politically at President Donald Trump and showcase this White House as less-than-capable of addressing America's societal ills and soothing social justice angst—so, too, all the Republicans.

The hate and fury and utter scorn of moral standards of behavior were flown on the wings of secularism, of unbelief in God, of outright rebellion to all things godly.

These are all seeds of socialism—ignorance, entitlement and victimhood mentalities, secularism and immorality, jealousies and frustrations born of lies, indoctrination of the greatness of government and weakness of the individual.

And it's all these seeds and more that grow cultural socialism, then political socialism, then a government of socialism led by card-carrying socialists. It's all these seeds and more that sprout, spread, stifle, and choke all concepts of freedom.

When it comes to socialism in America, it's not socialism, it's collectivism that must be fought. It's collectivism that must be stomped and killed and eradicated from US soil. It's anything that's *not freedom*. To do that, we must recognize the seeds of socialism when they're planted, where they're planted, how they're planted—so we can rip them from the soil before they sprout. It's the seeds of socialism we want to pluck.

And we need to do it quickly, with bold determination and fearless focus. Why? Because socialists don't sleep. Socialists don't quit. Socialists don't abandon the battlefield. So let's grab them early and stop their un-Americanism. These are their seeds. . . .

CHAPTER 1

FORGETTING
OUR ROOTS

The year was 1775. Just a few months earlier, American delegates meeting at the first Continental Congress in Philadelphia had been arguing and weighing and mulling the merits of striking a bargain with Britain's King George III, versus the dangers of declaring themselves a free people, separated from the crown.[1]

All in attendance had agreed on the principle of colonists' rights and on the premise that the king, via his "Intolerable Acts," or "Coercive Acts," as these punishments against the people became known, had overstepped his authority and unduly burdened the people. But not all saw separation from England as the only solution.

Not all thought crown-colonists' relations were irreparably severed. Some saw concessions and cooperation as still viable options—even though the king, in a speech to Parliament delivered shortly before the start of this Continental Congress, had openly condemned the colonists for a collective "daring spirit of resistance and disobedience to the law."[2]

To what "spirit of resistance" was he referring? From the stuff of elementary school textbooks to the stuff of American History 101, the stuff of the Boston Tea Party of 1773. That's when a band of colonists, angry at unfair and excessive taxation from Britain and organized under the umbrella of the Sons of Liberty, dumped an entire shipment of East India Company tea into Boston Harbor. Go America. Let freedom reign.

The British Parliament didn't react favorably, of course, ordering the Royal Navy to set up a blockade in the waters surrounding the city and for the British Army to patrol city streets. It wasn't long before massive unemployment shook the local economy.[3] And that was just one reverberation. Can you say "oppressors in the house"? Colonists nearly choked under the iron rule, particularly when Parliament pinched further and passed the Quartering Act, giving British soldiers, already hated for their arrogance, the legal right to take over any colonists' dwelling of choice.[4] The gall of it all!

Imagine the sufferings of the women with children, the families, the hard working men who simply wanted a taste of the free life the new country could offer—all being forced to sit down and shut up, and make way at their tables, kitchens, and bedrooms for the entitled soldiers of a faraway throne.

It's a wonder anyone in the colonies still considered the king a worthy enough ruler to follow. But they did. Some did.[5] In what's both a true and sobering commentary on the evils men will suffer so as to avoid open war, the fact is that in March 1775, at the Second Virginia Convention, some in the colonies—some of the 120 or so delegates who had gathered at Saint John's Episcopal Church in Richmond—were still willing to barter and bargain for freedom with the king.[6]

That is with the same despotic king who had just so coldly and over the course of so many years stripped them of nearly every freedom they could possibly hold.[7] They were loyalists, and by gosh, they didn't see the sense of taking on the most powerful force in the world over principles that could lose them their lives, their fortunes, their families, their comforts—waning though those comforts may have been.

Patrick Henry

Enter Patrick Henry. Enter Henry, toting reality by the big dose in his back pocket. Enter Henry, the well-respected lawyer from Hanover County in Virginia, who stepped into center stage at his state's Second Convention to unleash a hurl of rhetoric that still, to this day, sets patriotic hearts pounding.

> Shall we gather strength by irresolution and inaction? Shall we acquire the means of effectual resistance by lying supinely on our backs, and hugging the delusive phantom of hope, until our enemies shall have bound us hand and foot? . . . There is no retreat, but in submission and slavery! . . . Gentlemen may cry, peace, peace—but there is no peace. The war is actually begun! The next gale that sweeps from the north will bring to our ears the clash of resounding arms. Our brethren are already in the field. Why stand we here idle? What is it that gentlemen wish? What would they have? Is life so dear, or peace so sweet, as to be purchased at the price of chains and slavery? Forbid it, Almighty God! I know not what course others may take; but as for me, give me liberty, or give me death![8]

What a call to arms. What a breathless moment. It was a pivotal time; a pivotal speech. A fiery bit of rhetoric that knocked the heads of those disinclined to take decisive action and reminded: Guess what guys, we're already at war. That it may not have actually been delivered as history tells it is just one of those little quirks of research.[9] Sometimes, you just never know what you're going to find.

Unlike other founders, Henry didn't leave behind a long trail of written papers and copies of his speeches. So the main recording of this famous "Liberty or Death" speech came by way of a biography written by a young lawyer named William Wirt, who gathered his information from local newspaper accounts of the event, and through interviews with St. George Tucker,[10] a great legal mind who had been physically present at St. John's the very day Henry spoke.[11]

As such, historical nitpickers like to suggest there's really no surefire way to know, precisely, word for word, what Henry said that fateful day. But let the nitpickers nitpick. The case is overwhelming that Henry spoke either those exact words or something pretty darn close to those exact words.

Not only was Tucker—who in his life served as an attorney, judge, scholar, and writer—a highly esteemed source. But also, shortly after Henry's speech, the delegates passed a resolution to prepare for military defense against the British. A group of Virginians who volunteered for militia service wrote "Liberty or Death" on their shirts.[12] And a man named Colonel Edward Carrington who had listened to Henry's remarks from a window of St. John's was so impressed he actually said, "Let me be buried on this spot."[13] His widow, years later, honored that request.[14]

Boom, boom, boom. Something fired up these events. Something, or someone, sparked these actions. As one historical account put it:

> The convention ended on 27 March and less than a month later on 19 April the first shots of the American Revolution were fired at Lexington and Concord. Henry's speech was prophetic and has been credited as "the signal utterance of the Revolution, a speech whose eloquent and ringing defense of liberty best expressed the colonials' emerging will to independence." Henry's phrase, "liberty or death," became a rallying cry during the Revolution.[15]

Henry's famous "Liberty or Death" speech may or may not have been recorded in exact delivered form for today's pupils, for today's scholars, for today's historians. But it's irrefutable: His words buoyed the spirit of the colonists and compelled them to act. And in that, Henry's speech is very much like America itself: It's the spirit that matters most. We can dicker over words, we can substitute phrase for phrase, we can change out one line for another—we can cry "give me liberty or give me death" just as easily as shout "freedom at all costs, even death." It's all good. So long as the spirit soars—it's all good.

The fact is, America's great because Americans are irrepressibly free. Free to the point of preferring death over bondage. Free to the level where it's unimaginable to envision any other way. Free to the degree of taking it for granted. "Give me liberty or give me death." The words, so few, say so much. Even today.

America's great because Americans are irrepressibly, immeasurably, unapologetically free. It's why the world knocks at our gates—and why so few Americans go knocking on others. But that's just one aspect of America's exceptionalism. America's great because America's free, but America's great, too, because America is principled.

Thomas Nelson Jr.

Look at the life, the struggles, the inspiring successes of Thomas Nelson Jr., one of the signers of the Declaration of Independence, born December 26, 1738. Nelson was part of the Virginia aristocratic society—groomed for leadership, educated at Trinity College in Cambridge, connected by both birth and marriage to money and property.[16] He could've led a very comfortable life, soared high above the fray of politics, taken full advantage of his better-than-bourgeois opportunities. Had he desired. Had he only wanted.

But service to colony and service to country were his primary goals. He reached adulthood just around the time Britain's Parliament passed the Boston Port Act that closed the city's main gateway to trade;[17] just around the time Virginia's "House of Burgesses called for a day of fasting, humiliation and prayer in support of [these] people of Massachusetts," as one historical curator recounted;[18] and just around the time his own governor, John Murray, the fourth Earl of Dunmore, responded to this legislative expression of support and sorrow by dissolving the body.

Nelson didn't like what he saw. It stoked a righteous indignation. "To protest this action," the Society of the Descendants of the Signers of the Declaration of Independence wrote, "Nelson began spending some of his personal fortune, sending needed supplies to Boston. He arranged a Yorktown tea party and personally threw two half-chests of tea into the York River."[19]

That's not just bold. That's putting principle above personal cares. Imagine the reactions of the British—and of fellow colonists. Hated and loved, all for the same act.

Nelson was ultimately elected to the House of Burgesses in 1774 and became a member of Virginia's provincial convention in 1775, where he helped form and then command the Virginia militia. Subsequently, and through various health trials, including serious bouts with asthma, he served on the Second Continental Congress and in various leadership roles of the military, and finally as Virginia's governor, in 1781, succeeding Thomas Jefferson.[20]

Yet it was his character that shone brightest. Yes, he was a noted politician. Yes, he was a respected military leader. But it was his committed adherence to principles over the personal, country over self—even in the face of danger, even as the potential for great loss lurked—that truly earned him a highly esteemed place in the history books.

From the Society of the Descendants of the Signers of the Declaration of Independence:

In the spring of 1781, [when] Nelson was elected Governor . . . [t]he Virginia Legislature was on the run at the time, pursued by the British cavalry commander Banastre Tarleton into Albemarle County. By early September the American and French armies were closing in on [Lord Charles] Cornwallis who had decided to await evacuation of his army at Yorktown. When the French fleet arrived his fate was sealed. During the siege and battle Nelson led the Virginia Militia whom he had personally organized and supplied with his own funds. Legend had it that Nelson ordered his artillery to direct their fire on his own house which was occupied by Cornwallis, offering five guineas to the first man who hit the house. Either the cannoneers were inaccurate or the event never happened, but there are three cannon balls still lodged on the outer wall of the house.[21]

Myth? Legend? The stuff of boisterous tales over late-night campfires? Well, the National Park Service reports similarly—that "evidence of the damage" to Nelson's own home "exists to this day."[22] So does the Institute on the Constitution, which wrote: "A legend from the battle is that Nelson ordered artillery to direct their fire on his own house which was British headquarters. There are three cannon balls still lodged in the outer wall of the house."[23]

Amazing. Still, it's hard to decide which is most remarkable about Nelson—the tale of the cannon balls or the offering of his own money to battle the British. From the National Park Service:

In November 1781, poor health forced Nelson's resignation as governor. The war had ruined his business and his personal loan of over $2,000,000 to help finance Virginia's war costs was never repaid by the state. Nelson was left a poor man with a wife and 11 children. Living on the edge of poverty, he died of asthma eight years after the 1781 siege and was buried in an unmarked grave at Yorktown's Grace Church so that his creditors could not hold his body as collateral.[24]

By that description, one might think Nelson died a bitter man, regretting his sacrifices to colonists and country. And he'd certainly be forgiven for feeling that way, right? But fact is, he didn't. Not a bit. And this is just what's so awe-inspiring about Nelson, the man of unwavering principle. When asked if he felt anger or bitterness at how he was treated, Nelson said, according to National Park Service records: "I would do it all over again."

He would do it all over again. How many of us, reared with the finest of educations, accustomed to the finer things in life, padded with wealth, secure in property, and prepared to walk a road of ease and comfort—how many of us would not only sacrifice all for a principle, but also, when faced with the realities of broken promises and dashed expectations, including poverty, react with an attitude that says, "Oh, well"?

Nelson died on January 4, 1789, and in a tribute, his good friend Colonel James Innes wrote, in part: Nelson "exhibited a conduct untarnished and undebased by sordid or selfish interest."[25] Even that seems an understatement.

Americans Give

It's one thing to claim a spirit of "give me liberty or give me death." It's another thing entirely to claim that same spirit, but rather than die, continue to live for liberty in the face of unendurable hardship, in the throes of financial ruin, in the midst of unbelievable loss of material fortunes—and then look back and say it was all worthwhile; it was worth doing again. That's not just irrepressible freedom. That's utter selflessness. Saintly selflessness.

And only those ingrained with the highest order of principles can live at this level. Nelson, in life, in sacrifice, helped set a standard for what America could be, what America should be—and it's one, thankfully, that has stood the test of time. When times get tough, what do Americans do? They fight. They unite. They give.

What's more, they do so largely because of religious belief. This is the third, and greatest, trait of America: This country is great because this country is good. This country is good because it takes its definition of "good" from a moral compass shaped by God, dictated by the Bible, forged by Judeo-Christian ideals. Let the secularists laugh. Let the atheists mock and scorn.

If charitable works are a mark of faith—and they very frequently are—then America, even today, even today as yesterday, is a nation of faithful, God-fearing, Bible-believing, Judeo-Christian ideal-adhering patriots. Therein lies our hope. Americans, in 2018, gave more than $427 billion—that's billion with a *b*—to various charities, according to the National Philanthropic Trust. Of that, more than $20 billion came from corporations and almost $76 billion from foundations. But the largest givers, by far, with $292 billion worth of donations, were the individuals.[26]

Those are astonishing numbers. But hardly anomalies. In 2017, the revised total of American giving was a little more than $424 billion.[27] In 2016, American giving totaled more than $390 billion.[28] In 2015, it was just over $373 billion.[29] In fact, since 1977, with the exception of three years—1987, 2008, and 2009—"giving has increased in current dollars every year," making up a substantial portion of the national gross domestic product, Charity Navigator found.[30]

Prior to the 40-year period 1977–2017, total giving was consistently at or above 2.0% of GDP. It fell below 2.0% throughout most of the 1970s, 1980s, and 1990s. Total giving as a percentage of GDP rose to 2.0% and above through most of the 2000s, but then dropped to 1.9% in the years 2009 to 2011. Total giving as a percentage of GDP was 2.1% for four of the five years, 2013–2017.[31]

Americans, when it comes to helping those in need and donating to worthy causes, are some kind of bleeding hearts. But this makes sense. Giving is ingrained in the nature of Americans because ingrained in the nature of America is the spirit of freedom. These two statements are indisputably linked: Nothing says free like a limited government; nothing limits the scope of government's power like a people who refuse to turn to the government for fulfillment of every need.

If churches feed the poor, the poor don't need food stamps. If nonprofits help people with disabilities, the people with disabilities don't need government handouts. If volunteers help build homes for low-income families, low-income families don't need subsidized housing from the government. Simply put, a free citizenry is a self-reliant citizenry. Who knows that better than people of faith? Who puts wings behind those words more vigorously than the churchgoers of America?

America is different from all other nations this way. "Americans Are More Charitable than 'Socially Conscious' Europeans," reported the Foundation for Economic Freedom in February 2017. "Most of the supposedly compassionate welfare states have dismal levels of charitable giving."[32] Then there was this, from MarketWatch, in a December 7, 2019, headline: "The U.S. is the No. 1 most generous country in the world for the last decade."[33]

That headline came from a report from Charities Aid Foundation's 2019 World Giving Index that asked 1.3 million individuals around the world if, in the past month, they'd "helped a stranger," "donated money to a charity," or "volunteered . . . time to an organization"—and found: In all three areas, America topped.[34]

Impressively, notably, in all three areas for the past 10 years, in fact, America has topped.

> Consistently high numbers of Americans say that they helped a stranger, donated money or volunteered time and this has ensured its position as highest performer when we look at the last decade as a whole, with a score of 58%. Myanmar and New Zealand take second and third place. . . . *China has the lowest Index score over the 10 years at 16% and in fact is the only country that appears in the bottom 10 for all three measures we ask about; helping a stranger, donating money and volunteering time.*[35] (Italic added.)

China, land of the repressed. China, land of the communist. China, land of the godless. The fact this nation falls lowest on the list of giving is no surprise—just as the fact America, built as it was on Judeo-Christian principles and a quest for religious freedom, tops this list is hardly shocking.

Believers give. It's the nature of the faith. "People who are religiously affiliated are more likely to make a charitable donation of any kind, whether to a religious congregation or to another type of charitable organization," IUPUI Lilly Family School of Philanthropy reported, in an October 2017, study. "Sixty-two percent of religious households give to charity of any kind, compared with 46 percent of households with no religious affiliation."[36]

The point? Nobody knew better than this nation's own Founding Fathers and visionaries of American exceptionalism that the link between individual or personal morality and good governance was inextricable. It's why their writings and discussions were filled with caveats about the republic lasting only so long as its people were moral and virtuous. It's where they derived their vision of America as a place of rights coming from God, not government.

> We hold these truths to be self-evident," the Declaration of Independence reads. "[T]hat they are endowed by their Creator with certain unalienable Rights, that among these are Life, Liberty and the pursuit of Happiness. —That to secure these rights, Governments are instituted among Men, deriving their just powers from the consent of the governed . . .

Without a "Creator"—without God—this fundamental mission statement of America falls flat. America, absent God, is a piece of land with a bunch of people, nothing more.

Legend has it that Isaac Potts, a Quaker famer who lived near Valley Forge, happened upon George Washington praying, on bended knee, in the snow, asking God to watch over his men and protect his troops from British annihilation. The story goes on that Potts later recounted the scene to his wife, assuring that "all will be well" because he saw "General Washington on his knees" and therefore, "our independence is certain." It's that image of Washington that's been captured in paintings and pictures for decades.

Of course, the Potts legend is likely just that—a story absent historical proof. But it serves its purpose just the same. The reason why that story stands the passage of years and the painting, the test of time, is because it shows, at a glance, why America is so exceptional, where America gets its gift of exceptionalism, what roots America to good governance. The source of America's greatness, pure and simple, is God.

Patrick Henry believed this. "Henry," wrote Richard Beeman, in an article for JSTOR, grew "sorely distressed" when he observed, in the days of the American Revolution, the loss of civic virtue, "when the financial contributions of the states to the war effort seemed to lag and when individual self-interest seemed everywhere to be triumphing over the public good." Henry's recommendations? They were as bold as his fiery manner of speaking. At one point, he sought to instill George Washington as a "temporary dictator" in order to prod the states to fulfill their moral and practical obligations in fighting the British; at another, he countered the pressings of Thomas Jefferson and James Madison for a complete separation of church and state with a call for the "general assessment for the support for all Protestant denominations in the state."[37]

His motivations for either suggested course of action aren't entirely clear; this is yet one more example of where Henry's failure to write much down causes historical headache.

But it is certain," Beeman went on, "[Henry] was deeply disturbed by what he saw as the decline in virtue and morality among his fellow Virginians . . . about the decline in many Episcopal parishes in Virginia, the flight of many Episcopalian ministers from the state and, more generally, the tendency of many Virginians to ignore their public responsibilities . . . [H]e did believe—in true classical republican fashion—that it was the job of the church and state, working hand-in-hand, to promote virtue among the citizenry.[38]

Thomas Nelson Jr. knew this, too. Nelson was well aware of the link between faith and freedom, and how the scorning of the first would lead to the loss of the second.

The grave marker for Nelson reads, in part: "Gen. Thomas Nelson Jr. Patriot — Soldier — Christian — Gentleman."[39] He was an Episcopalian, a member of Grace Church in Yorktown, and, without a doubt, grew much of what Colonel Innes summed up as his "splendid and heroic parts of his character" from the seeds of godly instruction.[40]

The equation is simple. America plus God equals greatness. America is great because America was built on a foundation of God, on a rock of Judeo-Christian principles, on a belief that the talents and courage determinations of a properly morally compassed individual might translate into a nation of exceptionalism. America minus God equals despair. Freedom absent morality brings tyranny.

Freedom Can Fall in a Flash

This is where Democrats, today's euphemism for socialists, want to take us. If we forget what made America great in the first place, we're just helping the leftists work their destructive designs. And here's the red flag alert: It takes only a flash for freedom to fall. If conditions are right, it takes only a moment and the freedoms are gone.

In early 2020, as fears of coronavirus gripped the nation, Americans experienced the kind of government-imposed clampdowns more common to police states, not republics. Businesses were ordered closed, citizens were told to stay inside their homes, schools were shut down and classes canceled, churches—churches!—locked their doors and canceled worship services.[41] Police arrested pastors and recreational park-goers for violating social distancing dictates.[42] Police manned states' and cities' borders, ensuring drivers weren't trying to skip town, leave their homes, travel outside their jurisdictions—unless, of course, they were essential employees and could provide proof of that essential status.[43] Show me your papers, comrade.

President Donald Trump and states' governors unleashed the military and sent out the National Guard to assist where most needed.[44] "Trump authorizes call-ups of military reservists to fight virus," Politico wrote on March 28. The story went on to report how Trump, in an executive order, authorized the Department of Defense and the Department of Homeland Security the ability to activate as many as one million members of the military's ready reserves' units.[45] "Trump Says Thousands of Military to Be Sent to Help States Battle Coronavirus," Reuters reported on April 4.[46]

Americans started wearing facial masks outside, in stores, in their cars. National parks, recreational facilities, movie theaters closed.[47] Major sports' venues shut down; whole sports' seasons canceled.[48]

Toilet paper was impossible to find; store shelves were hauntingly bare. Facial tissues were impossible to buy—even online.[49]

If ever there was a taste of socialism to come to America's soil, the political response to coronavirus was it. Talk about total government control. Talk about loss of individual rights. Yes, government declared a national emergency, and yes, the virus was real, and, in some cases, deadly.[50] But the political and economic reactions to coronavirus were outright chilling to freedom.

"Hospitals say feds are seizing masks and other coronavirus supplies without a word," one *Los Angeles Times* headline read.[51] "Cuomo signs order for New York to commandeer ventilators, protective gear," one Hill headline read, in the aftermath of New York Governor Andrew Cuomo's mid-coronavirus April order.[52] Seizing private property? Commandeering privately owned products?

Then this, a headline from Politico: "[Jared] Kushner's team seeks national coronavirus surveillance system." Well, that's alarming. The story went on to report:

> White House senior adviser Jared Kushner's task force has reached out to a range of health technology companies about creating a national coronavirus surveillance system to give the government a near real-time view of where patients are seeking treatment and for what, and whether hospitals can accommodate them. . . . The proposed national network could help determine which areas of the country can safely relax social-distancing rules and which should remain vigilant. But it would also represent a significant expansion of government use of individual patient data, forcing a new reckoning over privacy limits amid a national crisis.[53]

How's that saying go—those who would trade liberty for security deserve neither liberty nor security? It's a line of thought that's often credited to Benjamin Franklin. But it's badly butchered and taken out-of-context. Still, the idea, reflecting on coronavirus chaos, serves well.

Barack Obama, in a tweet, essentially called for the same. "[I]n order to shift off current policies," Obama tweeted, on April 8, shortly after the Politico story on a national coronavirus surveillance system ran, "the key will be a robust system of testing and monitoring—something we have yet to put in place nationwide."[54]

National emergency, national health emergency, national pandemic emergency to the side—what resulted was a government crackdown on individual freedoms times ten. That it came courtesy of the advisements of unelected, unaccountable doctors, globalists, and billionaires, rather than by way of duly elected politicians, made the loss of individual rights all the worse.

At the heart of the issuance of federal policies regarding coronavirus was Anthony Fauci, the director of the National Institute of

Allergy and Infectious Diseases and an adviser to six White House administrations.[55] In an April interview on CNN, Fauci was asked by host Anderson Cooper, "Knowing the science, does it make sense to you that some states are still not issuing stay-at-home orders? I mean, whether there should be a federally mandated directive for that or not, I guess that's more of a political question, but just scientifically, doesn't everybody have to be on the same page with this stuff?"[56] And Fauci's answer: Yes.[57] "I think so," Fauci said. "I don't understand why that's not happening."[58] Fauci then gave a nod at states' rights, but then added, "If you look at what's going on in this country, I just don't understand why we're not doing that. We really should be."[59]

In a separate *Today Show* interview, Fauci said similarly—that a federal stay-at-home order was the best way to combat the virus. "I mean," he said, "I know it's difficult. But we're having a lot of suffering, a lot of death. This is inconvenient from an economic and personal standpoint, but we just have to do it."[60]

Then again, that's a doctor's order—not the Constitution's. In America, it's supposed to be the rule of law based on a concept of individual rights and protected by the voter-selected political class that guides and governs, not an unelected medical adviser. Not a guy who's been tapped to help explain the possible risks of a virus. Yet America pretty much quarantined.

The nation's top health official, Surgeon General Jerome Adams, called for a federal stay-at-home order for all citizens, as well. "My advice to America would be," Adams said, of guidelines that were mailed to the states from the feds, "these guidelines are a national stay-at-home order."[61] Well, which is it—an advisement or an order? The mixed messaging isn't just annoying; it's purposeful and bureaucratic doublespeak meant to serve as an order while giving government a shield to say, hey, it's just an advisement not an order.

But Fauci and Adams—they weren't the only two unelected figures in the 2020 coronavirus quarantining order. "Bill Gates says we need a nationwide shutdown for at least 10 more weeks to fight coronavirus: 'The window for making important decisions hasn't closed,'" *Business Insider* reported, in early April.[62]

Gates, of course, is the billionaire cofounder of Microsoft, and through his Bill & Melinda Gates Foundation, one of the world's leading philanthropists. He resigned his Microsoft board of directors' seat in March 2020, making his split from his company complete, and at the same time announced intent to "dedicate more time to philanthropic priorities including global health and development."[63] Part of that philanthropic priority included developing a vaccine for coronavirus. "Bill Gates says he'll spend billions on coronavirus vaccine development," MarketWatch reported.[64]

For that, Gates was widely applauded. After all, spending billions to help humanity is commendable, yes? But billionaires can be both philanthropic and self-serving at the same time. Gates is a guy who wields incredible influence at the World Health Organization, serving as one of that UN body's largest funders. In 2017, Politico reported:

> Some billionaires are satisfied with buying themselves an island. Bill Gates got a United Nations health agency in Geneva. Over the past decade, the world's richest man has become the World Health Organization's second biggest donor, second only to the United States. . . . This largesse gives him outsized influence over its agenda. . . . The result, say his critics, is that Gates' priorities have become the WHO's.[65]

The Politico-reported connection is all the more interesting when it's seen that Gates, according to a March 10, 2020, *Business Insider* article, had been "sounding the alarm on the COVID-19 coronavirus, calling it a 'pandemic,' though the World Health Organization ha[d] yet to give it that distinction."[66] The piece went on to report how the Gates Foundation, in partnership with a couple of other outlets, was donating $125 million in funding for companies actively engaged in developing a coronavirus cure.[67]

The Gates Foundation, meanwhile, in a separate announcement on its own web page, specified that some of that funding would go to the World Health Organization.[68] One day later, the day after the Gates Foundation announced this money for WHO, the WHO director-general, Tedros Adhanom Ghebreyesus, came out and said this: "We have therefore made the assessment that COVID-19 can be characterized as a pandemic."[69] On March 10, Gates announced money for WHO. On March 11, WHO made the announcement that Gates had long wanted—that coronavirus was a pandemic. Coincidental? Perhaps. Perhaps not.

Also at the height of the coronavirus crisis, when panic was shifting into full-blown mode, *Barron's* reported this: "The Bill & Melinda Gates Foundation Trust disclosed a large investment in The Mexico Fund, a closed-end fund that focuses investments in that country. The fund has withered in the face of the market disruption caused by the coronavirus pandemic."[70] Specifically, the trust bought a 5 percent stake, making it the fourth-largest investor in the fund, *Barron's* reported.

There's money to be made in a crashing coronavirus market, it seems. It's not as if Gates doesn't have a right to make money—or to recoup money invested for philanthropic endeavors, like vaccine developments that could protect people from sickness, even death. But just because Gates says he's a philanthropist doesn't automatically make him a saint. In fact, Gates, on vaccines in general, carries lots of curious conflicts of interest that seem to pit his do-good image against his influence peddling successes.

Take a look at this excerpt from a 2010 press release from The Gates Foundation:

> The World Health Organization (WHO), UNICEF, the National Institute of Allergy and Infectious Diseases (NIAID) and the Bill & Melinda Gates Foundation have announced a collaboration to increase coordination across the international vaccine community and create a Global Vaccine Action Plan. This plan will build on

the successes of current work to achieve key milestones in the discovery, development and delivery of lifesaving vaccines to be the most vulnerable populations in the poorest countries over the next decade. The collaboration follows the January 2010 call by Bill and Melinda Gates for the next ten years to be the Decade of Vaccines. The Global Vaccine Action Plan will enable greater coordination across all stakeholder groups—national governments, multilateral organizations, civil society, the private sector and philanthropic organizations—and will identify crucial policy, resource, and other gaps that must be addressed to realize the life-saving potential of vaccines.[71]

The Global Vaccine Action Plan, according to this same Gates Foundation press release, included the creation of a leadership council to oversee program implementation, a steering committee to take charge of putting the plans into action, an international advisory committee to help the leadership council in looking at the pros and cons of how the plan was implemented, and a secretariat to give the necessary administrative support.[72] It's all very organized and structured. And guess who was listed as a member of the leadership council? None other than Dr. Anthony Fauci, "director of NIAID, part of the National Institutes of Health." Gates–Fauci: The ties that bind.

If Gates had been Dan Cathy of Chick-fil-A fame spending billions on vaccines while pressing policy through WHO that tanked the US economy and while investing heavily in funds that had precariously dropped due to coronavirus stay-at-home orders—if it had been the openly evangelical Dan Cathy spending and investing billions while advising people to stay at home in the name of good Christian duty—the left would've gone nuts.

The media would've gone into hyper watchdog mode. The Democrats, the globalists, the socialist types would've cried about conflicts of interest and separation of church and state and the need to keep the Bible thumpers out of government.

Philanthropy, apparently, to the masses, is one thing. Christian aid is quite another. And we know this double standard to be true because we had a real-life example of leftist disdain of Christian assistance with coronavirus in New York. When evangelical Franklin Graham announced his Samaritan's Purse was going to set up a military-grade field hospital in Central Park, staffed entirely with volunteer medical experts and aimed at easing the burdens on nearby hospitals who were overrun with patients due to coronavirus fears, New York City Mayor Bill de Blasio had a conniption.[73]

"I said immediately to my team that we needed to find out what was happening," the Democrat mayor said, in response to Graham's charitable endeavor. "Was there going to be an approach that was truly consistent with the values [of] New York City?"[74]

Interesting. Questioning the motives of a Christian is A-OK. Questioning the motives of a billionaire philanthropist is a no-go. Questioning the motives of a medical scholar tied to the billionaire philanthropist is a no-go. Even when the computer modeling making all the frightening medical predictions that brought about the crackdowns in the first place was ridiculously flawed.[75] Even when the reported real-time deaths due to coronavirus were far from factual, because of spotty testing and the uncertainty of how all doctors were figuring in patients' accompanying, preexisting medical conditions.

"How does mortality differ across countries?" Johns Hopkins University of Medicine Coronavirus Resource Center asked. "Differences in the number of people tested: With more testing, more people with milder cases are identified. This lowers the case-fatality ratio."[76]

Just to put some context in the coronavirus matter: On April 12, 2020, Johns Hopkins reported 554,226 coronavirus cases in the United States.[77] Given there are about 330 million people in America[78]—that's just 0.17 percent of the population that tested positive for coronavirus. That same day, April 12, the death count due to coronavirus stood at 21,994, according to the same Johns

Hopkins tally.[79] That's 0.007 percent of America's population—actually, 0.00666 percent, to carry out the figures to an eerie place count.

For that, America shut down operations. For that, Americans let unelected wonks wield tremendous national influence with nary a pushback. For that, Americans, practically overnight, gave up their cherished freedoms.

It's in time of great distress or chaos when critical thinking is most needed. Think as you will about coronavirus; believe as you wish on the medical risks and health impacts and dangers to the citizens. But then push those thoughts to the side and consider this: The climate that came from the 2020 government-imposed coronavirus crackdowns was one of fear, and that fear was then played by some of the leftists and globalists and anti-American forces and sources to instill even greater fear and exert even greater government control. It gave the left some easy pickings. And no one knew that better than the leftists.

- "Will coronavirus launch the second wave of socialism?" the Hill asked, in a late March 2020 headline.[80]
- "Covid-19 Creates an Opening for Socialism (Also Barbarism)," *New York Magazine* wrote, in an early April 2020 headline.[81]

Freedom is a precious thing. If coronavirus shows us anything, it's that freedom is precious and can be whisked away at a moment's notice. Government can indeed crack down on individual rights for causes of greater goods. Citizens will abide the crackdowns if they believe in the cause of the greater good. And only those whose memories serve well on the history and founding greatness of our country will care enough to fight for a return to American normalcy—to an America the framers would have recognized as free.

"Why stand we here idle?" as Patrick Henry thundered.[82] Good question. Let's not. If we forget our roots, the socialists, the globalists, the leftists, the collectivists—they all automatically win.

CHAPTER 2

LETTING DEMOCRATS DISGUISE THEIR SOCIALISM

ctress Patricia Heaton, in a February 2020 Twitter post, questioned why anyone who's pro-life would want to align with today's Democrat Party. On that, she has an excellent point. "I don't understand why pro-life people want to know if they are 'welcome' to join the Democrat party," she wrote. "Why would any civilized person want to support a barbaric platform that champions abortion for any reason through all nine months funded by taxpayers?"[1]

That's today's Democrats, in a few short words. Secular. Godless. Secular and godless to the point of being communist. Even some of the party's own acknowledge that.

"Last night on CNN, Bernie [Sanders] called me a political hack," complained former Bill Clinton political operative James Carville, in a February 2020, telephone interview with *Good Luck America* Snapchat host Peter Hamby. "That's exactly who the [expletive] I am. I am a political hack. I am not an ideologue. I am not a purist. He thinks it's a pejorative. I kind of like it. At least I'm not a communist."[2] Left unstated: ". . . like Sanders is." And given the political winds Sanders flies, calling him communist is not that far off the mark.

Senator Bernie Sanders—who somewhat confusingly and deceptively wears an Independent button, caucuses with the Democrats, and self-identifies as democratic socialist or progressive, all the while simultaneously acting and speaking as a flaming socialist—said in a June 2019 presidential campaign speech at George Washington University in Washington, DC, that the Bill of Rights was good, the constitutional protection of certain individual freedom was fine, but that "now we must take the next step forward and guarantee every man, woman and child in our country [some] basic economic rights."[3]

Among those rights? "The right to quality health care," Sanders said. "The right to as much education as one needs to succeed in our society. The right to a good job that pays a living wage. The right to affordable housing. The right to a secure retirement. And, the right to live in a clean environment."[4] He added this: "We must recognize that in the twenty-first century, in the wealthiest country in the history of the world, economic rights are human rights. And that is what I mean by democratic socialism."[5]

Thud.

Economic Rights

The definition of "rights" in America has never been broader. And for big-government types, this broad definition allows for a sneaky way of sliding socialism into the nation without ever even having to use the dreaded "socialism" label. Once it's admitted into America's society and government that something is a right, rather than privilege, or luxury, or benefit, or hard-earned reward, then it easily becomes part of the American consciousness that it's government's job to provide that right. It oftentimes and easily becomes an expectation for the government to act and the individual to simply receive.

But this is not properly part of the American experience. Just because one breathes does not entitle one, say, to a four-year college degree at taxpayer expense. It doesn't even entitle one to a K–12 education, else how to explain the failure of third world countries to provide this level of education to all their children? The left, like Sanders, would argue that the rights of a child in sub-Saharan Africa, one of the poorest regions in the world, are one and the same as those of a child in Fairfax, Virginia, one of the wealthiest areas in America, and therefore, the two must be treated equally, must be provided the same housing, health care, same education, same job prospects, and so forth. But this is a red herring. This is a transference of morality for government.

There is morality, and there is government. While the two are not mutually exclusive and should not be—of course, we want politicians who are moral and virtuous—the first should always remain a matter of individualism so as to keep the second from serving as arbiter.

In other words, government is not the decider, or definer, of morality. God is. And while in the spiritual realm, in the eyes of God, all His children are certainly equal and worthy of lives of success, prosperity, joy, and yes, even college education, all are not owed these lives simply because they're born. There is a biblical concept of work. There is a Bible-based idea of reaping and sowing. There is a Christian ideal of reaching in one's own pocket to help others—but that Christian ideal stops short of demanding the reach-in of government's pockets to help others.

Economic rights are not human rights, no matter what Sanders says, no matter how politicians masquerading as do-gooders push it. Arguing this leads down a rabbit hole of deep, dark despair, absent ambitions, goals, and hopes, where the talents of the individual are stripped, the seeds of greatness ripped, and even the power to think with clarity torn asunder. It's a life of tasteless collectivism, robotic drudgery. It's a life where the dreams of a child are choked for the good of the aggregate. It's a life that looks at struggle as an enemy to obliterate, not a challenge to beat, and that therefore wipes away all opportunities and motivations for individuals to win. It's a life devoid of spirit, with minds conditioned to believe that's the way it ought to be. That right there is socialism in its truest form. So how does Sanders get away with calling for this evil—and winning hearts and minds of Americans in the process?

Truly, populism is a powerful political aphrodisiac. "For the people" is a phrase that can be twisted to mean mightily different things. Leftists learned long ago that making a case based on emotion not logic—of appealing to the morality of a situation, rather than relaying the fact-based consequences—can earn them big political wins, particularly with the low-information voters. After all, how to argue against giving "free" education to the poverty-stricken children of the world? Particularly when there are so many far-leftists in the media all too willing to play their own activist roles?

Sanders is just one in a long line of socialists who, through the years, through the decades, through the centuries, has taken the truth that it's unfair for one child to be born in misery while another is born into luxury, and turned it into the lie that it's therefore government's job to redistribute the luxuries—turned it into the lie that those who oppose the idea of government as cradle-to-grave caretaker are simply heartless and cruel.

Be not fooled. America's emphasis on individual rights runs both ways—as a gift to be received and as a personal responsibility to be shared. If citizens see only the blessing of the first and take, take, take, but refuse to accept the conditions of the second, and give, give, give, willingly, without reservation, when needs actually arise, then the doors to big government won't just open wide. They'll never shut.

Socialist with a Small *s*

This is where America stands today. President Donald Trump in his 2019 State of the Union address vowed: "Tonight, we renew our resolve that America will never be a socialist country."[6] A couple months later, at an April rally in Wisconsin, Trump said similarly that America "will never be a socialist country."[7] A few months after that, in a September speech before the General Assembly at UN headquarters in New York, Trump repeated the line once again: "America will never be a socialist country."[8]

After eight long years of Barack Obama, and the weighted fists of government controlling nearly every aspect of American productivity, creativity, and economic activity, Trump's remarks were soaring welcomes.

Yet Sanders is openly socialist. He has been since he started in politics in 1981. Yet Alexandria Ocasio-Cortez was elected in 2018 to serve in Congress on behalf of those living in sections of New York's Bronx and Queens' boroughs—as an open socialist. Rashida Tlaib was elected in 2018 to serve in Congress on behalf of those living in half of Detroit and several western suburbs outside of Michigan's main city—as an open socialist. The official Democratic Socialists of America (DSA) organization counted among its 2018 electoral wins another three dozen or so of state and local government seats. "We are building a pipeline from local positions all the way to national politics," the national political committee of the DSA wrote in a statement on the heels of the 2018 races.[9]

Maybe Trump is right—America will never be a "Socialist" country. But he's far too optimistic that America will never be a "socialist" country—meaning, a country comprised of individuals who value, favor, push, and legislate policies and ideas that embrace the collective over the individual, which in time lead to outright government controls on production and individual creations. Meaning, a country that's truly socialist in all but name.

Democrats, as a party, have already taken the country far down this socialist-in-all-but-name road. They've done it by sly means, pretending to be progressives, pretending to be social justice warriors, pretending to be populists who care for the little guy and the downtrodden gal. They've done it by open, strong-arm means, by taking over courts and judicial seats to press activist, anti-constitutional agendas into local laws, into local legislation. They've done it by vicious loudmouth means, by smearing and assassinating characters and reputations via their friends in the media. They've done it by using a combination of those tactics, a never-ending drumroll of those tactics, a wearying, fatiguing never-let-up all-courts press of those tactics. They've done it for decades, and they'll continue doing it for as long as they can get by with doing it.

The perils to the Constitution are real. Solving the problem requires seeing the problem—and seeing the forest, not just the trees. Fact is, there's been far too much attention paid to "Socialism" with a capital S and not nearly enough to the "socialism" with a small s—to the cultural changes that have brought on the entitlement mindsets and the national cravings for government to step in and solve all. This is folly. It's only from "socialism with a small s" that "Socialism with a capital S" springs. It's only by worrying about the "socialism with a small s" that the "Socialism with a capital S" can be discerned, then stopped.

Sanders shouldn't be allowed to shake fingers and declare, with scorn and outrage, that democratic socialism is not socialism—even as he then goes on to explain policies, viewpoints, and legislation he favors that are exactly that, socialism. Wonks at liberal rags and leftist publications shouldn't be allowed to lecture how socialism, by textbook definition, is a complete government takeover of a country's means of production, and that nobody in politics in America—not Sanders, not Ocasio-Cortez, not anyone in the Democratic Party—wants that, and that therefore, if nobody in politics in America wants that, my goodness, well then nobody in politics in America is really socialist.

The left shouldn't be allowed to define itself as it chooses without challenge. The left shouldn't be allowed to sell deceptive messaging about socialism. The left shouldn't be given an easy pass about its true nature—and true politics.

If it looks like a duck, walks like a duck, and quacks like a duck, it's a duck. If it looks like socialism, walks like socialism, and quacks like socialism, it's socialism—or a derivative thereof, and in which case, it still doesn't belong in America. None of it does. Intellectuals and scholars like to engage in lively debates about what's socialism versus what's progressivism, what's democratic socialism versus socialism, and what's soft socialism versus hard-core socialism, but in America, the debate should be much shorter, far sweeter.

There's the Constitution—and there's not. There's the God-given—and there's not. Those are the standards; those should stay the standards by which all political, economic, social, and societal programs and proposals in America should be measured. Short. Sweet. Clear-cut. Constitutional.

As philosopher and writer Ayn Rand wrote in a letter in 1945: "Fascism, Nazism, Communism and Socialism are only superficial variations of the same monstrous theme—collectivism."[10] As Rand also warned in her later "Conservatism: An Obituary," based on a lecture at Princeton University in 1960: "The world conflict of today is the conflict of the individual against the state, the same conflict that has been fought throughout mankind's history. The names change, but the essence—and the results—remain the same, whether it is the individual against feudalism, or against absolute monarchy, or against communism or fascism or Nazism or social-ism or the welfare state."[11]

Clarity of mind, in a world of clanging ideologies and clash-ing philosophies, is crucial to keeping our country free. Socialism doesn't come as an announcement from Congress, blasted by the speaker of the House across America's airwaves, "America is now a socialist country." If only. That would be easier to fight. Instead, socialism comes as a shadow—a seductive, creeping, shadowy fig-ure promising nirvana while distracting from the Ponzi scheme of redistribution impossibilities, while deceiving about the only end result that can come: government oppression. And my, how that shadow has crept.

In 1949, Gallup polling found that only 15 percent of Americans wanted to move the country in the direction of socialism, defined for the purposes of the survey question as a system in which the government owned and operated certain businesses, like banks and natural resource companies, but that still allowed citizens to vote for their politicians. Sixty-four percent said they opposed such a system.[12]

By the time 1964 rolled around, though, this same Gallup survey found that 48 percent of Americans agreed "there is a definite trend toward socialism in this country." A year later, 37 percent of American adults told Gallup the country's economic system was driven by capitalism—but 31 percent said "moderate socialism," and another 3 percent answered "pure socialism."[13]

That means in fifteen years' time, Americans went from outright opposing socialism to softly, quietly, widely embracing at least some of socialism's ideas. Fast-forward to 2018, and the nation's millennials, defined in one GenForward survey as those between the ages of 18 and 34, really began to embrace socialism—particularly those millennials who identified as Democrats.

Majorities of Asian Americans (56%) and white Millennials (54%) hold favorable opinions toward Capitalism, but only 45% of Latins and 34% of African Americans feel similarly. A significant majority (61%) of Millennial Democrats express favorable views toward Socialism. Less than a third of Independents (32%) hold favorable views of Socialism. Only 25% of Republicans report feeling favorably toward Socialism.[14]

The GenForward findings are interesting because they underscore the ramrodding of socialism into American society that's yet to come—as youth reach adulthood and assume positions of power and leadership—and because they provide a statistical point of argument for what the politically aware already know: Democrats have a natural predisposition for socialism.

Other pollsters have found just that, in fact. In 2010, in a study entitled "Democrats More Positive About Socialism Than

Capitalism," Gallup discovered 53 percent of self-identifying Democrats viewed capitalism in a positive light; 53 percent of this same group also saw socialism positively. Eight years later, those numbers had dramatically changed. In 2018, Gallup asked the same question of self-described Democrats and discovered that while 47 percent still favored capitalism, fully 57 percent gave thumbs-up to socialism.[15]

At the same time, those who identified as Republicans steadfastly through the years told Gallup pollsters they disdained socialism. By the numbers, in 2010, roughly 72 percent of Republicans favored capitalism versus 17 percent who waxed positive on socialism; in 2018, about 71 percent of Republicans stood strong for capitalism versus 16 percent for socialism.[16]

Democrats, Party of the Socialists

"What democratic socialists want," *Time* magazine quoted Michael Kazin, a Georgetown University history professor, editor of *Dissent* magazine, and former member of Students for a Democratic Society, as saying in an October 2018 article, "is a large welfare state in a capitalistic society."[17]

What democratic socialists want, *Time* magazine quoted Maurice Isserman, a history professor at Hamilton College and the author of a biography of the founder of the Democratic Socialists of America, *The Other American: The Life of Michael Harrington*, as saying in this same article, "is not a violent overthrow of capitalism, but working within the system through legal and peaceful means [such as] electoral and social movements."[18]

The first quote, from Kazin, could just as easily describe the political goals of the Democratic Party. The second quote, from Isserman, shows how the Democrats, walking a unified path with the democratic socialists, are doing it. And this—this third quote, from Helen Raleigh, an author who came to America after experiencing firsthand the horrors of Communist China—this is what we can expect from this clashing of economies, this melding of welfare state and capitalism:

> Today's DSA leaders not only share the same goals as socialists from the past, but also promise the same kind of socialist paradise that has been often promised but never realized. Neither [Joseph] Stalin, nor Mao [Zedong], nor other socialists ever declared that their goal was to bring starvation, mass murder, and unimaginable misery to their people. In the early days of their revolutions, just like today's democratic socialists, they painted a rosy picture for all: everyone will have adequate food, housing, health care, child care, and education.[19]

It's when the money runs out that things turn sour. It's when the government's ability to rob Peter to pay Paul comes to a grinding halt—because Peter has nothing left to rob—that the rosy picture turns black.

The important takeaway here is this: Today's Democrat is socialist. Today's Democratic Socialist is socialist. Today's progressive is socialist. And all of today's Democrats, Democratic Socialists, progressives—all of today's leftists—will, unchallenged, bring about the utter collapse of America, the total demise of individual rights, the choking communist fists of big government control. Who cares if they do it under the label of socialism or progressivism? It all leads to the same cesspool of despair.

"The academic debates about socialism's 'meaning' are huge and arcane and rife with disagreements, but what all definitions have in common is either the elimination of the market or its strict containment," said Frances Fox Piven, a former DSA board member, in an interview with *Vox*.[20] Well, let the academics have those stupidly distracting discussions. There's a country to save.

Democrats, in their 2016 party platform,[21] pressed to:

- Raise worker incomes and "restore economic security" for the middle class

- Create what they called "good paying jobs"
- Use government resources to "fight for economic fairness" and "against inequality" of all kinds
- Unite Americans of all walks of life, and guarantee opportunities for all
- Protect voting rights, "restore our democracy"
- Fight climate change, "secure environmental justice"
- Provide both high-quality and "affordable education"
- Secure "health and safety" of all

"Democrats believe health care is a right, diversity is a strength, the economy should work for everyone, and facts and truth matter," the party wrote, in its "Where We Stand" section of their website.[22] "Democrats believe that cooperation is better than conflict, unity is better than division, empowerment is better than resentment, and bridges are better than walls," the party wrote, in its platform summary statement.[23]

Well who doesn't? The words are meaningless; they're frill and lace and feel-good wishes, minus any details on fulfillment—which is where the big-government clampdowns occur, of course.

Progressives offer the same meaningless drivel:

- "Everyone deserves a living wage."
- "Money should be taken out of politics."
- "College should be free."
- "Everyone should have healthcare."
- "*All* immigrants should have a chance at citizenship & families should not be broken up."
- "Climate change is a huge threat facing our planet."
- Progressives believe "in equality for women, minorities and the LGBT community; in breaking up big banks; that wealth inequality exists."[24]

How nice. Now who pays? Who controls and ensures all these wish-list items are properly implemented? And by the way—how does the Constitution not already provide for much on this list?

Now for the DSA's democratic socialists, who openly admit their affiliation with progressives, and their overall goal to drive out capitalism from America. "The Democratic Socialists of America (DSA) is the largest socialist organization in the United States," the DSA's website states. "DSA's members are building progressive movements for social change while establishing an openly democratic socialist presence in American communities and politics."[25]

The DSA is not an actual political party, but rather an activist organization with a nonprofit tax tag. Citing the group's growth and growing influence, though, members in 2019 approved the development of formal platform by its national political committee, one to be adopted in 2021 that would strive for the likes of these specifics ideas:[26]

- Medicare for all; a nationalized health care plan
- The Green New Deal
- Universal rent control
- An end to mass incarceration
- Right-to-strike legislation

In more general terms, the DSA, in its own words, seeks to:

- Bring corporations "under greater democratic control," moving toward a time when it's possible to outright "eliminate" them
- Realize a "world without oppression"
- Run "both the economy and society" "democratically," so as to "meet public needs, not to make profits for a few"
- Cause "social and economic decisions" to be made "by those whom they most affect"

- Instill a system of "democratic planning" for "mass transit, housing and energy," while allowing "market mechanisms" to determine the demand for consumer products

What's interesting is the illogic. How a product manufacturer might seriously fill a consumer demand while relying on the bureaucratic, inefficient bloat of government to, say, ship that product on time, as promised, on budget to store shelves so as to enable the producer to still turn a profit is anybody's guess. If the US Postal Service weren't rapidly headed toward irrelevance, for example—sparking headlines like this, "The Shocking Incompetence of the USPS," in an *Oppositelock* op-ed from 2015[27]—there wouldn't be a market demand for FedEx or UPS. Now imagine small businesses everywhere having to rely on big-government types in Washington, DC, to get their products to shelf to sell.

Now imagine businesses across the country being told the trucks can't come, the pilots are on strike, the trains are out-of-order—their orders will have to wait, their buyers will have to be patient. Demand, schemand. All the "market mechanisms" in the world won't matter if, in the end, it's the bureaucrats who command the market. This is the gaping hole of cause-effect rationale that plagues the entire DSA's being, though. It's impossible to have "democratic planning" and "market mechanisms" survive in the same boat forever. One's got to jump ship for the other to survive. Saying otherwise is a lie.

And with socialism, it's always government, government, government is the solution—the free market, profits, the big evil. Banks are bad, businesses are worse, corporations and big businesses the worst of the worst. From the Populist Party, or Peoples' Party, platform out of Omaha, Nebraska, in 1892:

- Populists pushed for "direct democracy," where senators would be voted by the people, rather than by state

legislatures and where electors—the electoral ballot system—
wouldn't be needed.

- Populists pushed for a graduated income tax that would take
  more from the rich to give more to the poor.
- Populists pushed for government ownership and management of all the railroads, the main system of national transit
  at the time, as well as for the telegraph and telephone—and
  that "all land . . . held by railroads and other corporations in
  excess of their actual needs . . . should be reclaimed by the
  government."[28]

Sound familiar? Ending the Electoral College, using the tax
system to redistribute wealth, government ownership of private
industries for greater good of society—even to the point of outright stripping private property rights by regulation or force—are
all Democratic ideals. They're all democratic socialist visions.
They're all progressive principles. They're all leading to the same
communist ends.

From the Communist Party USA, which vows to "put people
before profits," and which bills itself as "of the working class, for
the working class, with no corporate sponsors or billionaire back-
ers,"[29] comes this:

- "Communists support a health care system that is compre-
  hensive and free"—free, of course, meaning tax-paid.
- The "mobilization of workers" is the "best way of protecting
  and promoting working-class interests."
- The "chronic problems working people face today are rooted
  in the birth and history of the capitalistic system itself."
- Capitalism oppresses and exploits minorities, women, youth
  and seniors, immigrants and the LGBTQ communities.
- America is inherently racist: "From its inception, the United
  States was built on racism."

- The "ultra-right ideological" community, in particular, is to blame for the oppression of women by "trying to force them to revert to a submissive role" in the home.[30]

Those could come right off the Democratic Party's website. Those are talking points that could come straight out of the mouths of today's Democrats. In fact, they do, they have, they are.

But it's not as if the communist ties to today's Democrats are that secretive. From the Communist Party's website: "The Communist Party USA is dedicated to the struggle for socialism in this country." And this: "The Communist Party has an unparalleled history in the progressive movement of the United States."[31] From the DSA's website: "[M]any of us have been active in the Democratic Party." And this: "We will continue to support progressives who have a real chance at winning elections, which usually means left-wing Democrats."[32]

What's Democrat is progressive is socialist is communist. Getting caught up on labels, proper definitions and scholarly discussions of what a socialist is versus a democratic socialist, what a progressive is as opposed to a communist, is a time-waster for freedom lovers. It leads to a never-ending argument of Leninism versus Marxism, of Scandinavian economics versus Norway policies, of historical truths of socialism versus modern-day denials of truths—and in the end, it really doesn't matter. In the end, there's America—and there's not America. And that's the only line that needs to be held.

Once again, the standard is the Constitution. Everything else should be held and compared to that standard—precedents and priors be danged.

Once again, the wall to preserve at all costs is God-given. Any political group or party or politically active organization working in the United States that doesn't recognize the existence of God, and the history of America's founding as based on Judeo-Christian principles—and that doesn't work to uphold these ideals, these visions, these core mission statements—ought to be regarded with suspicion, at best, and as an enemy, more likely.

From the Republican Party platform of 2016:

> We believe in American exceptionalism. We believe the United States of America is unlike any other nation on earth. We believe America is exceptional because of our historic role—first as refuge, then as defender, and now as exemplar of liberty for all the world to see. We affirm—as did the Declaration of Independence: that all are created equal, endowed by their Creator with unalienable rights of life, liberty and the pursuit of happiness.[33]

Not saying the Republicans get it right 100 percent of the time. But contrast that with the Democratic Party's 2012 vote to remove "God" from its platform.[34]

Contrast that with the atheism so typical of communist regimes—or the substitution of socialists of political pursuits like environmentalism for God. At least Republicans, as a party, haven't tried to openly rebel against God in America or openly attempt to tear at the fabric of America's system of God-given rights.

Where Republicans have faltered, however, is allowing Democrats to move the scale of political ideologies so that what used to be moderate conservatism is now far right, what used to shock as far left is now liberal mainstream. And knowing better—seeing the evil—while failing to fight can actually be a far worse crime against the Constitution than simply not knowing.

CHAPTER 3

GIVING REPUBLICANS A FREE PASS, JUST BECAUSE THEY'RE REPUBLICANS

I n early 2020, amid a global pandemic called coronavirus, America's economy came to a grinding halt.

President Donald Trump declared a national emergency on March 13, directing Health and Human Services to grant wide latitude in the regulatory requirements for providers and recipients of Medicare, Medicaid, and the State Children's Health Insurance, or CHIP, benefits.[1] Within a week, 48 states declared emergencies of their own, setting the stage for massive shutdowns of schools, businesses, retailers, and even, in some cases, churches and places of worship.[2] Unemployment surged: A record 3.28 million of Americans filed for jobless benefits in the final days of March—a significantly higher number than the 1.5 million claims forecasted by economists.[3] Even more filed in the weeks that followed.

Congress scrambled to put together a legislative package that would ease the financial burdens of the hardest hit and most vulnerable. Members passed Phase One on March 3, giving $8.3 billion to the medical field for testing and supplies, and to small businesses for loans.[4] Phase Two, worth about $100 billion, sailed through March 18, giving tax credits to employers and additional unemployment insurance to states for laid-off and furloughed workers. Then came the third phase, a $2 trillion plus deal—and Democrats stalled the process, in large part because of Speaker Nancy Pelosi's last-minute swoop to pass her own version. Pelosi's bill, spanning 1,400 pages—a real "you have to pass it to know what's in it" Obamacare-like monster of a document—proposed $2.5 trillion of tax dollars for New Green Deal provisions, Planned Parenthood, sanctuary cities, diversity training imposed on private sector businesses, and the Kennedy Center for the Performing Arts in Washington, DC, among other special interest causes.[5] It was a disaster of a political move, described by Republicans as a dizzying last-minute grab at power.

As House Minority Leader Kevin McCarthy put it, Pelosi "performed jiu-jitsu" on the bill that Democrats and Republicans had finally agreed upon, needlessly stoking tensions.[6] Hours later, probably feeling the political winds of coronavirus-induced panic, Pelosi pulled back on the pork-barrel legislation, biding her time to reintroduce it with more effective bite.

Airlines Bailout

Shortly after, Congress reached another agreement for around $2 trillion that Trump signed on March 27. The nation breathed a collective sigh of relief—barely pausing to think of the debt burden. It was a national emergency; no time to think.

The money, courtesy in large part of the Republicans, began to flow. Among the payouts:

- $250 billion in one-time cash payments to 150 million American households to help families afford essentials like food, utilities, gas, and medicines[7]
- $350 billion in loans to small businesses[8]
- A massive infusion of cash to state unemployment insurance coffers—enough so that each filer receives an extra $600 per week, above and beyond what the state pays, for four months[9]

- $500 billion for corporations, including the airline industry, to keep operations running—with the caveat that Treasury Secretary Steve Mnuchin, along with a congressional oversight committee and a newly established inspector general for Pandemic Recovery official, would control and monitor how those funds were allocated[10]

It was that last—the funding for corporations, the funding for airlines and Boeing, Inc.—that had proven one of the biggest sticking points to the bill's passage. As well it should. Taking tax dollars and giving them to private businesses isn't exactly a line item in the Constitution, no matter how great the need.

But once again, national emergency dawned; once again, no time to think. "We clearly need massive action very quickly and urgently," said Alexandre de Juniac, director of the International Air Transport Association, estimating the airlines would lose at minimum $250 billion in 2020 from lost flights due to coronavirus.[11] Clearly. But why would taxpayers be the go-to on that?

Democrats called the multibillion-dollar set-aside for corporations a "slush fund" and an unwarranted "bailout." They also professed outrage at the bill's original establishment of Mnuchin as the sole disburser of monies, calling the setup an egregious faceslap to taxpayers, entirely devoid of accountability.[12] Democrats refused to sign until Republicans agreed to add the Inspector General stipulation to the final version.

Republicans, meanwhile, pointed to the national security need to keep airlines operative, to keep Boeing—one of the airline industry's largest manufacturers, one of the military's largest contractors—in the black.[13] Hurry, they said. Pass the package before the airlines went under, before the industry completely tanked. "Airlines Are No. 1 Priority for Virus Relief, Trump Says," *Bloomberg* wrote in a headline.[14]

Then it was Trump who had an issue with the legislation. He signed the stimulus bill, the Coronavirus Aid, Relief, and

Economic Security (CARES) Act. But he expressed his disapproval with the Democrats' meddling and added a written interpretation of how he planned to carry out the new law. "I do not understand, and my Administration will not treat, this provision as permitting [the inspector general] to issue reports to the Congress without the presidential supervision," Trump wrote, in a signing statement alongside the bill.[15]

Now here's where the red flag of socialism starts to wave. At what point do necessary emergency stimulus dollars and other forms of financial assistance to the hardworking taxpayers and citizens of the country become big cash bailouts to corporations and favored government interests? At what point are we simply talking redistribution of wealth and quasi-nationalization of private business?

Yes, coronavirus was an unpredictable storm. Yes, coronavirus was surprisingly devastating to the economy. Yes, coronavirus proved a shock to the bottom line of many of America's biggest and most necessary businesses—including the airlines. But isn't that what good CEOs do—plan for the unplanned? Provide for the unknown? Prepare for the worst, while hoping for the best?

That's not what the airlines did. That's not how Boeing executives behaved. For years, the airline industry had taken plenty of profits, while giving little in return. So when Democrats raised a bit of a ruckus over these same airline officials crying for bailout money during the coronavirus crisis, truth be told, they had a point. A very good point that was lost amid all the panic-driven talk about the national security needs of keeping airlines and airline manufacturers up and running.

"Airlines are begging for a bailout," *Markets Insider* wrote in mid-March, "but they've used 96% of their cash flow on buybacks over the past 10 years. It highlights an ongoing controversy over how companies have been spending their money."[16] In bullet points, this news story summed up the basics:

- "The Trump administration has proposed $50 billion of emergency aid for airlines ravaged by widespread cancellations amid the coronavirus pandemic.
- "But critics are deriding it as a bailout to an industry that made bad financial decisions.
- "Resistance to the plan emerged among Democrats and even some Republicans. They're concerned that extra money will go straight to share buybacks, as they have in the past.
- "Their pushback is reminiscent of past criticism relating to how companies have spent excess capital."[17]

Yes indeed. For years, the airlines took in big bucks from stock buybacks that drove up prices-per-share—big bucks that certainly enriched the pockets of the industry executives and their investors, but did little to improve services for passengers. Frequent fliers know well the massive chops in seat sizes, cuts in meals services, reductions in legroom, and increases in bag fees the airline industry has imposed in recent years. Even first-class fliers will tell you—service is certainly subpar.

But this is the industry deemed worthy of focus for bailout? What a scam. Or maybe the better word is *sham*, especially when the federal government announced that as a condition of awarding the bailout money, it would be taking a stake in the privately owned airline industry. The scam-slash-sham deepens.

Larry Kudlow, the director of the National Economic Council, explained the process in a March 29 television interview on Fox News with Maria Bartiromo. Here's a pertinent excerpt where they discussed just that—the government's partial takings of the airline industry:

Bartiromo: But Larry, what about the government taking equity stakes in businesses? You are going to be taking equity stakes in the airlines? Secretary Mnuchin . . . told me that now the airlines are being looked at as national security? Is Boeing national security as well? Are you taking equity stakes in more than just the airlines? And that's long term, right? The government is going to be a shareholder? Is the government going to be an activist shareholder, wanting to tell these companies how to run their businesses, Larry?

Kudlow: I don't think we will be activist, but we are laying down some conditions, as I think you know—no stock buybacks, no executive compensation increases, things of that sort. But look . . . [y]ou cannot run a country with a vibrant economy like ours without the airline channels. You have got to have air channel. You have got to have truck channels. . . . [and] I think, in return for direct cash grants, which is what the airlines have asked for, I see no reason why the American taxpayer shouldn't get a piece of the rock. . . . I do feel, in return for the direct cash grants, which is somewhat unusual, we should have a piece of the equity there.[18]

This is all wrong. In America, private entities operate in a private market, where they're free to succeed or fail on their own doings. The government is not a backup bank—because in America, the government is the people. Why would Joe NeverFly want his tax dollars to be used to prop up an airline? Why would tax dollars go to save the airlines and not to save Betty BakesCakes? The only difference is the government has deemed one industry more important than another—but in America, in a free market, that's what the consumer is supposed to deem.

Governments and big businesses that cut deals to take tax dollars from one to give to another aren't working as free market partners. They're behaving more like oligarchies.

And what's most maddening about stripping consumers of their choices and setting the government and big business in charge of picking who's worthy of saving, who's expendable, and who's most needful of bailout is that it hands the socialists and far leftists an easy "in" to complain. It feeds into the leftist narrative that capitalism just doesn't work for the little people.

On the heels of CARES' passage, socialist Representative Alexandria Ocasio-Cortez railed against the stimulus and said: "What did the Senate majority fight for? One of the largest corporate bailouts with as few strings as possible in American history. Shameful."[19] It is shameful—just not in the way Ocasio-Cortez the socialist meant. It's shameful because every time a private business gets a tax-funded bailout, the concept of capitalism becomes a bit watery. The free market goes from free to mostly free to partly free to not so free at all.

Congressional members, presidents, White House staffers, and the like have no business taking tax dollars and distributing them to private businesses. If the private businesses cannot stay afloat, then the executives of those private businesses need to make the hard decisions about where to cut, where to trim, whom to lay off, and if none of that works, where to sell. Harsh? Yes. So is freedom. America is not Venezuela; White House staffers are not Nicolas Maduro bots. If America's airlines are all so important to national security—then perhaps the airlines ought to be nationalized for the common good of the people. And not just the airlines. Kudlow mentioned in his Fox News remarks that the trucking industry, as carrier of the products shipped by airplanes—as one of the "airline channels"—is a national security need, as well.[20] What's next, agriculture? Mining sectors? Clothing manufacturers?

Pandora, meet box. America is either free market, or not. The economy is either capitalist, or not. Consumers are either in control—or not. And if not, then that means government, alongside their special interest partners, like big business, will seize the control board and determine the winners, as well as the losers. Those seen as "too big to fail," or crucial to national security—those seen as providers of the greatest amount of good for the greatest number of people—will rise to the top of the winners' list.

This is Republican-driven socialism. Think about it. That we've been down this road before shows it's a trend, not an anomaly. Businesses that are supposedly "too big to fail" have been successfully dipping into taxpayer pockets for years.

Republican Socialism

In 2008, it was George W. Bush and the Emergency Economic Stabilization Act, bailing out the banks—the same banks that had fallen on tough times by doling out loans so unqualified buyers could purchase overvalued homes.[21] That was followed by the Troubled Asset Relief Program, passed by Bush but carried to full effect by Barack Obama.[22] Cha-ching, $700 billion here, $350 billion there. And what did that get the taxpayers?

Here's a taste of what ensued, courtesy Pro Publica, which did a marvelous job tracking the bailout expenditures, from beginning to payback end:

> On June 1, 2009, GM filed for Chapter 11 bankruptcy protection. As part of the restructuring, the U.S. government agreed to provide the company up to $30.1 billion more. In exchange, the U.S. received a 60.8 percent stake in the company when it emerged from bankruptcy protection about a month later. The remainder of GM's equity state was divided between the Canada and Ontario governments (11.7 percent), the UAW retiree trust (17.5 percent), and the bondholders and other creditors (10 percent). On Nov. 16, 2010, General Motors began to see its shares on the stock exchange. This investment resulted in a loss to taxpayers.[23]

Want more?

- There was the Housing and Economic Recovery Act of 2008 that distributed $191.5 billion of tax dollars to save homes from foreclosure. "On Sep. 7, 2008, Fannie [Mae] and Freddie [Mac] were essentially nationalized: placed under the conservatorship of the Federal Housing Finance Agency," Pro Publica wrote.[24]

- There was the combined $182 billion Treasury and Federal Reserve bailout of American International Group, AIG, insurers that gave the government the authority to fire the CEO and replace the company's board of directors and senior management. This bailout ultimately led to a court showdown over the Federal Reserve Bank of New York's attempt to take a 79.9 percent stake in AIG. Ultimately, FRBNY lost. U.S. Court of Federal Claims ruled the Federal Reserve had no lawful right to "acquire equity in AIG, and that the FRBNY's doing so effected an illegal exaction," *Harvard Law Review* reported.[25]
- There was the Targeted Investment Program under TARP that gave more than $25 billion to Citigroup and Bank of America, and then another $20 billion to Citigroup, and then some billions more to Bank of America.[26] Treasury eventually recovered these monies "through repayments, dividends, interest, and other income" that Treasury estimated would help "provide a lifetime positive return of approximately $20 billion to taxpayers."[27]

That last feeds into the argument of bailout supporters who would say doling out taxpayer dollars to save certain big businesses from going bankrupt and folding is actually good for taxpayers—that in the end, taxpayers gain. But making that argument is to miss the larger point. What right does government, in a free market, in America, have to save private businesses using tax dollars? What right does government have to choose which businesses are worthy of saving?

And here's a question the bailout supporters have yet to answer: What do taxpayers actually gain? Even when the bailed-out businesses pay back more than what they borrowed, it's not like Jane Q. Taxpayer gets a check in the mail. All excess monies post to the Treasury's account, or to the Federal Reserve's coffers. The very sources of the bailout dollars, the citizens, don't see any real returns on their investments—unless the fact the bailed-out business still exists counts as a return on investment for the citizens.

This whole "too big to fail" argument that's been floated alongside America's political wings for some time now has to stop. If Democrats do a good job of selling socialism on wings of entitlement, then Republicans, sadly, do nearly as good a job at pressing forth some socialist policies of their own on the wings of big business and national security. Just because Republicans don't intend to do that doesn't excuse the behavior. Conservatives are supposed to be the ones who watch out for the taxpayer, after all, and make sure the leftists in the room, the ones who would grow government until government can't grow any more, don't steamroll over small business owners, independent American families, and middle-class wage earners.

Remember the budget battles of yesteryear, when Republicans only all too docilely caved and crumbled to Barack Obama's debt ceiling will? "Has John Boehner surrendered on debt ceiling?" queried one *Christian Science Monitor* headline in October of 2013.[28] Why yes, America, yes he has. Not just once, either. Moreover, all while holding a Republican majority in the House. "Boehner offers debt ceiling increase in cliff compromise," the *Washington Post* reported in December 2012.[29] "GOP caves on debt ceiling fight—for now," MSNBC reported in January, 2013.[30] "House passes debt-ceiling increase with no add-ons," the Associated Press reported in February, 2014.[31] "Boehner considers raising debt ceiling without a fight," the *Los Angeles Times* wrote in October of 2015.[32]

Not to single Boehner out—but his political leadership on the debt ceiling issue was a major point of contention for limited-government conservatives around the nation. After all, debt, as noted money-man Dave Ramsey puts it, isn't just "dumb."[33] It's also slavery. That holds true whether the debt takes the form of household or national. Moreover, there's a good case that can be made that taking on more debt at a time of high indebtedness is immoral because it tricks debtors into believing everything is A-OK; everything will be A-OK—even as it leads down a path of slavery. Regardless, foisting more debt on a nation via secret meetings with powerful elites is always immoral.

Politico, in a 2013 story penned at a time Boehner was seeking reelection as speaker of the House, aptly captured the mood of many on the ideological right with this headline: "Conservatives rebel against Boehner."[34] Some excerpts that strike particularly hard at truths that were being murmured among conservative voters around the nation:

- "A small, but extraordinarily vocal group of conservatives sent Boehner a message: We don't trust you."
- "[Boehner] is now somewhat weakened leading into key showdowns with President Barack Obama over the debt ceiling . . . The debt ceiling in particular has become a rallying cry for conservatives as they seek to avenge themselves for the tax hikes imposed as a result of the fiscal cliff deal."
- "Even those who supported Boehner complain about how the leader operates, and the freedom he will have to negotiate with Obama and Democrats is likely to be severely restrained. . . . Boehner senses the tension—and is looking to find ways to ease it. He told House Republicans he's done negotiating behind closed doors with Obama."[35]

That last bullet point cuts to the core of dissatisfaction with Boehner—that he used his position of leadership to strike deals with the Democrats, with the president, without the advice and consent and majority approval of his fellow congressional party members. à la ruler, à la "I am zee law" style. In so doing, he slapped the faces of not just House Republicans, the ones who were supposed to be in the ditches doing the political fighting with him, but also, more horribly, more arrogantly, more egregiously, those of the voters.

What's more, he did it on an issue that, unlike any other, ushers in a big, bigger, growing even bigger government that can then use its power of the purse to control the people.

This is not the American way. Massive debt and high taxation aren't just markers of socialist governments. They're core characteristics of immoral governments. That Boehner helped bring this atrocity to life via closed-door dealings with Democrats only adds to the immorality of the situation.

Yet Boehner's hardly alone in breaking from basic conservative principles to cooperate with the left. Plenty more Republicans have strayed from the supposed Republican principles they told voters they supported. Plenty of other Republicans have failed to deliver, or even in some cases, staunchly defend, the very limited government values they said they represented and held dear. Plenty of Republicans have campaigned on one issue—and openly, insolently voted the exact opposite.

- "Obamacare Repeal Fails: Three GOP Senators Rebel in 49–51 Vote," ran one NBC News headline on July 28, 2017.[36]
- "Republicans Learn the Limits of Reconciliation with failed ACA repeal," ran another headline from the liberal-leaning Brookings Institute, reporting also in July of 2017 about the unsuccessful repeal of the Affordable Care Act, or Obamacare, in the Republican-controlled Congress.[37]
- "Why [John] McCain Screwed the GOP on Obamacare repeal—again," Politico reported, in September of 2017.[38]
- "[John] McCain Hated Obamacare. He also saved it," NBC News reported in August of 2018.[39]

Whatever the politics on Capitol Hill, whatever the justifications and causes and rationales and media sound bites, the optics of repeated GOP legislative failures on long-promised campaign hot buttons is often this: Republicans, party of the cavers. And when Republicans cave to Democrats, these days, given the far-leftist leanings of the Democratic Party, what they're really caving to is socialism.

Think about it. For about a decade, beginning with the 112th Congress, the House was dominated by Republicans.

- Between 2009 and 2011, in the 111th Congress, the House was run by Democrats, with 257 members versus 178 Republicans.
- The next election brought a massive upset, and between 2011 and 2013, in the 112th Congress, the membership makeup in the House was 193 Democrats, 242 Republicans.
- Republicans maintained the majority, and in the 113th Congress, between the years of 2013 and 2015, the House was divided into 201 Democrats and 234 Republicans.
- In the 114th Congress, between 2015 and 2017, it was more of the same: 188 Democrats, 247 Republicans.
- In the 115th Congress, between 2017 and 2019, Republicans again dominated. Democrats filled 194 seats; Republicans, 241.
- The Democrats took back the House in the 116th Congress, 2019-2021, with a 235-seat majority versus the Republicans' 199.[40]

On the Senate side, Republicans didn't have as long control as in the House—but they had some.

In the 114th Congress, Republicans controlled with 54 seats to the Democrats' 44; again in the 115th, with 51 seats to Democrats' 47; and yet once more in the 116th Congress, running 2019-2021, with 53 seats to Democrats' 45. In fairness, in all three Congresses, Democrats saw two extra votes from Independents. But Republicans still ruled the Senate roost.[41]

Trump Versus the Republicans

Meanwhile, on January 20, 2017, Trump took his oath of office to become the 45th president of the United States. Boom, boom,

boom. The Republican sweep was complete. Republicans held all the power positions. It was hammer time, for all the leftist, unconstitutional, socialist policies put in place by the Obama administration. Right?

Wrong. Where were all those ambitious political reforms? Republicans, so it seemed, dropped the ball. Republicans in the Senate complained and explained about the 60-vote threshold, they spoke of the filibuster, they went on national television and gave interviews to the national press to educate the people on why, even with a majority, they couldn't pass certain long-promised pieces of legislation. They even used the 60-vote threshold message to do a little sly campaigning, telling voters that if they only had more members in the Senate—say, 60—they could get these long-promised legislative goals to pass.

But conservatives, post-Obama, weren't really in the mood for the lesson. Conservatives wanted action, and they wanted it straightaway.

It may not be a fair shaming of the Senate, circa 2017, but this Trump tweet over his frustration with Obamacare repeal captures much of the conservative angst of the time: "The Senate must go to a 51 vote majority instead of current 60 votes. Even parts of full Repeal need 60. 8 Dems control Senate. Crazy!"[42]

Moreover, this excerpt from a *Los Angeles Times* story from December 2017 gives clues into why the Senate behaved as it did.

> [Senate Majority Leader Mitch] McConnell is known as an institutionalist, less a devotee of a defined agenda than to the traditions of the Senate, which he's aspired to lead ever since winning his first election in Kentucky more than 30 years ago.[43]

That speaks volumes. So did the fact that Republicans, when they held the clean sweep majority, didn't spend their time so much pushing full steam ahead with a limited-government legislative agenda—60-vote threshold be danged—as they did bucking Trump.

One of the most frustrating outcomes of Trump's successful campaign and ultimate win of the White House was the response of inner-circle, elitist Republicans.

- "GOP Senator Jeff Flake attacks 'reckless, outrageous and undignified' Trump," ran one headline from the *Guardian* in October 2017.[44]
- "Republican Senator John McCain said . . . Trump's administration was in 'disarray' and that NATO's founders would be alarmed by the growing unwillingness to 'separate truth from lies,'" the *Irish Times* wrote, reporting on the Arizona senator's speech to a Munich crowd in February 2017.[45]
- "Donald Trump is a threat to liberty in America," wrote Representative Justin Amash in August 2019, weeks after announcing he was leaving the GOP because of Trump. "He has grown government, centralized power and undermined rights. He appears increasingly unstable. In 2020, we must elect someone who will restore respect for our Constitution and each other."[46]

Even the liberal-leaning *New York Times* acknowledged the long-running vitriol Trump faced from his own party. "No One Attacked Trump More in 2016 Than Republicans," the *New York Times* wrote in a headline from August 2019, "It Didn't Work."[47]

It's one thing for Democrats to attack a Republican; it's expected. But Republicans attacking Republicans is simply a favor to Democrats. Democrats, as socialist as they are, don't need any extra boosts to their abilities to pass their agenda.

Trump, meanwhile, shouldn't have had to fight so hard to pass agendas that were clearly in line with small-government principles. Republicans should have rallied; instead, they engaged in petty infighting.

"President Trump said during the campaign that he would like to abolish the EPA or 'leave a little bit.' It is a goal he has and sometimes it takes a long time to achieve goals," said Myron Ebell, a climate scientist tied to the free-market Competitive Enterprise Institute who headed up Trump's EPA transition team, in an interview with the *Guardian* in February 2017.[48]

Abolishing the EPA—it was a conservative's dream come true, particularly given the previous Obama White House's penchant for using the environment to justify about any and all regulatory design that would come to mind. Want to force taxpayers to pay for new homes for the lower-income earners? Welcome to the US Department of Housing and Urban Development's Environmental Justice Strategy 2016–2020, tying subpar housing to carbon monoxide, lead, and mold—and making the case that individuals who suffer from these environments do so only because they've been unjustly treated by society.[49] Want to make taxpayers subsidize the construction of entire new communities where cramped living is the norm? Welcome to Smart Growth policies, "sustainable communities," and a new definition of "livability" for families that "means being able to take your kids to school, go to work, see a doctor, drop by the grocery or post office, go out to dinner and a movie, and play with your kids at the park, all without having to get into your car," said Ray LaHood, secretary of the US Department of Transportation from 2009–2013.[50] Truly, the EPA, under Obama, had been a tool of oppression—a means of inflicting top-heavy socialist-style controls on citizens and businesses alike.

Trump's campaign promise to rein in the Green zealotry from the fed, even going so far as to disband the agency responsible for the federal Green zealotry, was a welcome breath of fresh air. But it wasn't to be. Not all Republicans were on board, even though the idea of booting the EPA, along with the Department of Education, the Department of Commerce, and other big bureaucratic agencies—big bureaucratic socialist agencies, seen as brashly unconstitutional violations of the Tenth Amendment—had been talked-up GOP party wish-list items for years. Circa 2017, with the finish line in sight, with the Republicans in positions of power in the House,

Senate, and White House, the station suddenly switched. The tune changed. The Republicans sang a different song.

"I'm not one who says, 'Get rid of the EPA, abolish the EPA," said Virginia Republican Scott Taylor, who served in the House between 2017 and 2019. "I believe you have to have someone who is administering reasonable, responsible regulations to protect our environment."[51] It's an interesting view. By all appearances, Taylor was a conservative who served his country well in the military and as a Navy SEAL, and who also represented the 85th district of Virginia in the General Assembly for a time—though in his federal role on Capitol Hill, he did only eke out a somewhat dismal 52 percent rating in 2018 from Freedom Works on that group's legislative scorecard. His lifetime score on conservative votes, meanwhile, wasn't much better, at 59 percent.[52] But "R" button aside, his remarks completely bolster the Democratic agenda—and represent well the shifting face of too many in the Republican Party.

They're also a bit misleading. To suggest conservatives don't care about the environment is a leftist talking point. To suggest that only a big bloated federal EPA can take care of the environment is a socialist talking point.

The proper limited-government view of environmentalism, the one Republicans used to widely espouse, was that the key to preservation is private property rights, and that rightful, constitutional order of managing and overseeing natural resources should start with the private sector—meaning, individuals and businesses—followed by the local governments, followed by the states. On most matters of environmentalism, the federal government need not apply. So it used to be among the GOP.

But Republicans, as with so many other issues in recent years, have strayed into Democratic territory on environmentalism. The idea of private property owners taking care of natural resources better than the federal government has become radicalized. The notion of local and state governments overseeing environmental issues, rather than the fed, has become unthinkable. The shift in thinking has come by way of pressures from power-hungry leftists and nutty environmentalists who want to control the country—but Republicans, through timidity or concern about their political careers, have actually helped the movement spread. Worse, some have actually sown this socialist agenda with one hand, while playing good little conservative with the other.

> Judith Enck, an Obama appointee who served as the regional administration for the EPA's Region 2, which includes New York and New Jersey, recalled a conversation with a Republican congressman who told her how much he appreciated a program that removed PCBs from schools in his district, but vowed to "continue to blast the agency publicly." When she asked why, he shrugged and said, "That's in the talking points."[53]

It's an uncomfortable truth to accept that Republicans are oftentimes just as adept playing the political game as Democrats. After all, Republicans are supposed to be the good guys.

That the EPA was established in 1970 by President Richard Nixon, a Republican, only shows how far back the infiltration of leftist-styled politics into the conservative ranks goes.[54] This meshing of Republicans with Democrats, this softening of conservatism and morphing of the nation toward socialism, cannot go on indefinitely in the shadows. At some point, America's going to have to choose: socialism or democratic republic. God forbid it's the first. But if it's the second, then it's time to take a stand and fight—beginning with acknowledgment of how Republicans, the supposed defenders of limited government, have betrayed those principles.

US Chamber of Commerce

The US Chamber of Commerce spent $56.5 million on lobbying in 2019, making it one of the biggest political influencers on Capitol Hill.[55] The group also spent millions of dollars in recent elections for Republican candidates and for Republican causes—a total of $10.9 million in 2018, for instance, exactly zero of which went Democrats' way.[56] In addition, the Chamber's PAC, through the years, has given hundreds of thousands of dollars directly to Republican candidates.

- In the 2012 election cycle, the Chamber's PAC donated $222,500 to federal candidates, 89 percent of whom were Republican.
- In the 2014 cycle, it was a total of $227,425 from the PAC to federal candidates, fully 99 percent of whom were Republican.
- In the 2016 cycle, it was $209,500 total, with 96 percent going to Republicans.
- In the 2018 cycle, the PAC distributed $340,998 to federal candidates, 80 percent of which went to Republicans.
- In preliminary 2020 cycle reporting, it's more of the same: Of the $89,500 that was donated to federal candidates by January, 74 percent had gone the GOP's way.[57]

With all that, this is what the Chamber tries to buy: Open borders. Illegal immigration. Trade deals that favor corporations—even those in foreign markets—over individual American workers. "They ship their jobs, they ship their plants, and they keep their profits overseas," railed Fox Business Network commentator Lou Dobbs at the US Chamber of Commerce, in one 2016 segment.[58]

Meanwhile, on Trump and his "America First" agenda that promised, among other things, tighter borders and better trade deals, the Chamber, during campaign season and after elections, waxed critical, while warning of great gloom and doom.

In January 2016, the Chamber's president, Thomas Donohue, subtly, without naming names, ripped Trump's rhetoric on border control and business as one of the "loud voices who talk about walling off America from talent, from trade," a voice he went on to describe as "morally wrong and politically stupid."[59] A couple of months later, Donohue told Bloomberg that Trump "has very little idea about what trade really is."[60] A few months after that, the Chamber of Commerce sent out a barrage of Twitter messages criticizing, both directly and indirectly, Trump—in one, outright predicting that under his White House leadership, America would "see higher prices, fewer jobs and a weaker economy."[61]

My, how ridiculous that tweet showed to be. In October of 2019, the nation's unemployment rate, at 3.5 percent, dropped to the lowest level in almost 50 years.[62] On borders, meanwhile, the Chamber has proven itself the enemy of the Constitution—the ally of oligarchy. "The United States is fundamentally out of people," Donohue said in 2018, at a speech at Chamber headquarters in Washington, DC, against which sat this political backdrop: Trump announced the deployment of 5,200 U.S. troops to the border to curtail illegal intrusions from Mexico.[63] Donohue continued: "Immigrants have long been a vital part of our economy, and they can help fill those gaps now. . . . Our nation must continue to attract and welcome the world's most industrious and innovative people and finally fix our broken immigration system."[64]

In Trump's eyes, one huge way to that fix was building a border wall and clamping illegal border crossings. So, too, the frustrated millions who trekked to the polls with the headlines of sanctuary cities, killed citizens, and grieving fathers and mothers in their heads, had decided while voting for Trump: no more.

To the Chamber, though, tight border controls were something to fear because of the negative impact it could bring to businesses' bottom lines. "We oppose," said Neil Bradley, executive vice president and chief policy officer for the US Chamber of Commerce, in a statement issued on April 1, 2019, on the heels of a White House–announced crackdown at the border, "closing the border."[65] Three days later, when the White House softened its stance on the border and gave Mexico a year to clean up its drug-running incursions into the United States,[66] Bradley again released a statement on behalf of the Chamber. "We welcome the president's decision not to close the Mexican border," it simply said.[67]

Well, open borders might be good news for the Chamber and its alliances. After all, cheap labor from newcomers whose idea of decent pay is a few dollars a week certainly helps American businesses with their balance sheets. But company interests should not come before border security. Corporate interests should not be calling this country's shots. America is free in part because America is sovereign. And since a free America benefits business as much as it does the citizens, the Chamber ought to respect the call for tighter borders—even if it does mean fewer cheap laborers in the market to hire.

Instead, the Chamber of Commerce, with all its resistance to tight border controls, with all its opposition to trade fights that benefit or even equalize America's economic playing field, with all its lobbying of Congress for agendas that sometimes favor the global interests at US expense—the Chamber is a group that's done more Democratic bidding than Republican. Its immigration advocacy has outright helped the socialist agenda. Its sizable amount of money in politics has helped moved the politics of the country farther left.

The fact that nearly all the Chamber's financial gifts go to Republicans should be a clanging warning of one of two things: Either Republican recipients are on board with the Chamber's open-border, Democratic Party leanings, or the Chamber is actively seeking to expand its open-border, Democratic Party leanings by reaching out to moderate Republicans with money. Lots of money. Lots of influence peddling and vote-buying money.

Both scenarios, in a country like America where maintaining borders is key to maintaining freedom, are discomforting. Both scenarios lead to bigger government. The only difference is the speed by which that path to bigger government is traversed. Put it this way: It's hard enough to get today's batch of politicians to abide by the Constitution. Opening borders to those of nations that are already socialist will make that job of limiting government all the harder. And opening borders in the name of business profits is as short-range selfish as it is destructive and immoral.

Companies may gain. The economy may soar, for a while. But ultimately, it won't be just our government that crumbles. It'll be the free market, as well. "Freedom," said Supreme Court Associate Justice Antonin Scalia, speaking at his son's high school graduating class of 1988, "is a luxury that can be afforded only by the good society. When civic virtue diminishes, freedom will inevitably diminish as well."[68]

If Americans can't trust Republicans to stay true and keep the country free of socialism, who can they trust? Conservatives want cooperation, not capitulation. But more than cooperation, conservatives want the Constitution. And preserving the limited-government aspects of the Constitution requires leaders of strong and courageous moral characters to serve in both business and politics.

When greed usurps principles, and money, not the Constitution, becomes the engine that drives politics, the uneasy oligarchic outcomes hand progressive-slash-socialists like Senator Elizabeth Warren an easy opportunity to run for president on a platform of condemning big business. They give democratic socialists like Senator Bernie Sanders the golden ticket to decry the corrupt free market. They provide socialists like Ocasio-Cortez the fodder for pointing at all the failures of the corporate world.

The younger generations—the ones trained in the socialist way in public schools, taught to speak the language of entitlement, brainwashed in the messages of social justice—these youth pay attention and listen. Then they join in the voices from the far left and blame capitalism, the Constitution, and the country's very founding ideals for all that ails. Fact is, when it comes to corrupting even Republicans, the socialists are seeing wins.

CHAPTER 4

BELIEVING PUBLIC SCHOOLS ARE GOOD FOR CHILDREN

Wisconsin, year 2011, was in turmoil. Republican governor Scott Walker and Republicans in the legislature, facing what was estimated as a two-year $3.6 billion budget shortfall, proposed a bill that would cut public employees' benefits—including those for teachers and local governments—as well curb some collective bargaining rights and the accompanying means of paying for that service, the compulsory members' dues.[1]

Unions fast-forwarded into frenzy. "We're at a point of crisis," Walker said, explaining the financial tightening was necessary to save 6,000 or so jobs.[2] The unions didn't care. Tens of thousands of union-represented public employees rallied in the streets of Madison, while thousands more stormed the state capitol, noisily took up spots, and refused to leave. "The Statehouse filled with as many as 10,000 demonstrators who chanted, sang the national anthem and beat drums for hours," one Associated Press story read. "The noise level in the Rotunda rose to the level of a chainsaw, and many Madison teachers joined the protest by calling in sick in such numbers that the district had to cancel classes."[3] Actually, about 40 percent of teachers in the area called in sick, leaving students—leaving the children, the very ones the liberals always say they seek to protect—along with their working parents, in limbo.[4]

It's not as if the proposed cuts were outrageous. Indeed; public workers were only being asked to pay more into their pensions and at least 12.6 percent of their health care plans.[5] Given that private-sector employees rarely even have pensions these days—between 1975 and the mid-2000s, the number of workers with pensions in the private force dropped from 88 percent to 33 percent[6]— and given that private-sector employees also regularly pay for 50 percent or so of their work-based health care plans, Wisconsin's Republicans weren't asking a lot of their tax-paid force.

It was simply time to pay the piper for years of irresponsible fiscal living, two of which—2009 and 2010—came with Democrats in complete charge in the House, Senate, and governor's mansion.[7] Walker and the Republicans hadn't created the mess. They were trying to clean it up.

Besides, it's not as if teachers in Wisconsin were exactly poverty stricken. In the 2009–2010 fiscal year, public school teachers in the state earned on average $49,816 for a salary, and another $25,325 in benefits.[8] At $75,141, that's not too shabby, especially in a state that falls consistently on the lower end of national cost-of-living comparisons in the areas of housing, transportation, and groceries.[9]

Again: the unions didn't care. To union leadership, it wasn't just the extra pension and health costs that irked. It was the reality of losing their unfettered rights to bargain—meaning, their unfettered powers to hog-tie politicians and taxpayers and bend them to their financial will—that most galled. Collective bargaining, contrary to what the name suggests, is actually about as far from the table of equitable bargaining as can be. More truthfully, collective bargaining is the unions' way of forcing employers to make concessions—or else. It's not so much bargaining as it is extortion. And in a country like America, where markets are supposedly free and where citizens in the workforce can pick and choose and come and go as they please, the system of collective bargaining, like affirmative action, should have been killed long ago.

Well, Wisconsin's 175,000 or so public-sector employees, circa 2011, obviously disagreed.[10] Teachers and their union representatives banded together with other public-sector employees in disgusting shows of mob-style protests on the floors of the capitol, at the offices of the governor, outside the state buildings, and elsewhere—where they waved signs, demanded Walker's recall, chanted slogans, blocked doorways, and generally disrupted business.[11] Taxpayer-funded business, to be exact. They slept on the floors of the capitol building, despite laws prohibiting such action. Police were called to the scene to control crowds and, when and where possible, quiet outbursts.[12]

Meanwhile, Democratic representatives made themselves scarce. More than two dozen Democratic Assembly members, friends of the union all, simply skipped town and took up lodging in hotels just outside the state's borders.[13] Why? To deny the Republicans the necessary quorum to vote on the budget bill. Cowards. Crybabies. To Democrats, money is magic.

"I'm just trying to balance my budget," Walker said, in an interview with the *New York Times*. "To those who say why didn't I negotiate on this? I don't have anything to negotiate with. We don't have anything to give."[14] Teachers, apparently, didn't want to hear that reality. Neither did the fleeing Democrats.

Still, sanity prevailed. The Republican adults in the room stayed tough and steered straight. On March 10, after weeks of contentious hearings, the state Assembly passed the budget bill, 53–42, with all its curbs on costs, with all its curtailment of union powers.[15] A day later, Walker signed Wisconsin Act 10 into law.[16]

It was a big win for Republicans, one that reverberated across the nation. Truthfully, it was also a big win for taxpayers, who had been forced to provide funds so politicians could live above budget means for years. Yet all the Democrats saw was red. To this day, leftists, not just in Wisconsin but elsewhere, continue to fight for union control of the public education system.

Teacher Strikes

Welcome to America's schools. Welcome to the madness of today's public schools. The system is not so much about teaching our children to read, write, and compute as it is now a battleground for money, power, control, leftist indoctrination, and yes, outright socialist infiltration.

And if you think this is hyperbole, think again. On February 22, 2018, teachers in West Virginia kicked off a massive strike that impacted an estimated 277,000 students.[17] The strike was called because union leaders said Republican governor Jim Justice's budgeted 4 percent raises for teachers over three years didn't go far enough.[18]

So thousands of teachers across the state's 55 counties simply walked out of class and headed to the state capitol to protest in the streets and at the political offices of Charleston, leaving hundreds of schools emptied and closed in the process. The buildings stayed that way until March 7, when teachers ultimately won 5 percent raises and returned to their classrooms.[19] Actually, the unions won their 5 percent pay-raise concessions from the governor just a few days into the strike, on February 27, and he signed the deal a few days after that, on Tuesday, March 6. But teachers didn't want to return right away to school.[20] "Schools are called off on Wednesday [March 7] for a cooling off period and will resume on Thursday [March 8]," the West Virginia Education Association posted on its Facebook page.[21]

How nice for them. But for the taxpayers and parents who either had to take off work to stay with their children or pay higher day-care costs to occupy them during normal school hours? Cha-ching. What a face slap. After more than a week of striking, teachers were in essence treated to a paid emotional holiday.

That's not even the worst of it. Much as the left-leaners in the media would have it believed, this whole multiday walkout was not a groundswell moment of concerned teachers decrying a truly desperate situation. Yes, striking teachers were indeed paid below the national average. But the convenient failure of omission was this: West Virginia's cost-of-living, in comparison to other states, was and is below average, too.

Teachers making the average $45,642 in West Virginia may have wanted to be paid the average $84,227 of a New York educator, according to 2017–2018 National Education Association figures.[22] But that wouldn't really be fair to New Yorkers—or to taxpayers in West Virginia. In one estimate, West Virginia's cost of living was figured nearly 22 percentage points below the national average, with a median home cost of $96,400 compared to the $231,200 for the United States.[23] In another, from the West Virginia Department of Commerce, the state's cost of living was rated 5.6 percent lower than the average for the country.[24] Yet one more claimed the cost of living for West Virginia was 12 percent lower than the national average.[25] The discrepancies are due to different factors used to figure the lists, as well as the different times of figuring. But the conclusion's the same.

"Local experts: Despite rising costs of living, W.Va. remains among one of most affordable states to live," WVNews.com reported in August 2018.[26] So why should teachers in West Virginia expect or demand to make salaries that would put them on par with educators living in more expensive states? The answer is they shouldn't. But just as in Wisconsin, teachers in West Virginia didn't care about the financial facts. They wanted their money, and they wanted it now.

So they abandoned their classrooms, took to the streets—and this is the real hair-raiser: Their protests weren't just carefully orchestrated and strategically planned. They were completely socialist-driven. They were specifically crafted by socialists working within the school system. They were specifically designed by socialists who purposely tried to put those evil corporations in the crosshairs so as to gain the most public support for their protest buck.

From the website of the Democratic Socialists of America—an excerpt of a post "penned by DSA teachers of West Virginia," explaining the genesis of the strike movement in that state:

> A few DSA members that were teachers in West Virginia public schools began having conversations about new austerity measures facing public employees. Our wages had been stagnant for years—unlike our healthcare costs, which were climbing. We formed a reading group, held brainstorming sessions, and quickly agreed that winning our demands would require militant action.[27]

Militant action? Teachers as DSA members? This is not the rhetoric of kindly elementary-level instructors. These are not the people to be trusted with American children. DSA wrote:

> Our immediate win in West Virginia was a 5% raise for all public sector workers. . . . But crucially, our movement's demand was that the money come from highly profitable corporations that have long exploited West Virginia's natural wealth. . . . [Socialist teachers called to] raises taxes on the corporations and extractive fossil fuel industries that exploit our people. Workers began showing up to the Capitol holding signs like "Tax our gas!" and "MAKE A CHOICE: Tax cuts for big business or healthcare for WV workers." The revenue battle is ongoing, but our popular campaign against corporate interests will make it harder for the ruling class to drive a wedge between public employees and other working class West Virginians.[28]

Big business bad, big corporations bad-der, sacrificial teachers always looking out for the children—good. Right? It's a lie. Be not deceived. Socialists will use distraction and deception to create the kind of chaos that wins them influence, power, and control.

Look at this admission, also on the DSA website, in the section describing why socialists should consider entering the field of education:

> [D]espite attacks on schools and teachers unions in the recent past, teaching is still one of the most stable professions in the United States. In most states teaching pays a living wage with benefits, including health insurance. *Even in West Virginia, where teachers experienced some of the lowest pay in the nation, they were sometimes the highest-paid workers in their communities.*[29] (Italic added.)

That's a heck of an admission, given the troubles the strikers generated.

Yet this is what socialists do: They foster a narrative of victimhood at the hands of anyone with money, and they do it to lay the groundwork for the government to come in and strip those with money of their money, and redistribute it elsewhere. That's the narrative of Senator Elizabeth Warren from the 2020 presidential campaign trail. That's the narrative of Representative Alexandria Ocasio-Cortez, near-daily in the House.

And apparently, that's the narrative coming from public school teachers in a state, West Virginia, that voted the Republican for president between 2000 and 2016[30] and that polled, in 2017, overwhelmingly in support of President Donald Trump.[31] In fact, as Gallup reported, "at the state level," support for Trump throughout the United States in 2017 "ranged from a high of 61% in West Virginia, to a low of 26% in Vermont."[32]

But socialists don't sleep. They're coming for your children. They're not stopping until they achieve their goals—the complete takeover of America's public schools. Their own words give testimony to that fact.

From the DSA website, once again:

> The West Virginia strike didn't happen by chance. It was the result of creative shop floor organizing by teachers with socialist politics. These teachers introduced a fundamentally different vision of their state than what was on offer from either elected officials or union leaders. And they were able to do this because they had organic connections to their co-workers. Rather than shouting socialist messaging at workers from afar, these teachers were able to alter the direction of the movement from within. If DSA members become active in workplace organizing for the long term, we can wage fights similar to West Virginia . . . [S]ocialists should take jobs as teachers (and other school-based workers) for the political, economic, and social potential the industry holds.[33]

If this is horrifying—it should be. These are America's schools we're talking about, after all.

Education is a key target for socialists because (1) it's a system that's already highly unionized—meaning, the masses are easier to shepherd; (2) education isn't going anywhere—meaning, it's not a business that will just pick up and move to an area less friendly to unions; (3) the system is ingrained in communities nationwide— meaning, students and families regularly interact with teachers, and compassion-for-cause is therefore more easily gained; and (4) teaching is a relatively stable job—meaning, the socialists within the system will be better able to root their messages and spread their influence, because the workforce won't be in constant turnover. Their ultimate end game is not better education for the children. Their ultimate end game is agitation, with the purpose of gaining greater, ever greater power. The schools—your children—are just tools to achieve this goal. In the words of DSA:

> The rank-and-file strategy is not only concerned with recruiting our co-workers to socialist organizations. . . . The aim of the

rank-and-file strategy is to build organizations of working class people that challenge the power of capital. Organizers on the shop floor [the schools, for instance] with a socialist political vision can help build struggles that draw in large numbers of workers and raise the class consciousness of many. It is out of these struggles that new socialists will arise.[34]

They're taking the lessons learned from their failures of Wisconsin and their successes of West Virginia, and applying them to their plans for the future. They're learning from their "mistakes" how to better implement socialism in the schools.

The strike in West Virginia didn't end in West Virginia. Shortly after that campaign was settled, teachers in Oklahoma, in Arizona, and other parts of the nation kicked off their own protests for pay— and, taking a memo from the West Virginian strikers' playbook, they pointed to the higher teacher salaries in other states as cause for their calls, while outright ignoring cost-of-living comparisons. In 2019, it was more of the same. Teachers in Los Angeles went on strike in January 2019; weeks later, teachers in Denver walked out of classes; shortly after that, teachers in Oakland, California, organized to follow suit.[35] In February 2019, meanwhile, teachers in West Virginia, for the second time in about a year, simply walked off their jobs and closed schools.[36] This time, their protests weren't for pay, but rather against the Republican-led legislative effort to privatize education.[37] Privatizing education, obviously, strips the unions, strips the socialists, of their primary source of bargaining: the children.

"Kill that bill," chanted thousands of striking teachers who crowded the state capitol in opposition to legislation that would've opened the first charter schools in the state.[38] A brief video posted on Twitter from one of the protest participants showed the ugliness of the scene. "We aren't using our indoor voices," the Twitter poster wrote, above a video of a noisy congregation of protesters as they screamed within the hallways of capitol and waved signs with messages like, "The power of the people is stronger than the people in power." And that was a post from a woman who self-identified on Twitter as "Committed to Christ and His call. Wife. Mother . . . Pastor. English teacher . . . Activist."[39]

What about the children? What about the supposed top priority of teachers to educate the youth? If nothing else, get this message: It's not about the children. It's about weaponizing the schools to gain socialist strongholds across the nation.

If nothing else, realize this: These are not the schools of America's yesteryear. They're not even the schools from America's yesterday. These are political breeding grounds of anti-American activism. From the website of Socialist Alternative, a group that seeks to spread socialism throughout the country:

[T]he 2018 West Virginia teachers' strike now serves as an important instance of rediscovering the strike weapon and shows what could have been achieved in Wisconsin. Schools were shut down in all 55 counties in an illegal strike. . . . In very different ways, the Wisconsin defeat and the West Virginia victory created ripples across the country. While the defeat in Wisconsin embold-ened other right-wing politicians to launch further attacks on workers, the ripple effect of West Virginia was to inspire teachers across the country, spreading to Kentucky, Oklahoma, Arizona, and North Carolina. This shows the importance of struggles being won. Working-class people and socialists don't struggle against the capitalist class just to prove a point but to win real gains. Victories increase working people's confidence to fight for more. These struggles are laying the ground for a new, more militant, leadership in the unions . . .[40]

The lengthy quotes from the socialist websites are important. It's imperative to see, in their own words, socialists' plans for America's public schools. Otherwise, it's hard to believe. It's tough to see those kindly teachers who send home report cards with specially prepared notes about your child's progress in marching, militant formation.

That's not to say all teachers in the public schools are socialists. By no means are they all socialists. Some, in fact, are wonderful people with hearts set on teaching children the basics, and seeing today's youth blossom into tomorrow's patriotic, purposeful American leaders.

But as a group, as a unionized organization, far too many teachers and administrators have set aside the core values that were supposed to have guided them into the field of education in the first place—actual teaching—and instead, thrown in with the socialist mindset of victimhood and entitlement. Far too many have joined the socialist movement spreading through America's public schools and picked up protests signs and marched on legislators, making unreasonable demands year after year that burden taxpayers and parents alike.

Sadly, the good teachers, soon enough, catch on and get sifted. They either suffer in silence, patiently awaiting retirement, or quit for more fruitful pastures. Either way, along the way, they're treated to the socialist special: attack and intimidate.

"Teacher unions still have a stronghold on our education," wrote Rebecca Friedrichs, a California public school teacher who came under union fire for bucking the system from within and calling for more freedom in education.[41] She later wrote a book about her experiences, *Standing Up to Goliath: Battling State and National Teachers' Unions for the Heart and Soul of Our Kids and Country*. In a Fox News opinion piece in December 2019, she insisted that while the Supreme Court had, in its *Janus v. AFCME* decision, overturned the 40-year state practice of forcing public workers to pay union dues,[42] the nation's public school systems were still in peril. "[Unions have] harshly bullied great teachers into silence for decades and are chasing many of the greatest teachers right out of the classroom," Friedrichs wrote.[43]

Red for Ed

It's a movement all right. "Inspired by West Virginia, Teachers Spread Red for Ed Movement Across Arizona," read one Labor Notes headline in March of 2018.[44] What's Red for Ed? Red for Ed is a campaign that was started, at least in part, by a 24-year-old music teacher from Arizona named Noah Karvelis as a means of getting fair pay for teachers, of getting the schools properly funded, and so forth and so on. The campaign began locally, but spread nationally. Photos of numerous teachers' strikes held in recent months underscore Red for Ed's rapid-fire emergence as the go-to campaign for protesting teachers. How so? Most participants can be seen wearing the signature red shirts of the movement.

How fitting. Red is, after all, the color of choice for socialists, Marxists, communists, and leftists. And the dirty secret of Karvelis—who otherwise appears a sensibly speaking, clean-cut young education advocate—is that he's a socialist.

Maria Mazzeo Syms, who served as an Arizona legislator between 2017 and 2019, tried to point this out in the early portion of 2018, but was promptly attacked. From the *Arizona Daily Independent*:

When Rep. Maria Syms boldly stated that the #Redfored movement organizers were socialists, she was jeered. When the leader of #Redfored, Noah Karvelis, spoke at the Socialism 2018 event in Chicago this month he was cheered. Karvelis scrubbed his social media presence and denied that he was leading a radical movement at the time. He and his supporters, including many in the mainstream media, went on the offense and took umbrage with Syms' simple observation. The media was largely complicit, or they got played. In either case, Karvelis' appearance at the Socialism 2018 Conference in Chicago from July 5–8, indicates that he and his "fellow militants" no longer care to hide their agenda, and it exposed the degree to which the media again failed to report on simple truths that would have profoundly altered the coverage of a major event (the #Redfored strike and rallies).[45]

Or would it have? Given today's leftist leanings of many in the media, maybe the socialist roots of the very teachers' strikes taking place around the nation in the 2018–2019 time frame wouldn't have resulted in "altered" coverage—wouldn't have resulted in watchdog warning pieces about the true nature of Red for Ed.

Red for Ed supporters took to social media by the thousands to post pictures of smiling teachers in red shirts at protest sites; they filled scores of Internet blog space with appeals for the public to support their teachers, alongside hashtags or icons of Red for Ed; they paired their Red for Ed–referenced posts with happy stories about student learning—all as a means of inextricably linking the socialist tag with public schools in a way that doesn't scream "socialist." That way, those who called out Red for Ed as the socialist movement it was, and is, could easily be dismissed as conspiratorial.

Crazy. Delusional. That way, Red for Ed opponents could easily be silenced. And that way, Red for Ed organizers could grow their socialist movement further. Domestically and globally. "Wear red to support public ed," read one Facebook page with more than 48,000 followers that described itself as a "grassroots movement started by parents and teachers as a way to stand up for Public Education . . . in America."[46] Other Facebook pages—"Wear Red for Public Ed," "Red for Ed: Educators Solidarity Network," "Red For Ed"—advocated similarly.[47] "This is the first time in over 20 years that all 4 education unions," tweeted Elementary Educators, a Canadian outfit, in January 2020, "have moved into a legal strike position. We are united and proudly #RedforEd."[48]

The National Education Association, on its NEA Today webpage, dedicates a whole section to calling for Red for Ed supporters to organize and recruit. "We're joining together to demand the public schools our students deserve," NEA wrote. "We are Red For Ed."[49] But slapping a snappy slogan atop a purely socialist endeavor does not change the socialist nature of the endeavor. Neither does throwing in some photos of smiling children.

Our nation's public schools aren't just in trouble. They've become utterly corrupted by anti-American forces who are wickedly using the most vulnerable and most innocent, the children, to stage an internal takeover of the country's government, culture, and societal foundations.

They've become no place for the children. Yank them out now, homeschool them, put them in private and charter schools, enroll them in places of learning affiliated with the church—or suffer the coming generations' onslaughts on all that patriotic Americans hold dear. When possible, where possible, run hard-core conservative candidates with traditional views of family, culture, and politics for school board positions so as to fight back, formally, against the far leftists who want to shove far-leftist agendas as deep into the education system as they can. Petition the locals and states to open more charter schools and open doors wider for educational choice for children. And every time a teachers' union brings forth a demand for higher pay, make sure the political powers-that-be have at their disposal a cost-of-living comparison report that shines light on the truths of teachers' salaries.

And finally, remember this: Just because your child's teacher is nice doesn't mean your child's teacher isn't socialist. Socialists smile, too. Especially if they think it'll help their cause.

CHAPTER 5

ALLOWING WOLVES IN SHEEP'S CLOTHING TO TEACH SOCIALISM AS BIBLICAL

I t's a dangerous thing to make the case in America—a country built on Judeo-Christian principles, a nation founded on the concept of individual rights—that big government is moral. But that's exactly what leftists in the church do when they argue Jesus was a socialist.

They're in effect saying that it's government's moral responsibility to take care of all the needs of society's citizens, even those needs that have been traditionally left for the individuals to take care of themselves. And if that's the case, they're also arguing, by logical extension, that in a country with as large a population as America, the bigger the government grows, the better it is for all—because it's only a big government that can take care of all the citizens. Voilà, socialism becomes the moral form of government. Limited government becomes cruel. And since Jesus didn't preach cruelty, Christians who oppose socialism must be cruel.

From Sojourners:

Virtually from the day she assumed office, Rep. Alexandria Ocasio-Cortez (D-N.Y.) and her avowed democratic socialism have been under attack. Much of the condemnation is from the same crowd that so vigorously insists that America is and always has been a "Christian nation." This is quite ironic, because democratic socialism and the Bible share a strikingly similar vision of what constitutes a fair and just society. Capitalism, however, does not share that vision.[1]

This is the big lie of the twenty-first century—which is actually a recycled lie from decades past. But now, as then, the line of logic goes that all good Christian soldiers believe in fair economies, social justice, equality, housing, food, health care, and education for all, and that these things are not just civil rights, but basic human rights, and that as such, it's the duty of a properly morally compassed government to provide. Bucking that viewpoint or deviating from it in any way means to support unequal governance, unjust social systems, an unfair economic model and ultimately, an un-Christian social and political structure.

Or as Sojourners goes on to say:

The Bible and democratic socialism preach that governments should enact policies that address the needs of the poor, provide equal access to opportunity, and legislate policies that curb inequity. Both believe that any government that ignores the interests of the poor is an unjust government in need of correction.[2]

Sure. But it's how you get there that makes the difference.

Jesus Wasn't a Socialist

No way, no how, was Jesus a socialist. Christians who buy into the belief of a socialist Jesus are either well-meaning but naive, fooled, led astray—or they're wolves in sheep clothing.

It's the latter that's more concerning. Far too many wolves run the church circuit these days, corrupting true biblical principles, undermining the actual Word of God, creating a chaotic message that advances a dangerous far-left ideology in a country where far-left ideologies have no right to exist. *Jesus wasn't socialist.* Truth be told, Jesus wasn't a member of any political party; he didn't preach on any political belief. He didn't call on governments to take from the rich to give to the poor—or for individuals to campaign their governments to redistribute and equalize and implement tax structures to take from the rich and give to the poor. Rather, Jesus was all about the individual.

"Each of you," wrote Paul in 2 Corinthians 9:7, "should give what you have decided in your heart to give, not reluctantly or under compulsion, for God loves a cheerful giver." That's the picture of Christian giving—a one-on-one relationship with Jesus, prompted by love and the Holy Spirit to help another less fortunate.

Christian giving is voluntary. Socialism is force. That's the big difference. If government is compelling the giving, it's force—no matter how kindly the force is being implemented. The left likes to cause confusion on this because confusion is easier to exploit and confused people are easier to control.

Here's a good example of how the confusion begins. "[L]et's be clear about what socialism is," wrote Robert Freeman, in a piece entitled "Teaching Democrats to Talk About Socialism," published by Common Dreams. "Socialism is when people come together in an economy to solve common problems that none of us could solve on our own. Does that sound radical?"[3] Of course not. But that's the groundwork for the big lie. From Freeman, once again, at Common Dreams:

Anybody here ever driven on an Interstate highway? That's socialism. . . . Anybody here ever used the Internet? That was created by a government agency . . . That is socialism. Anybody here ever been made safer by the military, or felt safer knowing that police or fire or first-responder services were there? That's people coming together to solve problems that none of us could solve on our own. Socialism. Anybody here ever fly on an airplane? Guess what, your safety was guaranteed by thousands of standards set by the FAA, and by air traffic control, run by the same agency. Socialism. Anybody here ever used prescription drugs, or drunk water or breathed air or eaten food that was made cleaner or safer by government rules and standards? Guess what? That's socialism.[4]

This is the mental gymnastics of the left: Nothing created under the sun comes by way of individual achievement. Everything is groupthink; everything is collective thought; everything ties back to the greatness of government. "You didn't build that," as Barack Obama would put it.[5]

This is ridiculous, lazy thinking. Government spending is not one and the same as socialism; government services, paid by tax dollars, are not automatically socialist programs. First off, the Constitution allows for government, as granted by the people, to provide for the general welfare of the citizens. It's only when the general welfare clause, as it's commonly called, is stretched beyond the rightful role of what founders envisioned—a limited government with the emphasis on individual freedoms—that socialism enters the picture. It's only when government services and programs that better belong in the hands of the locals and states wind up in the control of the heavy-handed federal authorities that socialism enters the picture, too. It's only when the Ninth Amendment and the Tenth Amendment are stripped of all meaning and relevance that socialism enters the picture, as well. "The enumeration of the Constitution of certain rights shall not be construed to deny or disparage others retained by the people," states the Ninth. As for the Tenth: "The powers not delegated to the United States by the Constitution, nor prohibited by it to the states, are reserved to the states respectively, or to the people." But roads, bridges, police and fire fighting departments, the military—these are all examples of government structures, systems, and services provided with the approval of taxpayers, by the duly elected.

Second, simply calling for more and more big government spending is not one and the same as socialism; rather, it's advocating for big government, or a welfare state. Socialism, at root, is forced government takeover of private property and the means of private production. Socialism stems from the thinking that government is the only source that can provide for citizens' needs; that individuals naturally rely on government for all their needs. But that's just step one. For socialism to move from thought to reality, some form of government force must occur—some form of taxation, or regulation, or legislation that stretches beyond the scope of the Constitution and impedes the individual's ability to private produce, privately own, privately buy and sell. Big government, burdensome as it is, is not one and the same as socialist government. It just happens to frequently lead there.

It's imperative to keep these distinctions clear, else socialism can actually be sold to the people as something that's as American as apple pie. And indeed, that is how it's being pressed and woven into American society. It's the failure to take into account the dangers of *socialism* with a small *s* until it's too late, until *Socialism* with a capital *S* becomes a reality.

"How Socialism Made America Great," wrote Jack Schwartz, in an opinion piece for the Daily Beast in mid-2019. It's a title that advances the lie of Robert Freeman, the lie of Obama, the lie of all those on the left who conflate government services with socialism, and socialism therefore with American exceptionalism.

> Ronald Reagan famously warned that Medicare would lead us away from freedom and toward socialism. Barry Goldwater considered Jack Kennedy a socialist and called Lyndon Johnson one as well. America did not lapse into a collectivist dystopia with access to Medicare nor embark on the road to serfdom under the tenures of Kennedy and Johnson. Reagan's fears and Goldwater's fancies serve to remind us that "socialism" is in the eye of the beholder.[6]

Blur the lines long enough, and yes, it's true, the definition of socialism gets watered down, debated, and debunked—and then, softly and almost imperceptibly, implemented. This is what's taking place in America's political world.

The real insidious deception, the real evil, is the socialism that's being pushed through America's primary religion, Christianity. In the name of Christianity, no less. Christian wolves are taking such lines of logic and twisting them into biblical duties. Christian wolves are using their pulpits and platforms to take advantage of immature believers and trick them into taking the commands from the Bible that are given to the individual and applying them instead to the government as a body, and then—with the handy-dandy assistance of a skewed definition of socialism—press forward a vision of American society that is far from free. Remember: In America, our rights come from God.

Each and every individual is endowed by the Creator to certain rights. To socialists, though, individual rights are only what the government grants, after taking into consideration the good of the society. To socialists, government becomes the god. Once that's established, there are no limits to where government can tread. There are no boundaries government must respect.

Remember this, from Hillary Clinton, from her speech at the 1996 Democratic National Convention?

And we have learned to raise a happy, helpful, hopeful child, it takes a family, it takes clergy, it takes business people, it takes community leaders, it takes those who protect our health and safety. It takes all of us. Yes, it takes a village.[7]

A couple decades later, while speaking again at the Democratic National Convention, only this time as a candidate for president against Donald Trump, she said pretty much the same.

Twenty years ago, I wrote a book called *It Takes a Village*. And a lot of people looked at the title and asked, "What the heck do you mean by that?" This is what I mean. None of us can raise a family, build a business, heal a community or lift a country totally alone. America needs every one of us to lend our energy, our talents, our ambition to making our nation better and stronger. I believe that with all my heart. That's why "stronger together" is not just a lesson from our history. It's not just a slogan for our campaign. It's a guiding principle for the country we've always been and the future we're going to build.[8]

It's just that type of ideology espoused by Clinton—that families can't raise children, but only government; that communities, not individuals, are the source of America's power—that's become the stuff of spiritual warfare for the left.

The Bible teaches the opposite: First comes the personal relationship with God, then comes the foundation of God's creation, the family. From the family springs all else; from a biblically strengthened, morally solid family comes the community, the politics and government, the culture, the country, the church.

The left sees it top down; the Bible teaches bottom up, one-on-one. The left sees government; the Bible preaches individual. Get that wrong and an entire worldview is wrong. Miss that truth and it's easy to see how government supplants God in society, even in the churches.

This is where America's at, right now, present day. Our churches have become corrupted by leftists. They're bringing unbiblical messages, teaching and preaching about God and the Bible in ways that accommodate the flesh rather than convict with truth. "North Texas Conference ordains openly gay pastor," ran one headline from *UM News*, a publication of the United Methodist Church, in mid-2019.[9] "First Openly LGBTQ Pastor Ordained in Southern Conferences," United Methodist Insights wrote, in June of 2019.[10] "Presbyterian Church Ordains First Openly Gay Pastor,"

PRRI reported in 2011.[11] "One year in, young pastor breathes fresh life into progressive Towson church," the *Baltimore Sun* reported in 2018, about "the Rev. David Norse, who is 32 and openly gay," on his one-year anniversary leadership of Maryland Presbyterian Church.[12] "Married lesbian Baptist co-pastors say all are 'beloved,'" wrote Religion News Service in March 2017.[13] "Lutherans Welcome Seven Gay Pastors," the *New York Times* reported in 2010.[14]

This is how far America's churches have fallen from Bible basics that teach homosexuality as a sin, marriage as between one male and one female, and sexual contacts and affairs outside of marriage—outside of biblically defined, God-ordained marriage, that is—as secular and ungodly. This is not the Christianity of truth. This is not the truth of Christianity. This is humankind designing a god of convenience and comfort.

Now look at what church leaders have done to the Constitution. In December of 2019, the Claremont United Methodist Church in California displayed a nativity scene that featured Jesus, Mary, and Joseph in cages.[15] Why? To make the political point against President Donald Trump's administration that illegals crossing into America don't belong in detainment centers. "Cages," as the left liked to call them. On Facebook, the Reverend Karen Clark Ristine explained the display as a crucial commentary on the social justice issue of the day.

> In a time in our country when refugee families seek asylum at our borders and are unwillingly separated from one another, we consider the most well-known refugee family in the world. Jesus, Mary, and Joseph, the Holy Family. Shortly after the birth of Jesus, Joseph and Mary were forced to flee with their young son from Nazareth to Egypt to escape King Herod, a tyrant. They feared persecution and death. What if this family sought refuge in our country today? Imagine Joseph and Mary separated at the border and Jesus no older than two taken from his mother and placed behind the fences of a Border Patrol detention center as

more than 5,500 children have been the past three years. *Jesus grew up to teach us kindness and mercy and a radical welcome of all people.*[16] (Italic added.)

That last line about Jesus is the spiritual perversion that's being used to tear down all the Constitution represents, all that the Founders foresaw for this great nation. Yes, Jesus taught kindness, mercy, and an embrace of all people. But when did Jesus teach to break the law? "Do not think that I came to destroy the law or the prophets," Matthew 5:17 cites Jesus as saying. "I did not come to destroy but to fulfill."

Harping on the love of Jesus but ignoring the law is an aberration of the Word. This is where the wolves in the church get their steam—by preaching a type of love that carries zero expectations. Borders are not unbiblical; as a matter of fact, God set the first borders when he booted Adam and Eve from the Garden of Eden and established a security force to keep them from entering: cherubim and a flaming, turning sword. God also set borders and gifted specific lands for His chosen people at several points in Bible history—Israel, for one. Further, biblical history also teaches that strangers in God's lands, called sojourners, were expected to abide the rules and laws and customs of the places in which they temporarily stayed.

To believe in the messaging of the Claremont United Methodist Church and its reverend, Ristine, is to believe that God himself is wrong and unjustly cruel. But here's where leftist church leaders reveal the true depths of their ugly partisanship: The very "cages" that drove the left to hysteria during Trump's leadership were the same put in place by the previous Barack Obama administration. Where was the outrage then? "[Joe] Biden said the Obama administration 'didn't lock people up in cages,'" PolitiFact wrote in September 2019. "Immigration policies of Obama and Trump are very different. Trump's administration implemented a policy that led to the separation of thousands of children from their parents.

Obama did not have that policy. But for Biden to say that Obama's administration did not put people in cages is inaccurate. . . . We rate Biden's claim as false."[17]

Liars and deceivers and partisan hacks and progressive-minded spiritual leaders who twist the Bible to fit modern society and human desires are infiltrating our nation's churches. They're teaching love means tolerance for everything—even sin. They're pushing a god that automatically forgives, no confession needed. They're selling a religion that ignores repentance, because after all, there's nothing to repent—their god of love forgives all. They're wolves. They're devouring America; they're devouring the souls of the misled, misinformed, the misguided.

It's one thing to embrace all, knowing that all sin and fall short of the glory of God. That's the Christian way: a genuine love and respect for God's creations. It's another thing entirely to embrace all and pretend as if sin isn't sin. You can love a liar without pretending lies are OK. You can love a thief but still express outrage and dismay at the stolen property. You can love the poor and downtrodden and express that love with personal donations of money or necessary items—but still enforce national borders, and laws that mandate certain criteria for entry to America. Love is not the absence of law.

Church leaders who press this type of unbiblical love destroy the truths of the Bible—and in America, where freedom hinges on the ability of the people to self-govern, and the ability to self-govern hinges on the people's adherence to Judeo-Christian teachings, this type of unbiblical love leads to socialism. If god is a god of anything goes, then so, too, can be the culture. So, too, can be the government. Take away biblical-based standards, morals, and expectations of behavior, and you take away rule of law and rights and wrongs. Take away rule of law and rights and wrongs, and you take away the Constitution.

What's left is progressivism-slash-socialism-slash-communism. What's the difference in ideology, really? All roads lead to ultimate government control. A democratic republic that devolves into a democracy, then into democratic socialism, then into outright socialism isn't far from falling into outright communism. Maybe it won't be called communism, at least at the outset. But there are God-given rights and God-given individual freedoms—and there are *not*.

Pope Pius XI and Pope Francis

The church, throughout history, has often served as a battleground where freedom for the individual has been tested by calls for collectivism. In 1937, at a time of rising communist infiltration and pressures at spots around the world and in America—that latter, through the labor movement—the Roman Catholic Church, in a papal letter from Pope Pius XI, called out communism as a "satanic scourge" of humanity, brought in large part by atheists and "groups of 'intellectuals' [who] formed in an arrogant attempt to free civilization from the bonds of morality and religion."[18] Another quote? Try this, from the same Roman Catholic Church encyclical:

> The Communism of today, more emphatically than similar movements in the past, conceals in itself a false messianic idea. A pseudo-ideal of justice, of equality and fraternity in labor impregnates all its doctrine and activity with a deceptive mysticism, which communicates a zealous and contagious enthusiasm to the multitudes entrapped by delusive promises.[19]

Here's another, most pertinent to today's political climate and to the unbiblical teachings of many of today's churches: "[T]he class struggle with its consequent violent hate and destruction takes on the aspects of a crusade for the progress of humanity."[20] And one more, from this same letter: "Communists hold the principle of absolute equality, rejecting all hierarchy and divinely-constituted authority."[21]

Absolute equality is an impossible standard—yet this is what the left, the Democrats, progressives, socialists, and more aspire to bring upon America. The failure that results affords them even more opportunity to bring down the big government guns as a solution to the inequality.

In 1937, the Roman Catholic Church recognized these evils.[22] Pope Pius XI, in fact, delivered several encyclicals outlining the anti-Christian tenets of totalitarian regimes—notably, in 1931,[23] warning of the dangers of fascism in Italy and again, in 1937, a piece entitled, "With Deep Anxiety" about Nazi Germany.[24] Of course, this is the same pope who also signed the Lateran Treaty of 1929 with dictator Benito Mussolini, the fascist who, interestingly enough—given America's present day morphing of the Democratic Party into progressivism and democratic socialism and barely masked socialism—briefly flirted with the Italian Socialist Party, before going full-blown "Partito Nazionale Fascista" militant parliamentary member.[25] The Lateran Treaty gave the pope sovereign control of the Vatican and surrounding areas—the State of Vatican City—provided all members of the church would cease and desist from participating in political actions.[26] In other words, the church got its land and independence; Mussolini got his fascism, free of church opposition. It was a devil of a deal. But at least Pius XI, at points in time, in his encyclicals, spoke a good game against tyrannical governments.

Now compare his more unequivocal statements against communism, against dictatorial governments, against even fascism, to those made by Pope Francis in his letter to "Young Economists and Entrepreneurs Worldwide," sent from the Vatican in May 2019. In an entreaty for an "inclusive," "not exclusive, humane and not dehumanizing" economy—one that also "cares for the environment and does not despoil it"—Francis described a type of biblically based financial system that was more "covenant" than market-driven.[27]

It's a confusing read, to say the least. At least for those expecting more precise language, in the vein of economic shop talk and factual figuring and financing. Among the excerpts:

- He called on followers of the faith "to give a soul to the economy of tomorrow."
- He suggested the best way to "reanimate" the economy was to follow in the footsteps of St. Francis of Assisi, who "stripped himself of all worldliness in order to choose God as the compass of his life, becoming poor with the poor, a brother to all," and who decided "to embrace poverty [which] also gave rise to a vision of economics that remains most timely."
- He characterized this self-imposed poverty as a "vision" for the "poorest of the poor," the "entire human family" and the "fate of the entire planet . . . our sister Mother Earth."
- He said each individual is called by godly principles to "rethink his or her mental and moral priorities, to bring them into greater conformity with God's commandments and the demands of the common good."[28]

He gently stroked, rather than openly stoked, the flames of socialism. You can almost hear the come-hither hiss of forked tongue social justice. Francis wrote:

Your universities, your businesses and your organizations . . . are workshops of hope for creating new ways of understanding the economy and progress, for combating the culture of waste, for giving voice to those who have none and for proposing new styles of life. Only when our economic and social system no longer produces even a single victim, a single person cast aside, will we be able to celebrate the feast of universal fraternity.[29]

The full context of this letter was to promote the church's March 2020 Economy of Francesco event in Assisi aimed at forming a "covenant" among the emerging business leaders and entrepreneurs of the world to "build a more just and beautiful world" and to "cultivate together the dream of a new humanism responsive to the expectations of men and women and to the plan of God."[30]

Call it Economics 101, Pope Francis style. There's nothing about free market ventures; nothing about capitalistic creations; zero about production versus demand, competitive spirit, trade, profit and loss statements, or even sowing the seeds of God given talent to build a fulfilling business. Rather, it's all about creating equality out of inequality—about creating good citizens of the world who would set aside the quest for evil profits in favor of slaving for the "common good" and giving souls for the "economy of tomorrow" because, by gosh, that's just what good followers of Jesus do. If this language doesn't disturb, it should. It's all a soft-sell socialism.

What's worse, it's all deviously couched to sound as if the Good Book teaches that a hunger for success, a desire to succeed, a quest for a booming business are wrongful pursuits, and that only those entrepreneurs who completely scorn personal profits to give to the poor are the blessed and favored by God.

This is a prime example of how religion is pushing the socialist message into American society. And truly, nobody knows it better than the pope. If Francis truly believed his own words, he would empty the very substantial coffers of the Vatican, and tear out the very gold in the chapel walls, and distribute—or redistribute—to the poor right outside Vatican City walls. Instead, the church sends out the public relations people to do some quick damage control.

"Top Vatican official says Americans misunderstand pope's social agenda," the Crux reported,[31] a couple of weeks after Francis released his "Young Economists and Entrepreneurs Worldwide" letter. The story went on to report how one of the pope's chief advisers, Cardinal Peter Turkson, said that every time he traveled to the United States, he had to clarify that Francis wasn't communist or socialist, but rather just someone who favored a "social economy." Rather, an economy driven by "fraternity, solidarity and the common good."[32] Rather: "Not Adam Smith's" type of economy. But "an economy which is able to serve all members of the community well."[33] Come again?

The decoding's simple: socialism. If Adam Smith is the "father of capitalism,"[34] as he's called, and the type of economy envisioned as best by Pope Francis is one that's "not Adam Smith's" but rather one that focuses on the collective—that is, fraternity and solidarity—and advances the "common good," then ding, ding, ding, the bells ring loud for socialism. No matter what clarifications, or clarifiers, say otherwise.

In religion, it seems, as in politics, the tendency might be to call socialism something other than socialism. But that doesn't take away the socialism. It only serves to deceive the people. And shame on churches and leaders of faith, in particular, for using God's Word to deceive in such manner.

Not all religious-based callings for socialism are so subtle. In the *Catholic Herald*, for example, one writer is actually quite open in making the case that capitalism is a blot on humanity and that socialism, and only socialism, is the moral political and economic system.

By "socialism" I mean two things essentially: the rejection of the liberal, capitalist view of private property, and consequently the abolition of an economic order predicated on the exploitation of those who do not have property by those who do. Socialists desire a society of the common good, in which citizens collaborate for mutual advantage in enjoyment of peace and security; a society where the public authority is empowered to correct injuries to the common good, rather than standing by indifferently, as if it were powerless in the face of evil. . . . What a socialist means by the abolition of private property is nothing more than the use of that property in the service of the common good, rather than property used only in the service of those who happen to possess it.[35]

Now let's unwind the lies.

- Capitalism does not "consequently" lead to exploitation. This is the language of dictatorial revolutionaries—of Marxists, actually.
- The dream of socialism as a society that benefits the "common good," where all "collaborate" to bring about a peaceful and secure country is one that can just as easily be sold as the dream of capitalism. As a matter of fact, this was the dream of American founders who sought a free nation that offered the "common good" of freedom to all individuals, absent the king's disruptions to peace and security.
- The idea of socialism as a system that combats "injuries to the common good" has no basis in historical fact. In fact, just the opposite. Socialism brings misery and death and its legacy for doing so is well documented.
- The argument that a socialist government is a better steward of private property than the private property owner is an outright evil that not only dismisses the roots of private property—hard work, production, planning, achievement, and determination to succeed—but that also kills the spirit of humanity: the drive to create. It's no coincidence socialists are often godless; creation itself comes from God.
- Property that people "happen to possess"? As if homes fall from the sky; as if businesses simply grow from thin air, and money on trees. This is the scorn of the socialists for individual achievement; this is the utter disdain of socialism for the seeds of God planted at birth.

Christian Socialism

Such condemnations of capitalism and free markets aren't confined to the Catholic religion—nor do all calls for Christians to be socialists come explicitly from those in church leadership. Members of the media, for instance, often cite portions of Acts 2 and Acts 4 as the basis for Christian socialism, where "all those who had believed were together and had all things in common," and where "all things were common property to them" who believed.

Other Bible passages used to further the socialist cause include 1 Timothy 5:8, which states that "anyone who does not provide for their relatives, and especially for their own household, has denied the faith and is worse than an unbeliever," and Ephesians 4:28. "Let the thief no longer steal, but rather let him labor, doing honest work with his own hands, so that he may have something to share with anyone in need," this passage of Ephesians states. But all these biblical teachings speak to the individual, not the government. They are voluntary Christian compliances, not top-down regulatory commands.

They are examples of individuals in the faith coming together to show agape love—not of a government acting with force and regulation and demand. It's not just the Catholic Church, of course. "Why a Southern Church Is Hosting Socialist Meetings," ran one headline in Sojourners in 2018 about Calvary United Methodist Church in Durham, North Carolina.[36] "Why These Young American Christians Embraced Socialism," ran another in Religion & Politics in 2020 about the growing links in American between church teachings and socialist politics.[37]

Moreover, at the turn of the century, the largely Protestant social gospel movement has been both interpreted and misinterpreted as a religious-based press for socialism in American government. Walter Rauschenbusch, 1861–1918, was a Baptist pastor who focused his ministry for a time on helping the poor in New York City's depressed Hell's Kitchen, and after an 1891 trip to Germany, began to push for better protections for laborers and more public ownership of property.[38] He believed more in the views of a Fabian socialist, in the vein of, say, what today's democratic socialists like to promulgate—that socialism does not destroy individual rights but rather serves the common good and that peaceful reform is better than violent revolution.[39] Nonetheless, as historian Jacob

Dorn wrote, he actually "contemplated [socialist] party member-ship,"[40] even as some in the party promoted more a more aggres-sive approach to societal reforms. Ultimately, Rauschenbusch joined with a couple of Baptist ministers, Nathaniel Schmidt and Leighton Williams, to form a group dedicated to advancing the cause of Christian socialism. Rauschenbusch also wrote the still-famous best-seller *Christianity and the Social Crisis*, used even today by those of left-leaning political persuasion as proof of the Bible's bent toward socialism.[41]

But chalking the Social Gospel movement as purely socialist in nature would be inaccurate. Truly, as many of this mindset who outright embraced socialism as the only system that could possi-bly be acceptable to Jesus, just as many saw otherwise. Or, at least more moderately.

Lyman Abbott, for instance, born 1835 in Massachusetts and died 1922 in New York, was a lawyer, then Congregational minis-ter, then editor of several religious publication. Distressed by what he saw as the lingering community divisions from the Civil War and of the injustices of the Industrial Revolution, he used his pul-pit and platform to apply Christian principles to social problems.[42] Still, Abbott, as much as he disdained capitalism, wasn't a socialist, but rather a more moderate, Theodore Roosevelt–supporting pro-gressive/pragmatic of the time.[43]

Washington Gladden, born 1836 in Pennsylvania and died 1918 in Ohio, was an American Congregational minister, journalist, author, and editor who investigated and outed the corrupt "Tweed Ring" of politicians who took over New York City's government and robbed millions from its coffers.[44] He advocated on behalf of unions and called out wealthy John D. Rockefeller money as "tainted."[45] But Gladden was a progressive and outright opposed socialism.[46]

There were more, many more, who came from this social gos-pel chapter of American church life to cite Christian duty as cause to tackle social problems, and Bible principles as solution to what ails society. But it would be a false narrative to characterize these social gospel types as card-carrying socialists. The movement was multifaceted; the beliefs, diverse. Dare say that then, as now, *socialism* could be seen as with a capital *S* as frequently as with a small *s*. This just shows the insidious creep of socialism and how on guard American citizens in general, and churchgoing patriots in particular, need to remain to halt the ideology at its inception.

In 1838, English theologian and author Frederick Denison Maurice, 1805–1872, wrote *The Kingdom of Christ*, making the case for a united church body that transcends earthly factions.[47] In 1848, Maurice joined with Anglican novelist Charles Kingsley and attorney and activist John Malcolm Ludlow, as well as with judge, politician, and author Thomas Hughes and others, to formally found the Christian Socialist movement.[48] And since, Maurice's writings have been frequently used by socialists to deliver messages that are, in fact, opposite to his original meaning.

As John Spargo, one of the founders of the Socialist Party of America, acknowledged:

> To one familiar with the writings of Frederic[k] Denison Maurice, the founder of English Christian socialism, it is evident enough that he was not in sympathy with the great fundamental changes contemplated by the socialist of today. His desire was to "christianize socialism," by which he could not have meant more than to supplant socialism by Christianity. The spirit of Maurice largely prevails in the Christian-socialist movement today, and to find prominent Christian socialists opposing the socialist candidates at election time, and supporting anti-socialists, is not unusual.[49]

The lure of socialism is that it promises what the Bible teaches will only come in the afterlife: a state of true love, true equality, true justice, true peace. So perhaps it's only natural that socialists would look to religion as a means of spreading their views into the political and economic spheres, and that Christians—either knowingly in their deceptions or unwittingly in their nescience—would seize hold of these messages and teachings as the true will of God, as true signs of a socialist Jesus.

But here's the test: Jesus places the burden, the responsibility, the task of feeding the poor, housing the homeless, providing for the less fortunate, and so forth on the individual. The framers of the Constitution, meanwhile, similarly based their vision for America on the ability of a moral people, principled in the ways of Judeo-Christianity, to run a limited government and warned that absent virtue, the democratic republic would fall. Any church that teaches contrary to those two principles is neither biblically sound, nor protective of the Constitution. Any church leader who says Jesus wants socialism to rule on earth is either serving up a side dish of immature biblical interpretation or using Bible knowledge to purposely teach lies. The first may be excusable; the second is utter evil. And one test to decide which it is to look at the church purse. Preaching for socialism atop a perch of gold and financial comfort, removed from the misery of the poor, while demanding government take care of the downtrodden, is hypocritical. Jesus was hardly a hypocrite. Even socialists using the Bible as cover to enact their anti-American designs wouldn't dare suggest that.

CHAPTER 6

PRETENDING AS IF SOCIALISTS CARE ABOUT THE YOUTH

I f socialists so recklessly use the Bible to advance their wicked ways, how much more so do they use the children? And just as they claim a love for the Bible while tearing apart the fabric of biblical teachings, so, too, socialists claim they love children, while mistreating the youngest and most vulnerable. Socialists say they love the children. But their actions, causes, policies, motivations, and missions actually destroy what they say they love—and sadly, what's worse, what's more horrific, is these socialists actually train America's youngest to play a crucial role in this cycle of destruction. They train the youth to ruin themselves.

Nationally syndicated columnist Cal Thomas wrote in a 2018 piece that it's the youth, who reap the most benefits from capitalism, who also seem to bite the hardest against the free market hand that feeds them. Aptly enough, the piece was titled, "It's the Spoiled Children of America Who Are Drawn to Socialism." Why is that? He suggests a variety of reasons, all for which ignorance is the base.

[First, it's] likely most of those [youth] who favor socialism have never lived in a country where it is practiced. A few months in Venezuela might be the perfect cure. Second, people who claim to prefer socialism to capitalism are probably reaping capitalism's benefits. This group of misinformed comrades includes parents who gave their pampered millennials a lifestyle they likely would never have enjoyed under a socialist regime. [Third] is that those who favor socialism over capitalism and socialist countries over America are spoiled rotten. They are part of a generation that has never had to serve in the military and, I would venture to guess, do not know anyone who is serving or has served, other than maybe a grandparent, whose values many seem to have rejected.[1]

They don't understand the sacrifices that went into the building of this nation. So they don't embrace the core virtues and principles that keep this nation's freedoms afloat. So they don't grasp the delicate nature of a democratic republic and the absolute uncompromising need for its people to maintain a solid moral compass to keep the country steered in the right direction. So they think, eh, what's the harm in a little socialism; after all, helping people is good. Helping people is godly.

Socialists swoop in to use the youth to further their agenda. That's tragic in itself—but the even bigger tragedy is the cycle of ignorance that develops. These youth are trained to hate the one economic system—capitalism—that's truly freeing, and told instead that socialism is the equalizer, the fairest of the fair. They're blinded by social justice promises. They're led into redistribution-of-wealth hell. They're enslaved by pie-in-sky falsehoods. Ultimately, they're beguiled into forgoing free markets for socialist slavery. Their children, raised in these deceptive ways and reliant on the government for handouts and subsidies and entitlements, never even have a chance.

"My people are destroyed for lack of knowledge," Hosea teaches from the Bible. Oh how true, the downward slope of socialism.

Greta Thunberg

Greta Thunberg, the teenage Swedish girl who rocked international headlines with impassioned pleas to please save planet Earth, addressed world leaders at the UN climate action gathering in New York and said, among other eyebrow-raising bits of rhetoric: "This is all wrong. I shouldn't be standing here. I should be back in school on the other side of the ocean."[2]

Well, why wasn't she? The answer is simple. The left saw in Thunberg, then 16, a once-in-a-lifetime opportunity to push a radical environmental agenda via a girl who (1) was a cute pigtailed child and (2) has Asperger's,[3] a neurobehavioral impairment that until 2013 was listed as one of five pervasive development disorders in the *Diagnostic and Statistical Manual of Mental Disorders* (*DSM-5*). As of 2019, it's been more generically considered a subtype of autism spectrum disorder.[4]

That being said: Thunberg was a golden egg to climate alarmists. She gave the radicals what they craved to drive their message deeper—that is, an irrefutable spokesperson. Criticize Thunberg's ridiculous assertions at peril. Those who did were immediately vilified for attacking a poor girl; for attacking a young girl simply trying to speak her mind; for attacking a poor, young, autistic girl; for brazenly, cruelly, and outrageously lashing out at a poor, young, autistic girl who was trying to make the world a better place for all. And so forth and so on.

She became the face of the climate cause. It didn't matter that Thunberg's parents, trained in theatrics and drama and opera as they were, likely passed along their best stage advice to help their daughter deliver her lines with feeling, to feed the media beast and to create the marketing magic.[5] It didn't matter that Thunberg hadn't a lick of scientific training, scientific knowledge, even meteorological schooling, or anything that gave her the credentials to make such wild assertions as:

- "People are suffering. People are dying. Entire ecosystems are collapsing."
- "We are in the beginning of a mass extinction."
- "For more than 30 years, the [climate change] science has been crystal clear."
- "The popular idea of cutting our emissions in half in 10 years only gives us a 50 percent chance of staying below 1.5 degrees [Celsius] and [that still leaves] the risk of setting off irreversible chain reactions beyond human control. . . . But those numbers do not include tipping points, most feedback loops, additional warming hidden by toxic air pollution or the aspects of equity and climate justice."
- "To have a 67 percent chance of staying below a 1.5 degrees global temperature rise . . . the world had 420 gigatons of CO_2 left to emit back on January 1, 2018. Today that figure is already down to less than 350 gigatons."[6]

Those were all excerpts from her September 2019 speech before the United Nations. But honestly, did she have a clue about what she spoke? That's highly doubtful. In fact, Thunberg pretty much admitted as much when she went to Congress that same month to weigh in on the perils of climate change, but rather than offer her own remarks simply submitted a copy of the United Nations "2018 Intergovernmental Panel on Climate Change" (IPCC) report. That's the report that called for "unprecedented" and sweeping global regulatory clampdowns on carbon emissions else the atmosphere would warm to 1.5 degrees Celsius above "pre-industrial" levels.[7] That's the report that blamed "human activities" for causing "approximately 1.0 degree Celsius of global warming above pre-industrial levels, with a likely range of 0.8 degrees Celsius to 1.2 degrees Celsius" and that warned "global warming is likely to reach 1.5 degrees Celsius between 2030 and 2052 if it continues to increase at the current rate."[8] That's the report, spanning hundreds of pages, Thunberg dumped on the desks of the House Climate

Crisis Committee and a House Foreign Affairs subcommittee, with the simple message: Read it and learn. "I am submitting this report as my testimony because I don't want you to listen to me, I want you to listen to the scientists," she said. "I want you to unite behind science. And then I want you to take real action. Thank you."⁹

Bam. That's showbiz, folks. Leave 'em wanting more. The problem, of course, is that climate science, much as the left wants it believed, is far from "settled." Most suspiciously, climate alarmism language and tactics have changed substantially over the years. What was once global cooling became global warming; what was once the greenhouse effect became the polar vortex. Science, and scientists, can't seem to make up their mind if looming environmental devastation is rooted in too much heat or too much cold—or too many hairspray cans with ozone-depleting chlorofluorocarbons on the market.¹⁰

Ultimately, science seems to have settled upon the more generic and all-encompassing, "climate change"—a phrase that gives no small measure of leeway with fact. After all, warming temperatures in the face of predictions for cooling are obvious proofs of scientific errors. But "change" is such a vague term. It can mean whatever the scientists want, whatever the politicians need. And it can bring a veritable cornucopia of linked-in outcomes, from droughts and flooding to hurricanes and tornadoes—all of which serve as headline-grabbing crises that underscore the frenzied need to do something, anything, just do something quick, to fight climate change.

Meanwhile, not even all in the scientific world buy into the IPCC's findings. More than 31,000 American scientists—9,000-plus with PhDs—have signed on to the Global Warming Petition Project that states, in part, there is "no convincing scientific evidence that human release of carbon dioxide, methane or other greenhouse gases is causing or will, in the foreseeable future, cause catastrophic heating of the Earth's atmosphere and disruption of the Earth's climate." At the same time, this petition continues, "there is substantial scientific evidence that increases in atmospheric carbon dioxide produce many beneficial effects on the natural plant and animal environments of the Earth."[11]

Why didn't Thunberg file that petition as part of her testimony to Congress in 2019? The petition only includes those with the minimum of a bachelor's degree in pertinent fields of science, including meteorological, atmospheric, environmental, astronomical, geophysical, and biological.[12] Moreover, only American scientists are approved as signatories—meaning, there are probably hundreds or thousands more physicists, chemists, biologists, engineers, and others with degrees of higher scientific learning in other nations who would gladly sign, if allowed. Why didn't Thunberg offer that viewpoint as part of her presentation before the United Nations?

Here's another red flag of the whole environmentalism movement: The IPCC science is wildly exaggerated—and often, outright misinterpreted. Forbes contributor Michael Shellenberger, in a 2019 piece entitled, "Why Apocalyptic Claims About Climate Change Are Wrong," does an excellent job of presenting the fact versus fiction rhetoric that often undercuts some of environmentalism's most hysterical warnings. He wrote:

> First, no credible scientific body has ever said climate change threatens the collapse of civilization much less the extinction of the human species.
>
> "Our children are going to die in the next 10 to 20 years. What's the scientific basis for these claims?" BBC's Andrew Neil asked a visibly uncomfortable XR [civil disobedience environmental group, Extinction Rebellion] spokesperson last month.
>
> "These claims have been disputed, admittedly," she said. "There are some scientists who are agreeing and some who are saying it's not true. But the overall issue is these deaths are going to happen."
>
> "But most scientists don't agree with this," said Neil. "I looked through IPCC reports and see no reference to billions of people going to die, or children in 20 years. How would they die?"

"Mass migration around the world already taking place due to prolonged drought in countries, particularly in South Asia. There are wildfires in Indonesia, the Amazon rainforest, Siberia, the Arctic," she said.

But in saying so, the XE spokesperson had grossly misrepresented the science. "There is robust evidence of disasters displacing people worldwide," notes IPCC, "but limited evidence that climate change or sea-level rise is the direct cause."

What about "mass migration?" "The majority of resultant population movements tend to occur within the borders of affected countries," says IPCC.[13]

It's a fascinating exchange that shows quite aptly how the leftists like to blame every fire, every human migration, every drought, everywhere, on climate change—and who then, even in the face of factual opposition, extend that viewpoint to emphasize the need to stop these natural disasters by regulating human activity.

It's just the type of exchange you'd think Thunberg would address in her presentations before the United Nations and Congress, if only to show her rebukes of the adults of the world for bringing on this "mass extinction" were rooted in sensible, tested, tried-and-true science.

But on countering viewpoints, Thunberg has been radio silent. Why? Obviously, it's because the people pulling Thunberg's strings don't want her to give any credibility to the scientists who question the far left's lines on climate change. Obviously, it's because Thunberg has come too far to reverse course now.

Echoing socialist Representative Alexandria Ocasio-Cortez's warnings of 12 years until environmental, earthly doom, Thunberg, in her 2019 book, *No One Is Too Small to Make a Difference*, predicted that "around 2030," absent momentous political and policy change, "we will be in a position to set off an irreversible chain reaction beyond human control that will lead to the end of our civilization as we know it."[14] We'll see. Right? We will see. A close reading of the words reveals lots of wiggle room with those predictions.

Meanwhile, Thunberg continues as a puppet for the socialists who want to use environmentalism as a means of redistributing wealth, of corralling power into the hands of a few, of stripping the world's nations—particularly, America—of their resources and sovereignty, and of clamping down on the ability of governments, businesses, and individuals to produce at will, create at will, and sell and consume at will. Environmentalism is a socialist's dream tool because it can be used to control everything on land, air, and sea, and on everything that comes into contact with land, air, and sea—and, more important, on everyone who lives, works, and breathes within the boundaries of the land, air, and sea. It's their idea of heaven on earth.

Jeff "Free" Luers, an ecoterrorist who was convicted of 11 felony counts and sentenced to more than 22 years in prison for setting on fire three Chevrolet SUVs in Eugene, Oregon, said it was actually love that drove him. In 1998, when he was just 19 years old, he said he traveled to the Willamette National Forest in Oregon, gazed upon the Douglas firs, Western hemlocks, and red cedars, and came away with the thought: "Standing before them is a humbling experience, like standing before a god or goddess."[15] For far too many, environmentalism has become a religion. And when a tree becomes a god, saving that tree becomes an act of martyrdom and worship. The impact of such ideology on children, the very people who are supposed to benefit from the whole protect-the-earth-at-all-costs movement, is destructive.

In Thunberg's case, this is a girl who struggled with depression, anxiety attacks, and eating disorders, going so far as to refuse food for fully two months at the age of 11. When she did begin to eat again, she only allowed herself certain foods. In fact, her mother had to prepare pancakes filled with rice for her to take to school every day, else she wouldn't eat. And if the container in which the pancakes were placed had a sticker with her name on it, Thunberg would fall into an obsessive-compulsive disorder (OCD) episode, and turn aside from eating again.[16] That's all according to the 2018 autobiographical *Scenes from the Heart*, written by Thunberg's parents—her opera singing mother, Malena Ernman, and her professional actor father, Svante Thunberg—and by Greta and her younger and similarly disturbed sister, Beata, who suffered at the time of the book's writing from OCD, attention deficit hyperactivity disorder, and Asperger's syndrome.[17]

Yet leftists didn't hesitate to hold Thunberg in high regard and elevate her pseudo-scientific call for environmental reforms to international status. One has to question the wisdom. In fact, one did: Paulina Neuding, in a piece entitled, "Self-Harm Versus the Greater Good: Greta Thunberg and Child Activism," wondered aloud at the sense of using a child with such widely acknowledged disorders as a voice for hotly contested political goals. This is what she concluded:

[A]dults have a moral obligation to remain adults in relation to children and not be carried away by emotions, icons, selfies, images of mass protests, or messianic or revolutionary dreams. Greta was recently named "Woman of the Year" by a Swedish newspaper. But she is not a woman, she is a child. It is time we stopped to ask if we are using her, failing her, and even sacrificing her, for what we perceive to be a greater good.[18]

Certainly the left is using her. Maybe her parents, as well. But the older she gets, the more certain it is, too: She's allowing herself to be used and exploited as a tool of the left. She's becoming part and parcel of the cycle of destruction that socialist thought, socialist ideology, socialist infiltration inevitably brings.

Fear as a Tool for Change

"Stop Scaring Children Witless About Climate Change," blared one 2019 headline from a column in Spiked.[19] There are plenty more of the same—and from other news outlets that aren't by any means to be confused with being conservative mouthpieces.

"Psychologists Warn Parents, Climate Change Alarmists Against Causing 'Eco-Anxiety' in Children," *Newsweek* reported.[20] From the *New York Times*, in mid-2019: "Climate Change Is Scaring Kids. Here's How to Talk to Them."[21] From the *Telegraph*, in September of 2019: "Parents told not to terrify children over climate change as rising numbers treated for 'eco-anxiety.'"[22] From the *Washington Post Magazine*, in early 2020: "Eco-anxiety is overwhelming kids."[23]

The American Psychological Association, in 2017, described "eco-anxiety" as a "chronic fear of environmental doom," and it's become so widespread, mental health professionals have carved out an entire new field of study to better address its symptoms.[24] They call it ecopsychology—the exploration of humans' relationship with nature and the study of the effects of natural disasters, climate change, and the environment on their mental states.[25] And failure to properly treat the affected can lead to a host of horrible-sounding conditions.[26]

Like what? Like post-traumatic stress disorder, for one. Like trauma, shock, depression, substance abuse, aggression, along with reduced feelings of autonomy, and a heightened feeling of fatalism, dread, and fear.[27] Good Lord. But wait. As *Newsweek* notes—it gets even worse:

> Researchers at the University of Bath and members of the Climate Psychology Alliance (CPA) in the United Kingdom say children are commonly being subjected to a barrage of concerns about the future of the planet and "environmental doom." Psychologists speaking with *The Telegraph* . . . said a rising number of kids and young adults are being treated with psychiatric drugs in order to reduce the emotional stress and exhaustion caused by "eco-anxiety," or, a fervent fear that humans will go extinct as a result of their own pollution and damage to the environment.[28]

Think about that for a moment. Radical socialists have seized so lustily on environmentalism as a political tool of power and created such an atmosphere of fear with their ridiculously wild doomsday warnings that children now need psychiatric drugs just to function. These children have become the acceptable casualties of the far left's longer-term causes. Has the left no shame at all?

But this is how socialism works: It's the collective that counts, it's the greater good that matters, it's the end, not the means, that's of greatest concern. And if that means a few children are harmed in the process, so be it—just so long as the political, policy, legislative, cultural, societal reform is moved one step closer to success. Just so long as the socialist dream is pushed a bit farther down the road.

Fear is a terrific tool for change. So is feigned love and brotherly and sisterly concern and compassion. Socialists do the same with gun control, creating deceptive messages about the dangers of nonliving firearms, rather than focusing on the true source of crime, murder, and mayhem—the blackened state of the human heart. They then take those lies, package them as love for the children, and sell them wherever and whenever they can bring the biggest bang for the buck. School shootings, anyone?

They do the same with birth control and abortion—or reproductive freedom, as they call it—and rather than teach accountability and abstinence, or godly virtues and values, scream shrilly about the rights of women to do with their bodies as they see fit, and the rights of young girls to have sex as freely as the young boys. They talk about sex in terms of recreation, not procreation, and then react in fury when biological truths are raised. Abortion is their equalizer. Abortion is the socialist woman's way of leveling the sexual freedom playing field with men.

They do the same with traditional definitions of the family unit, despising centuries-long normalcies and the biblically based in favor of elevating the broken, the dysfunctional, the psychologically damaging, even. Who needs a father? Really, who even needs a mother? These are the shoulder-shrugs of the socialists who say in one breath how much they care for the fate of the nation, for the future of the emerging youth, while in the very next call for the very cultural reforms that kill, spiritually, emotionally, and yes, physically—think gang violence, think drug addiction deaths— these same emerging youth.

They do the same with the LGBTQ movement, elevating mental illness to a stage of normalcy that completely wipes out any chance these poor victims, these poor sufferers, may have of receiving help. It's not a kindness or act of tolerance to tell a young boy he can be a girl simply by switching out clothing or undergoing medical treatment. It's not an act of love and compassion to pretend a teenage girl can simply stop referring to herself as a "she," and demand everyone else call her some sort of made-up gender neutral term, and there you have it—it's done. Out with the "she," in with the "ze."

What a cruel, cruel lie. But these are all examples of cruelty perpetrated by far leftists, by Democrats, by socialists, by the social justice zealots of the radically progressive movement, onto vulnerable, sick, wickedly secular, or otherwise disturbed individuals, and ultimately, onto society as a whole.

It's not like socialists don't know the cycle of destruction they're visiting on these people, either. There are just too many studies and reports and statistics out there that show the damage done to children raised in instable environments, absent discipline and enforced behavioral boundaries, for the left to maintain plausible deniability.

- The US Census Bureau in 2017 reported 19.7 million children in America were being raised in fatherless homes.[29]
- The Annie E. Casey Foundation reported in 2016 that 25 percent of US children were being raised in households with only mothers present.[30]
- The Centers for Disease Control and Prevention reported that in 2017, women between the ages of 15 years old and 19 years old gave birth to a total of 194,377 babies—a birth rate of 18.8 per 1,000 women in this age bracket.[31]

- Meanwhile, DoSomething.org reported that in the United States, roughly "750,000 women under the age of 20 become pregnant every year, meaning that about 750,000 men are also involved in teen pregnancies," and that "8 out of 10 dads don't marry the mother of their child."[32] More fatherless homes.

The situation is dire. According to the National Fatherhood Initiative:

- These children were four times more likely to suffer poverty than those raised in homes with fathers.
- They were twice as likely to drop out of high school.
- They were much more likely to have behavioral problems, more likely to abuse alcohol or drugs, more likely to end up in prison, more likely to suffer abuse and neglect from their caregivers.
- And girls raised in homes without fathers were seven times more likely to become pregnant during their teenage years.[33]

Then there's this, reported by Fathers.com, which cited 2012 figures from the federal Health and Human Services agency: "Children living in female headed families with no spouse present had a poverty rate of 47.6 percent, over 4 times the rate in married-couple families."[34]

Then there's this, reported by LiveAbout.com, which cited US Department of Justice statistics: "Children from fatherless homes account for . . . 63 percent of all youth suicides . . . 90 percent of all homeless and runaway youths . . . 70 percent of juveniles in state-operated institutions . . . 75 percent of adolescent patients in substance abuse centers . . . 75 percent of rapists motivated by displaced anger."[35]

Blacks and minorities are particularly impacted. In one report that used US Census data, it was found that almost 58 percent of black children and more than 31 percent of Hispanic children were raised in 2012 in homes without fathers, compared to just under 21 percent of whites.[36]

This is despicable. The Minnesota Psychological Association noted years ago:

> A high percentage of gang members come from father-absent homes . . . Gaining that sense of belonging is an important element for all individuals. Through gangs, youth find a sense of community and acceptance. In addition, the gang leader may fill the role of father . . . Having a father in the child's life greatly reduces the likelihood of a child joining a gang.[37]

That's just common sense. But there's little common sense that goes along with leftist visions. The dirty little secret of socialism is that its adherents will express horror at such brokenness of homes, while quietly using the brokenness to their advantage. Socialists will pretend to care about the victims of the broken homes, all the while ignoring that it's their very policies and cultural designs that bring about the brokenness—all the while exploiting the brokenness to dig socialist talons even deeper into society. They create the degradation, then exploit and expand the degradation by pretending to be the solution for what's become a new desperate, needy class of society.

In 2013, the Guttmacher Institute found "the proportion of pregnancies among 15–19-year-olds ending in abortion (i.e., the abortion ratio) was 29%."[38] In 2011, Guttmacher reported 42 percent of unintended pregnancies ended in abortion.[39]

In 2019, the Associated Press reported a story of a "man"—actually, a woman who identified and presented as a man—who went to the emergency room of an unidentified hospital with stomach pains. The admitting nurse noted the patient was obese and had stopped taking blood pressure medications and therefore, performed triage along those nonemergency lines. Several hours later, doctors discovered this "man" was actually pregnant, and her baby stillborn.[40] "It is unclear from the article, but the facts suggest that the life of that baby might have been saved if not for the confusion and intentional obfuscation of the mother's 'gender identity,'" Massachusetts Family Institute wrote in a blog post of the incident.[41]

Meanwhile, here's an interesting tidbit the leftists in the LGBTQ camp promoting such ridiculous ideas as male menstruation, at-will sex switches, gender-by-choice, and surgery for sex changes won't tell you: those who partake, often wish they didn't. "Gender-confirmation surgeries—the name given to procedures that change the physical appearance and function of sexual characteristics—increased by 20 percent from 2015 to 2016 in the U.S., with more than 3,000 such operations performed last year . . . Now, at least one surgeon [urologist Miroslav Djordjevic] is reporting a trend of regret . . . [and says] that those who want the reversal [surgery] display high levels of depression, and in some instances, suicidal thoughts," *Newsweek* reported in 2017.[42]

The Williams Institute reported similarly.

> Those [transgenders] who had "de-transitioned" at some point, meaning having gone back to living according to their sex assigned at birth, were significantly more likely to report suicide thoughts and attempts, both past-year and lifetime, than those who had never "de-transitioned." Nearly 12 percent of those who "de-transitioned" attempted suicide in the past year compared to 6.7 percent of those who have not "de-transitioned."[43]

Then there are the general societal upheavals that result from pretending boys can be girls, and girls can be boys, as simply as wishfully thinking—the bathrooms and changing rooms that have to be reconfigured, the school policies that have to be reconsidered, the identity documents that have to be rethought, the military and government security papers that have to be redone. And for what? Often, the end result is to harm the very people far leftists say they support. "Girls sue to block participation of transgender athletes," the Associated Press reported in early 2020, about a group of Connecticut high school female runners who were fed up with their rightful first-place ribbons—and accompanying college scholarship gifts and opportunities—going to boys who pretend to be girls.[44] "Trans Athletes Destroy the Meaning of Women, Then Ask 'What Is a Woman?'" wrote the Federalist in 2019.[45] Confusion is good for socialist business, even if it ends up destroying what used to be a foundational support for the socialist business itself—women's rights.

The real horror with this whole LGBTQ movement comes, once again, to the children. Sex-change surgery for children is growing. The Associated Press, in 2012, reported on the case of one California girl who, at the age of eight, was deemed by Los Angeles doctors a typical candidate for sex reassignment surgery because she had told her parents, when she was 18 months old, she was a boy. The girl's parents were on board with the idea; the mother told AP she was closely monitoring closely her daughter's growth so they could give her hormone treatments and puberty-blocking drugs at the right development stage.[46]

For the children, socialist style.

In a recent paper, "Growing Pains: Problems with Puberty Suppression in Treating Gender Dysphoria," endocrinologist Paul Hruz, biostatistician Lawrence Mayer, and psychiatrist Paul McHugh . . . note that approximately 80 percent of gender dysphoric children grow comfortable in their bodies and no longer experience dysphoria, and conclude that there is "little evidence that puberty suppression is reversible, safe, or effective for treating gender dysphoria." Thus, scientific evidence suggests that hormone-induced puberty suppression is harmful and even abusive.[47]

This is the atmosphere where socialism breeds and thrives. Chaos, confusion, a flip of normalcy for the abnormal, a destruction of tradition, a scoffing of what's lawful, a turning from all that's good to all that's not so good—these are all the means by which big government grabs a root and grows, turning a free society toward a socialist mentality, and finally, toward an outright, openly socialist political system. Authoritarian system. Godless, communist system, even.

It all stems from low morals, loose morals, or no morals. It ultimately leads to the exploitation and destruction of the very people who need the most protections. It inevitably creates a cycle of exploitation and destruction with a most predictable outcome: the utter collapse of any semblance of a free society.

Masquerading all this destruction as a benefit to youth is nothing less than pure evil.

CHAPTER 7

FAILING TO GRASP THAT NOT ALL DO-GOODERS DO GOOD

f America was founded on a principle of rights coming from God, not government—which it was and which is clear in the very Declaration of Independence's foundational recognition of "certain unalienable rights" coming from the "Creator"—then sovereignty is precious. Borders are crucial. The Constitution, as based on these individual and unalienable rights, is imperative to preserve.

Enter the United Nations, in all its global governance glory, with all its missionary talk of peace, with all its promises to bring about worldwide standards of equality. Well, the United Nations may talk a good game of peace and goodwill, of freedom to all of humankind. But our nation's founders most certainly would've regarded the global body with suspicion just the same.

"No title of nobility shall be granted by the United States: and no person holding any office or profit or trust under them, shall, without the consent of the Congress, accept of any present, emolument, office, or title, or any kind whatever, from any king, prince or foreign state," Article 1, Section 9 of the Constitution reads, as a check against foreign influences. Article 1, Section 10 applies similar standards to the states, prohibiting executives serving in these political offices from singling out favored citizens by granting them "titles of nobility."[1] The spirit of these clauses is clear: It speaks to the need to beware the influences and entrapments of foreign states. Beware of Greeks bearing gifts.

Other nations, foreign governments, global governing bodies—no matter how enticing the policies, no matter how tempting the platforms, no matter how worthy-sounding the proposals, fact is, they all must be regarded and approached with caution, judged first and foremost for their alignment with the preciousness of America's freedoms. It's the trust-but-verify way. It's the "America first" way.

United Nations

If big government breeds socialism, then all the more so global government. It's no coincidence leftists love the United Nations and want to spread its influence deep into America's politics.

President Donald Trump, thankfully, has delivered a refreshing slice of humble pie to this global body, earning himself a reputation as a "disrupter in chief" in the process. For instance—this excerpt, from a November 2019 *Foreign Policy* piece:

> Less than two weeks before Syrian Foreign Minister Walid Muallem was scheduled to arrive in New York City in September to attend the annual United Nations General Assembly debate, his staff received a message from the State Department. The United States would not provide the protective security detail customarily offered to the heads of foreign delegations. But the U.S. government did assign federal police to protect a delegation of Syrian opposition leaders attending the high-level summit, according to a complaint by the Syrian government to a U.N. committee that oversees U.S. relations with the U.N. community.[2]

The globalists gasped; they don't like being snubbed. And truly, what a switch that was from the previous administration, the era of

Barack Obama, when diplomacy wasn't so much the word that best described US associations with foreign heads of state, as butt-kissing. Butt-kissing and apologizing for America—for simply being America.

In 2009, Obama said this to the members of the General Assembly, in a speech at UN headquarters in New York: "In an era when our destiny is shared, power is no longer a zero-sum game. No one nation can or should try to dominate another nation. No world order that elevates one nation or group of people over another will succeed. No balance of power among nations will hold."[3] It was a thinly disguised slap at American exceptionalism—at the idea that when it comes to freedom and individual's rights, America is the best, America is the standard bearer. It's the ideology that gave rise to Ronald Reagan's reference to this nation as the "shining city upon a hill"[4]—which was actually the phrase uttered by John Winthrop, governor of the Massachusetts Bay Colony, during delivery of a sermon in 1630 about his hopes for the new country, entitled, "A Model of Christian Charity."[5]

All the Obama years were outright concessive to the United Nations, at America's peril, no less. In 2015, Obama said this to the UN General Assembly, in a speech in New York: "It is this international order that has underwritten unparalleled advances in human liberty and prosperity."[6] In 2016, Obama said this at the same UN venue: ". . . [T]here's another path—one that fuels growth and innovation, and offers the clearest route to individual opportunity and national success. It does not require succumbing to a soulless capitalism that benefits only the few . . ."[7] See the seeds of socialism as they were being planted?

Trump delivered both a refreshing and long overdue reality thump to the United Nations. But his influences were fated to be temporary, at best. White House administrations change; so, too, the levels of White House cooperation with the United Nations. From Jimmy Carter to Ronald Reagan; from Barack Obama to Donald Trump: one administration's UN butt-kissing is the next administration's insistence on US sovereignty.

More than that, though, no matter who's in the White House, the United Nations will never change. It will always put forth the idea of a global good over a sovereign nation good. And that makes its threat to America an inherent trait of the body. The United Nations will never be a friend to America—no, not even when it pretends to have America's interests at heart. Globalists, like leopards, never lose their spots. Socialists, always on the hunt for ways to increase their power, never sleep.

"Can Trump's Successor Save the Liberal International Order?" wondered Stewart M. Patrick, the James H. Binger senior fellow in global governance and director of the International Institutions and Global Governance Program at the Council on Foreign Relations, in a February 2020 essay.[8] This is a must-read for patriotic Americans. It spells out well the globalist takeover and globalist lust to take over America, America's government, and ultimately, all the world's governments. In other words: This is not conspiracy theory. This, as Patrick put it, is "no mirage."

Only Patrick, in his essay, wasn't warning; he was pining. He was pining for the end of the "Make America Great Again" and "America First" years, yearning for the return of pre-Trump times, when the White House was complicit with the international order. If only Trump hadn't been able to shake off impeachment so easily; if only the US economy, under Trump, weren't so solid; if only the Democratic Party had better candidates on the White House campaign trail, Patrick lamented, in the opening sentences of his piece. He then went on:

> [S]hould one [of these Democrats] pull off this audacious feat [and win against Trump], the new president will face another colossal challenge: reviving the liberal international order that Trump has done so much to disparage and dismantle. . . . The liberal international order was no mirage, and it did not arise by accident . . . During World War II, Presidents Franklin D. Roosevelt and Harry Truman laid the foundations for an open,

multilateral system under international law . . . Successive U.S. administrations believed that it was in America's enlightened self-interest to promote an open, rule-bound order governed by international institutions. Thanks to their efforts, the seven decades after 1945 saw hundreds of multilateral organizations and treaties emerge to govern everything from trade in services to the allocation of slots for satellites in orbit. . . . That order is now in grave crisis. Trump has abandoned any aspiration to global leadership in favor of a nationalist, transactional and hyper-sovereigntist mindset.[9]

This Patrick piece is breathtakingly honest, yes? What's more, with the dawn of Brexit and the election of Boris Johnson as UK prime minister, this very "hyper-sovereigntist mindset" has spread, giving the elites in power even greater cause to worry.

Rarely do those mocked as tin-foil-hat-wearing nutcases sputtering about a new world order receive so open an admission of the longtime push for just that—for a new world order of global governance—as well as a simple acknowledgment of the "whens" and "hows" the New World Order movement gathered steam. No wonder F.D.R. is held in such high regard by the progressives-slash-socialists of America. As Patrick made clear, it was Roosevelt's work that laid the groundwork for much of the global attacks against US sovereignty that take place today.

Hillary Clinton was supposed to take these international reins and run with them. But she failed. She failed to win the White House. It was a glitch of high order, an unexpected wrench thrown global elites' way.

Of Patrick's 2008 book, *The Best Laid Plans: The Origins of Multilateralism and the Dawn of the Cold War,* John Gerard Ruggie, the Kirkpatrick professor of international affairs at Harvard University and the UN secretary-general's special representative for business and human rights, wrote: "A timely and important book which shows convincingly how and why the twenty-first century quest for a viable global order is linked inextricably with the ongoing political struggle for the heart and soul of America itself."[10]

Clinton's loss was a sudden and shocking departure from the best-laid plans of the internationalists. Trump's win stayed the globalists' struggle for America's heart and soul—in much the same way Reagan, with his love for America and humble regard for the preciousness of America's freedoms, turned back the clock on the socialist-like devastations of Carter's policies and economics. But in both cases, it was for a time, for only a time.

Globalists always lurk. Communists always lust. Collectivists always scour for ways to seep into society.

They're in America's politics, on America's soil, pressing forward their socialist views in the worst, most deceptive ways possible—as charity for the poor and downtrodden. Exploiting misery can be quite lucrative.

The worst kinds of socialists, morally speaking, at least, are those who disguise their control-freak, power-grabbing, selfish designs as charitable efforts, aimed at helping the less fortunate, the most in need, the least able to take care of themselves. The United Nations is expert at playing that game—the United Nations and its many nonprofit offshoots, nonprofit partners, nongovernmental group consorts and affiliated nonprofit foundations, all with missions of helping people.

The sheer size of the bureaucracy guarantees corruption. The do-good nature of the bureaucracy makes it difficult to investigate without facing a barrage of outrage. Yet every now and then, signs of the corruption surface just the same. In August 2019, *Foreign Policy* ran with a headline that said, "Greed and Graft at U.S. Climate Program." The story went on to report how whistleblowers accused the United Nations Development Programme (UNDP), a body that touts a mission of eradicating poverty around the world, of misusing monies that were intended to fight climate change in Russia.[11] The foundation for the piece was a warning from Dmitry Ershov, a Russian national who oversaw the Standards and Labels program for the UNDP's greenhouse gas projects in his home state before turning informant on the graft he observed.[12]

In a December 2018 recorded statement, Ershov said to the project's overseas' funders: "Donors, please do not let the UNDP get away with stealing your money and covering it up for years and years."[13] This wasn't the first time Ershov complained about UNDP. Nor was he the only one.

> Ershov is one of nearly a dozen former U.N. employees, auditors, and consultants who have been flagging concerns for nearly a decade about mismanagement and alleged misappropriation of millions of dollars in international funds from the Global Environment Facility, or GEF, which are intended to reduce greenhouse gas emissions in Russia. But their concerns about irregularities in the program—which were first reported internally back in 2011—were largely dismissed or ignored for several years by their superiors in Istanbul, New York, and Washington, as well as by donor governments, including the United States.[14]

That, even as a quiet 2017 audit, shared only with New York and Istanbul officials affiliated with the UNDP—until *Foreign Policy* broke the news, that is—concluded that millions of dollars that were supposed to be used for the Russia project had been redirected to other hands. Specifically, auditors said there were "strong indicators of deliberate misappropriation" of funds, between the years of 2010 and 2014.[15]

Nothing was done, of course. The UNDP said its internal investigators found the misappropriations of funds allegations to be untrue—though a spokesperson reportedly told *Foreign Policy* that the UN Office of Audit and Investigation determined "the project management had not met expected standards."[16] The UN and donor governments similarly denied or ignored or dismissed the accusations. Meanwhile, Ershov was pressured to leave his UN-tied post.[17]

But as for the elites—they protected their own. They secured their interests. They kept the money. And that's how the big behemoth of bureaucracy called the United Nations operates: by creating such a behemoth of bureaucracy that it's ridiculously easy to kick the can of accountability down the road, to another office, and then to another and another. It's practically impossible to pin responsibility on any single person, on any specific manager or leader. When whistleblowers do whistle, even well-placed whistleblowers, they're easily ignored.

"Because I was closely involved in the EU operations in Russia," Ershov said in an interview with Newsroom, "I knew all these procedures. I sit in the evaluation committees; here I see that there is no control . . . there was no international expert nearby or above."[18] That's the United Nations. Big government, big money, zero accountability. Big tentacles. The flowchart looks like this: Atop the actual UN body is the Chief Executives Board for Coordination, or CEB. The CEB includes the United Nations, as well as 15 organizations that were created by various governmental agreements, a dozen funds and programs established by the General Assembly, and another three "related" groups—the International Atomic Energy Agency, the World Trade Organization and the International Organization for Migration.[19]

The 15 agencies created via intergovernmental agreements are the International Labour Organization, the Food and Agriculture Organization, the UN Educational, Scientific and Cultural Organization, the World Health Organization, the World Bank Group, the International Monetary Fund, the Universal Postal Union, the International Telecommunication Union, the World Meteorological Organization, the International Maritime Organization, the World Intellectual Property Organization, the International Fund for Agricultural Development, the UN Industrial Development Organization, and the World Tourism Organization.[20] The dozen funds established by the General Assembly include the UN Conference on Trade and Development, the UN Development Program, the UN Environment Program, Office of the United Nations High Commissioner for Refugees, the UN Relief and Works Agency for Palestine Refugees in the Near East, the UN Children's Fund, the UN Population Fund, the World Food Program, and the UN Office on Drugs and Crime.[21] Those are just the organizations under the umbrella of the CEB, controlled by the various organizations' executives and chaired by the UN secretary-general, all of whom meet twice each year to "consider policy and management issues impacting" the UN system.

There are also other bodies connected to the UN bureaucracy but separate from the CEB—bodies that include the UN International Computing Centre, the Organization for the Prohibition of Chemical Weapons, the Office of the UN High Commissioner for Human Rights, and the UN Framework Convention on Climate Change, to name a few.[22] There are also regional commissions—the UN Economic Commission for Europe, the UN Economic and Social Commission for Asia and the Pacific, the UN Economic Commission for Latin America and the Caribbean.[23] There are also research and training institutes established by the General Assembly, to include the UN Institute for Disarmament Research, the UN Research Institute for Social Development, the UN University, and humorously enough, the UN Institute for Training and Research.[24]

There are more—that list is incomplete. But the takeaway is this: How in the world can anyone track the United Nations? How in the world can anyone hold the United Nations accountable? More important, from an American perspective: How can a democratic republic with a Constitution that recognizes the God-given rights of the individual survive in the face of such monstrous interlopers?

The multitudinous offices of the United Nations invite the globalist influence into every aspect of human life. And that simply affords the United Nations innumerable opportunities to press its socialist visions onto the governments of the world—onto America. How can America, free and sovereign America, survive?

"Incoming UN Chief a Career Socialist," the Daily Signal reported in 2016, about the confirmation of Antonio Guterres to a five-year term as secretary-general.[25] As the United Nations itself noted, Guterres for years "was active in the Socialist International, a worldwide organization of social democratic political parties. He was the group's vice president from 1992 to 1999, cochairing the African Committee and later the Development Committee. He served as president from 1999 until mid-2005."[26] That was after South Korea's Ban Ki-moon held the secretary-general position for two terms, from 2007 through 2016. Though far less overtly socialist, Ban nonetheless pushed big redistribution of wealth programs, most notably the Climate Change Summit's radical environmental provisions and the Millennium Development Goals' poverty eradication programs.[27] Once again, note the messaging— note the do-gooding messaging: it's all for the betterment of society; it's all for the greater good of humankind. Participate, pay up, or be deemed a problem, not part of the solution.

HAPPYTALISM

"United Nations NEP calls on all people and all nations to adopt 'HAPPYTALISM' over Capitalism/Socialism on occasion of July 4 US Independence Day 2019," the PR Newswire reported, in reference to the global body's New Economic Paradigm Project, the NEP.[28] What's that? It's pure crazy, that's what it is. "HAPPYTALISM" and the UN New Economic Paradigm Project came into being in 2009, on the heels of global financial insecurities, as a means of imagining, envisioning and ultimately, working toward fairer international financial systems for all. Like all socialist programs, it sounds wonderful—on paper. From PR Newswire:

> HAPPYTALISM [is aimed at] solving siloed crises and issues, such as poverty, inequality, the mental health crisis, climate change, discrimination, freedom and slavery, gender inequality, sustainable economic growth . . . HAPPYTALISM answers the broader need

for a bold new economic and human development system and paradigm that addresses systemic and legacy issues, which exist as a result of the tyranny of the status quo and obsolete mindsets and ways of thinking, and envisions a totally new world where all human beings thrive and are free to live happy and fulfilling lives. HAPPYTALISM uniquely goes above and beyond old world and obsolete economic and political systems, such as capitalism and socialism, by proposing and advancing a philosophy that responds directly to the root causes of global crises . . .[29]

Oh, please, make it stop. As if the United Nations, with a simple declaration, could suddenly, magically and magnificently erase all the bad of the world and bring about only the good. As if coining a catchy word akin to nirvana and putting it in all-caps guarantees its outcome—happy, happy, happy all around.

As if the United States didn't already have an economic system that already addressed all the points of "HAPPYTALISM."

It's capitalism, after all, that brings the desire, opportunity, and freedom to produce, create, buy and sell, problem-solve and grow, both individually and as a society. Government-controlled economies, even those tailor-made for T-shirts and bumper stickers with the word *happy* in the title, are failed economies-in-waiting. "HAPPYTALISM" isn't just absurd. It's a slick UN social media marketing campaign designed to capture the attentions of the low-information voters, the useful idiots, the social justice crusaders, and the like, who can then hashtag a redistribution of wealth idea to infinity and beyond, all the while pretending they're working hard to combat societal ills. All the while driving further and further into the public consciousness and public discourse the idea that capitalism is bad, global governance is great, socialism shows concern for the poor, and only those with cruel and selfish hearts would disagree.

So much of what the United Nations pushes is antithetical to America, a country rooted in concepts of self-governance, self-sufficiency, and limited government. Yet so much of what the United Nations pushes, America funds. The Council on Foreign Relations reported in 2019 that America funded the United Nations to the tune of $10 billion in 2017—about a fifth of the global body's total budget. Most of that money was voluntarily provided, rather than assessed.[30] That means the United States isn't just paying what it agreed to pay to support UN operations, but also coughing up extra money for those UN bodies and programs and missions that aren't funded out of the agency's general operations' pot. We volunteer far more than we're assessed. More, from CFR:

> [M]andatory contributions help fund the United Nations' regular budget, which covers administrative costs and a few programs, as well as peacekeeping operations. In 2018, the United States paid 22 and 28 percent of these budgets, respectively . . . . The U.S. government contributed more than $10 billion to the United Nations in 2017, the most recent fiscal year with full data available. About $7 billion of this total was voluntary and $3.5 billion was assessed. This represents roughly one-fifth of the $50 billion the United States spends annually on foreign aid, which, by comparison, is about what the government allocates annually to the U.S. Coast Guard.[31]

America could easily use its power of the purse to exert substantial influence over the United Nations. America could start by pulling back the $7 billion purse of voluntary contributions that go to the likes of the UN Children's Fund, the UN Population Fund, and the World Food Program, and instead, provide the same resources and offer the same sorts of assistance using only those mechanisms that are more accountable to the US taxpayer and less contrary to American principles. Why use the United Nations at all? America has churches, nonprofits, charities, and a willing and compassionate citizenry. If American tax dollars are going to be

used to help foreigners, it seems that a simple solution to UN corruption and socialism would be to cut out the UN middleman, so
to speak. Send the money currently going to the United Nations
to US nonprofits instead. Let the charitable professionals within
US borders handle the overseas' outreach to feed families, educate
children, build homes, and develop infrastructure.

Here's a real kicker, too: UNDP is one of those UN offshoots
that relies on voluntary contributions, not assessed fees. "The
United States has contributed US $80 million a year since 2012 to
UNDP's core operating budget," UNDP reported. "This voluntary
contribution funds work that is vital to advance US foreign policy, national security, and economic interests around the world."[32]
Sounds do-gooding enough. But remember: Whistleblowing Russia
national Dmitry Ershov, along with a dozen other UN-tied officials, testified otherwise. Far too often, a peek behind the curtain of
UNDP doors reveals more wealthy elites working toward the same
borderless, anti-sovereign, statist global governing system as the
United Nations at large—than it does truly charitable minded individuals, seeking to serve in humble compassion to the world's poor.

Gifts of Money Don't a Saint Make

The Open Society Institute run by world renowned anti-American
philanthropist George Soros gave $3.4 million to UNDP in 2010;
that was after giving $2.3 million in 2008, and other amounts
totaling into the millions in other years.[33] The Soros Foundation
network, another George Soros organization, gave more than
$2 million to UNDP between the years of 2004 and 2010.[34] The
Bill and Melinda Gates Foundation, the Ford Foundation, the
Rockefeller Foundation—these are all organizations with far-left
ideologies that have donated, collectively, millions of dollars to
UNDP.[35]

The left loves to showcase these nonprofits and these billionaire foundation examples of goodness as compasses of virtue and
generosity. But gifts of money don't a saint make. Charity doesn't

always come from love. Sometimes, charity is motivated instead by desires to spread influence, stretch one's power—sow seeds of socialism.

The Gates Foundation was in large part responsible for bringing America the disastrous, top-down, heavily bureaucratic and federally mandated—for schools that wanted substantial funding, that is—Common Core education program.[36] The Ford Foundation has an entire Center for Social Justice building in New York City dedicated to bringing "social good" to the world—meaning, the far left's vision of social good, by taking from one to give to another—and to honoring "the courageous people who devote their lives to achieving it."[37] The Rockefeller Foundation counts among its causes the 2015–2017 Transform Finance project in Virginia, a $150,000 endeavor aimed at "empower[ing] investors to make capital allocation decisions based on an enhanced understanding of racial justice."[38]

The coursing of dollars from the elite flow widely from foundation to organization to UN mission to globalist cause. It's a seamless transference that makes for some of the world's most powerful socialist-minded elitists all traveling the same massively bureaucratic circles, all funding the same sorts of bureaucratic causes—all falling under media and watchdog radars by cloaking their socialist, collectivist designs in altruistic wrappings.

What's wrong with the Ford Foundation helping UNDP provide financially for poorer nations? Nothing.

Nothing at all—so long as Americans aren't caught in the trap of believing all these billionaires' do-goodisms are simply acts of charity, no strings attached. Nothing—so long as American tax dollars aren't used to bolster and pad the endeavors of the global bodies, and therefore, either directly or indirectly, the agendas of global-minded billionaires.

When Bill Gates in 2020 pushed hard for Americans to stay home, stay away from work, stay on the stimulus check dime until his foundation, working in partnership with the World Health

Organization and other groups, could develop a vaccine for coronavirus, members of the media fawned; big government types cheered. This is the same World Health Organization, mind you, of which Politico wrote in 2017: "Some billionaires are satisfied with buying themselves an island. Bill Gates got a United Nations health agency in Geneva."[39]

Watchdogs in the press should've been all over these connections. Watchdogs should have barked up that age-old follow the money tree and called out the inherent conflicts of interest with a guy who on the one hand runs a foundation with a stated mission to develop vaccines for the world and on the other pushes the WHO to declare coronavirus a pandemic—thereby opening the doors to global need for a vaccine. Watchdogs should have hesitated more in offering a guy with a vested financial interest in developing vaccines for the world a national and even international platform to talk about the dangers of coronavirus, and the need for a globally administered vaccine. But they didn't. "Bill Gates Might Save the World. Or Waste Billions on Vaccine Hunt," one April headline from The Daily Beast read.[40] Watchdogs were too busy carrying water for Gates—simply because Gates seemed so giving of his time and money and attention for a cause that he said would save lives. From CNBC, in late April: "Bill Gates is the top target for coronavirus conspiracy theories." The story quoted Mark Suzman, chief executive of the Bill & Melinda Gates Foundation, as saying that "it's distressing that there are people spreading misinformation when we should all be looking for ways to collaborate and save lives."[41]

Well, what's really distressing is the carte blanche way globalists are able to tout "for the good of humanity" as cover for their own personal agendas. That's not to say Gates doesn't have a love or compassion for humanity and a true desire to help. It is to say, though, that when billionaires working with globalists and foreign governments get involved, it's not always an America-first type of attitude that dominates. It's not always an America-first outcome that's guaranteed. And Americans shouldn't be afraid to call out these conflicts of interest, or at least question these perceived conflicts of interest, out of fear of offending billionaires and globalists with power. That's what the left counts on as a means of spreading its leftist views and agendas.

Look at these UNDP projects, examples of where U.S. tax dollars are commonly spent:

- A $436,913 consulting and construction project in Aruba[42]
- A $650,000 catering job at the UNDP facility in Bonn, Germany[43]
- A near-$2.6 million purchase of information technology equipment for the National Election Board of Ethiopia[44]
- A $957,819 payment for a garbage compactor and other vehicular needs in Lebanon[45]
- A $5 million-plus "procurement of Biometric Citizen Registration kits, software and related services for citizens' registration process in Honduras"[46]
- An $18 million bill for "travel services to U.N. agencies"[47]

These are but a handful of the most recent of hundreds of procurement notices from UNDP billed to or paid by America's Joe Q. Taxpayer. These are but a fraction of the expenses that UN globalists bill and that US taxpayers pay. When it comes to foreign aid in general, the pool of frivolously spent US tax dollars is deep. And honestly, it's tough to track the money as it travels.

Moldova

Here's an example of how complicated it gets to track foreign aid and to hold recipients responsible for the proper use of aid they get from US coffers. The nation of Moldova is small, landlocked, agriculturally based, and squeezed as it is between Ukraine and Romania, a geographical and political battleground of significant proportions. It's truly the crossroads of the east and west. While Moldovans rely on Russia and Ukraine for most of their energy, the state also benefits from a steady infusion of American dollars. Its future is still on shaky ground, however. "Since declaring independence following the collapse of the USSR in 1991, Moldova has made great progress toward becoming a strong, independent and market-oriented democracy," USAID reported, in a release about its 1992 aid-to-Moldova program "to support [the] transition" and to help establish "health and social safety" nets, democracy, and an economy based on private investments.[48]

Unfortunately, Moldova also has a corruption problem. "Politicians all along the political spectrum in Moldova have a reputation for being corrupt. . . . Endemic corruption, lack of transparency and accountability coupled with a high public debt and low business confidence has severely affected the country," Transparency International reported.[49] And from Reuters: "Moldova has been dogged by political instability and corruption, especially since a scandal known as the 'theft of the century' emerged in 2014–2015 in which $1 billion, around an eighth of its economic output, was pilfered from three banks."[50]

Forbes initially reported Vladimir Plahotniuc, one of Moldova's wealthiest and most powerful businessmen—and a former chairman of the country's Democratic Party, a leftist political group that was granted full membership status with Socialist International in 2009[51]—had a hand in orchestrating the theft of what ultimately amounted to half the reserves of the nation's National Bank. Plahotniuc denies the theft; he denies, too, all the other accusations that have plagued him for years. Forbes wrote in 2016:

Interpol has had a case ID involving Plahotniuc's activities throughout Western Europe since 2007 and think he is loosely associated with one of Russia's biggest mafias, the Solntsevskaya Brotherhood. Plahotniuc denies this . . . [H]e is not the easiest guy to defend. He was banned from running for prime minister by the president because of his spotty past. A July 26 arrest of a former associate in Ukraine who's looking to talk to the Federal Bureau of Investigation is the most recent example of how cohorts of his keep getting in trouble. To put it simply, Plahotniuc is Moldova's man behind the curtain, an A-list businessman who owns everything from luxury resorts to media outfits . . . A *New York Times* headline calls him Moldova's most "feared tycoon."[52]

To regard Moldova, and Moldova's richest politicians and most successful businessmen, in any other way than suspicious is to play the fool. Yet amid the known corruption, amid the known controversies about Plahotniuc, is this, from Joe Biden, who made a historic visit to Moldova while vice president in 2011, and said:

As you continue on this journey [of reform], I promise you, America will be your partner. Over five years, the United States . . . will provide a quarter of a billion dollars—$262 million—to support your agricultural industry. This assistance, God willing, will improve your roads to help your farmers get their goods to market, will make it easier for your farmers to secure the loans they need to buy better equipment. . . . And by the way, Moldova has made its own contributions, significant contributions, to American society and to American culture.[53]

Biden then referenced Barack Obama's former White House chief of staff, Rahm Emanuel, who said "that he has inherited his legendary toughness from his Moldovan grandfather" and Hollywood actress Natalie Portman, who "told us she carries in her wallet a picture, a photograph of her Moldovan grandmother."[54] And Biden wrapped his address by once again vowing, "America will walk with you on this journey" because "a successful Moldova" will "benefit" both Europe and the United States.[55]

Well and good. Fine and dandy. A chugging Moldovan economy, filled with chugging-along financially savvy and successful Moldovan citizens, is good for global business—good for Europe, good for America, good for Democrats and Republicans, both.

But using US tax dollars to bolster countries known as cesspools of corruption isn't sound fiscal policy that puts America first. Particularly, when the money's given over and over again. And saying the money's needed to help the poor and downtrodden doesn't make the corruption go away.

"Vice President Joe Biden," the White House reported in June of 2014, "announced during his meeting with Moldovan President Nicolae Timofti on June 7 an additional $8 million in assistance to Moldova, pending consultations with the U.S. Congress. This assistance will support Moldova's European choice and mitigate vulnerabilities to external pressure."[56] A few months later the United States, under Obama's administration, committed to spending another chunk of US taxpayer cash in Moldova, this time, as part of the two countries' assistance agreement "to support good governance" and economic growth. "Under these agreements, the United States . . . represented by the United States Agency for International Development (USAID), has agreed to provide about $27 million dollars for activities which will help Moldova create a more effective and accountable democratic governance system," the US Embassy in Moldova reported.[57]

Where's the accountability? Accountability is the one feature that appeared to be lacking during America's ongoing aid to Moldova, a country known as corrupt, a country known for staging the "theft of the century," a country known to be swimming in socialist influence. Plahotniuc fled Moldova in the summer of 2019, in shameful dodge of allegations of money laundering. But there's an interesting difference between US Democrats and Republicans in how his flight is being regarded. "As Plahotniuc fled the country," the *Washington Times* reported in January 2020, "the authorities were justifiably concerned that Plahotniuc's supporters in the United States, such as former Obama-era Assistant Secretary of State Victoria Nuland, may have attempted to influence the Trump Administration to offer the notorious oligarch political protection and enable his eventual return to power in Moldova."[58]

Compare that with this, from Radio Free Europe, also in January 2020.

> Moldovan oligarch and former head of the Moldova's Democratic Party (PDM) Vlad Plahotniuc has been banned from entering the United States "due to his involvement in significant corruption," the U.S. State Department said in a statement on January 13 . . . "In his official capacity, Plahotniuc was involved in corrupt acts that undermined the rule of law and severely compromised the independence of democratic institutions in Moldova," Secretary of State Mike Pompeo said in the statement.[59]

Interesting. This is interesting because the big justification for taking US dollars and sending them Moldova's way was, once again—drumroll, please—for the good of the country, for the good of America and Europe, for the greater good of society at large.

Interesting, too, because of the Biden tie. Joe Biden's son Hunter received tens of thousands of dollars each month for sitting on the board of the natural gas company Burisma Holdings, located in Moldova's neighboring country of Ukraine, at a time when the company was embroiled in corruption allegations.[60]

This is not to allege illegalities on any one's part, but rather to show the curious ties that often accompany foreign aid and the complicated paths the money can travel. If socialism breeds on redistributions of wealth, it seems key to keep abreast of how America's wealth is being spent. Sending money through foreign entities that promise to use it for good should be a last-case scenario for American taxpayers, particularly when there are so many other courses to consider for helping the world's downtrodden. The United Nations is not a natural ally of the United States, and often works at cross-purposes to Americans. UN bureaucrats and globalists are socialists and communists, busily working to strip US taxpayers of money and trashing the Constitution, seizing at our sovereignty.

Billionaires should never be given a free pass just because they call themselves philanthropists. Do-gooders need to be watch-dogged, too. It's a mistake to think that just because someone does some good, that means they're good for America—or even at all that good. After all, even the devil can go to church.

CHAPTER 8

BEING BLIND TO THE GLOBALIST SNAKES IN THE GRASS

In 2016, Politico, an outlet that can hardly be confused as a conservative news source, ran with a headline that went like this: "George Soros' quiet overhaul of the U.S. justice system." That's an attention grabber, yes? The contents, all the more so.

"The billionaire financier," Politico reported, "has channeled more than $3 million into seven local district-attorney campaigns in six states over the past year—a sum that exceeds the total spent on the 2016 presidential campaign by all but a handful of rival super-donors."[1] That's not all. In subsequent campaign seasons, he continued the practice. He expanded the practice.

In the 2018–2019 cycle, Soros pumped more than $2 million into three commonwealth's attorney races in Northern Virginia that normally would've gone forth as barely a blip on campaign budget sheets.[2] He tossed another $2 million into a Philadelphia district attorney race.[3] Between 2014 and 2019, in fact, he spent somewhere in the vicinity of $17 million on local law enforcement races in scores of states across the country, $2 million alone of which went toward the sheriff's seat in Maricopa County, Arizona, to get rid of longtime tough-on-crime conservative Joe Arpaio.[4]

Soros Funding Local Races

Why local law enforcement? That's an easy question to answer. In 2010, Tea Party types saw huge successes in their political races, winning in every region of the nation, most interestingly in the liberal enclave of the Northeast, where 229 state seats went Republican, and in the longtime Democrat-controlled South, which fell to GOP hands. As Rasmussen noted in 2010:

> What was probably most striking at the regional level [in 2010] was the symbolic tipping point that Republicans achieved in the South. For the first time since 1870, there are now more GOP legislators in the South than Democrats, punctuating a decline of Democrats in the region that has been steadily taking place since the late 1950s. Prior to 1994 . . . there was not a single legislative chamber in the South with a majority of Republican members. Now, 19 chambers in the South belong to the GOP, including five which switched [in 2010]: the House and Senate in Alabama, the Louisiana House, and the House and Senate in North Carolina.[5]

Other states saw historic changes, too. In New York, a Republican won a hotly contested District 7 state Senate seat by 451 votes, handing control of the Senate to the GOP.[6] In Oregon, Republicans won enough seats to tie with Democrats in the state House.[7] By the numbers, 22 state legislatures changed political direction in the 2010 election cycle, all from Democrat to Republican.[8] Democrats had to do something to counteract this massive Republican uptick in influence. Federal races are expensive; the logic, to the left, was this: Why not look local?

So George Soros did. He started aggressively spending on local law enforcement races via his Justice and Public Safety Political Action Committee, and through its various state offshoots—the Illinois Justice and Public Safety PAC, for instance.[9] And the New York Justice and Public Safety PAC.[10] And the Virginia Justice and Public Safety PAC.[11] And the Texas Justice and Public Safety PAC.[12]

And the Arizona Safety and Justice PAC. And the Colorado Safety and Justice PAC. And one in Florida. And one in Louisiana. And in Mississippi, Missouri, New Mexico, and California and the city of Philadelphia.[13]

Soros also spent on other PACs that would, in turn, spend on local and state judicial and law enforcement races. For example, his main Justice and Public Safety PAC headquartered in Washington, DC, gave:

- $25,000 to New Virginia Majority on May 7, 2019
- $50,000 to the same group about a month later, on June 17, 2019[14]
- $70,000 to the New York State Committee of the Working Families Party on June 20, 2019[15]

The New York State Committee of the Working Families Party, just two days before receiving that infusion of cash, had announced its endorsement of 32 candidates for various local governing offices, one of whom was named Tiffany Cabán, running for district attorney for Queens.[16] In a three-week period between 32-day and 11-day mandated filing deadlines, Cabán raised $233,469—in large part to a frantic fundraising push from none other than Representative Alexandria Ocasio-Cortez, the socialist who had just won her own upset against the entrenched Representative Joe Crowley, and by using the same batch of leftist activists and donors.[17] "Cabán was backed by the Democratic Socialists of America, billionaire activist George Soros, and a political action committee with ties to Bernie Sanders," Politico reported.[18] Cabán, in a tight primary race that pitted her against several other Democrats, initially declared a win. But a recount—and subsequent court challenge to the recount— proved her the loser. Queens Borough Melinda Katz won by a handful of votes and went on to beat her Republican challenger, Joe Murray, in November.[19] But who knew a simple district attorney race had so many socialist snakes slithering about, right?

That's just one small race; one small example. And from just one man, Soros. And Cabán was just one small loss, among a sea of wins.

The New Virginia Majority, the Soros-backed nonprofit with a mission to spread "racial, gender, environmental and economic justice," helped usher in a new Democrat-controlled General Assembly in Richmond by taking part in massive get-out-the-vote campaigns.[20] The $75,000 from Soros, coming as it did in the weeks and months right before the elections, certainly funded those efforts. "In 2019," said the group's political director, Maya Castillo, "we knocked on over 500,000 doors, and we talked to voters about protecting their healthcare, and ensuring their children are safe in their neighborhoods and schools."[21]

Then there were these:

- "George Soros poured nearly $2 million into the Philadelphia District Attorney candidacy of Larry Krasner. As we all know, Krasner won," the *Philadelphia Inquirer* wrote in November of 2019.[22]
- Buta Biberaj won the Loudoun County, Virginia, commonwealth's attorney race in November, 2019, with the help of $861,039 of Soros PAC funds, including a separate $18,000 from New Virginia Majority.[23]
- Steve Descano won the Fairfax County, Virginia, commonwealth's attorney race that same month with the aid of $601,369 of Soros funds.[24]
- Parisa Dehghani-Tafti won the top prosecutor job for two Virginia jurisdictions, Arlington and Falls Church, in November 2019, using $621,145 of Soros funds.[25]
- Jim Hingeley defeated Republican incumbent Robert Tracci by nearly 5,000 votes in November 2019, to take over another Virginia seat—the Albemarle County Commonwealth's Attorney office—with the help of $8,000 of Soros dollars.[26] And a month later, he hired four new assistant commonwealth's

attorneys to bring what he described as a more "community" involved feel to the prosecutorial office.[27]

- Geneviéve Jones-Wright won the seat of the San Diego County district attorney's office in 2018 with the help of $402,000 from Soros contributions to the California Justice and Public Safety PAC—an amount that was roughly twice as much as she raised by her own campaign efforts.[28]

- Aramis Ayala, in a win that shocked the community, ousted incumbent Jeff Ashton from office in a 2016 primary to then become the new Orange-Osceola state attorney. How'd she do it? In large part, with an infusion of $1.4 million into her campaign, courtesy the Florida Safety and Justice Group funded by, you guessed it, George Soros.[29]

Those are but a few of the Soros-funded wins in local judicial and law enforcement races in recent years. And if you're not clear on the significance of a district attorney office or a commonwealth's attorney seat, think "first line of defense."

- If sheriffs arrest a black man for selling heroin, only to see the local prosecutor's office insist on leniency and cashless bail because of perceived disparities over black-white incarcerations—that's a travesty of justice.

- If local police pick up a drunken driver only to learn he's an illegal with a long criminal history and several previous deportations, but it's widely known the commonwealth's attorney favors sanctuary policies, not tough border controls—there's going to be a travesty of justice.

- If local prosecutors see their primary role as serving as facilitators to build a more community-oriented, socially just legal system that takes into consideration skin color and race and gender and various other demographics—and not just at law and order and strict constitutional provisions—well, then there are going to be frequent and ongoing travesties of justice.

Aramis Ayala

The story of Ayala demonstrates this well. In 2017, just days after Ayala was sworn into office, Orlando police lieutenant Debra Clayton was shot and killed while trying to apprehend a man, Markeith Loyd, who was wanted for the murder of his pregnant girlfriend. Loyd was sentenced to life in prison for the killing of his girlfriend, but Ayala balked at seeking the death penalty. The outrage from the community was hot and swift.[30] The *Orlando Sentinel* gives a good overview:

> [Ayala] said her initial thought was to seek the death penalty against Loyd . . . But after extensive research, Ayala said she found the death penalty to be a costly process that drags victims' families through years of appeals and is not a deterrent to crime—a stance she had not publicly expressed during her campaign.
>
> "The reason we're doing this is for retribution," she said. "I never wanted to be a vehicle of injustice and death."[31]

The explanation didn't sit well with Governor Rick Scott—and why should it? Loyd fatally shot a pregnant woman, for which the jury found him guilty and sentenced him to life, and a police officer who was simply trying to carry out her duty to get him off the streets.[32] Scott's Republican-run office stepped in and reassigned 30 death penalty cases away from Ayala's control. Ayala sued to get back her cases, but five of seven Florida Supreme Court justices found in Scott's favor.[33] And here's the main punch part: Justice Alan Lawson, writing for the majority, said Ayala's "blanket refusal" to consider the death penalty was not a right she could claim as part of prosecutorial discretion.[34] That's code for, "Can it, lady—you're going rogue."

But guess who does favor blanket refusals of the death penalty? George Soros. George Soros and his Open Society Institute, dedicated to "ending the death penalty."[35] George Soros and his Open

Society Institute, which started the Gideon Project in 2000 to bring about the "reform and abolition" of the death penalty, among other actions.[36] George Soros and his Open Society Foundation, which gave $50 million to the American Civil Liberties Union in 2014 to "elect progressive prosecutors in cities with large jail populations," to change and reform how justice is implemented, as the *Sacramento Bee* put it.[37]

This is how the Soros funding mechanism works; this is how the Soros money weaves into local legal and justice systems. It's a huge problem for Americans who believe in the Constitution and in the concept of law and order and in the principles of blind justice. "We're just recognizing how powerful district attorneys are in shaping criminal justice policies, both at the local level, but also at the statehouse," said Taylor Pendergrass, a senior campaign strategist for the ACLU's Campaign for Smart Justice, in a 2018 interview with McClatchy DC for its "Impact 2020" section. "The lobbying power of prosecutors is really a substantial force almost everywhere we want to see change made in the criminal justice system."[38]

What's more, most of these local prosecutors' races are small potatoes on the funding scale—meaning, pre-Soros, races usually cost in the tens of thousands of dollars to run, not hundreds of thousands. Soros and his billions have upset that cart. In 2015, Caddo Parish, Louisiana, attorney Dhu Thompson lost his race for district attorney to James Stewart, a guy who was funded to the tune of $930,000 from Soros-tied organizations.[39] In August of 2016, Ayala sat on nearly $1 million in campaign donations from Soros-tied sources; Ashton, on the other hand, reported $112,445.[40] Ayala's campaign promptly turned that money into television ads and mailers attacking Ashton for race-based prosecutions—the social justice tagline lie of the Open Society types.

And that, ladies and gentlemen, is how you upset a local system of law and order. Soros, remember, is a globalist who wants to abolish sovereign states, crack wide and destroy capitalism, and instill an order, worldwide and in America, which has nothing to do with individual rights and everything to do with elitism and collectivism—where only the wealthiest would have the power to decide and govern. How is that the least bit in line with American limited government ideals?

On reports that Soros in 2019 had funneled $100,000 to Democrat Jack Stollsteimer in the district attorney race of Delaware County—dubbed Delco, and located by Philadelphia—newspaper columnist Christine Flowers wrote in *Philadelphia Inquirer*:

> I don't know either of the DA candidates well, and my objec-
> tions to Soros' involvement in this race is not about picking one
> candidate against the other. . . .This is about a man who has no
> connection to my corner of the world attempting to impose his
> agenda on a crucial local race without any real understanding of
> how that will impact the people who have to live with the fallout.
> This is about diminishing the voices of voters who could see
> their choices heavily influenced by a man they don't know and
> money they can never hope to earn in three lifetimes. . . . There is
> something concerning about a stranger placing his very weighty
> thumb on the scales of a local state race where he will not bear
> the consequences.[41]

Yes, there is. And there should be to anyone with concerns about the fate of law and order in this country. President Donald Trump can appoint all the conservative, constitutionally minded, limited government types to the US Supreme Court he wants—if leftists like Soros are able to take over the local prosecutors' offices, the legal system in America will be tipped and toppled regardless. Not everything can be challenged in the higher courts; not every citizen has the ability to take their cases to the next level for redress. Buying district attorney spots, for socialists like Soros, gives good bang for the buck.

Michael Bloomberg

Michael Bloomberg has jumped into the action, as well. In December 2017, a writer for the online *Marcellus Drilling News* posted a brief that went like this:

> Somebody needs to sue the New York University (NYU) School of Law and 10 state Attorneys General to stop a grievous practice—a bastardization of our justice system. We are floored to learn that NYU is paying to hire attorneys to work inside the offices of the Attorneys General in 10 different states— Pennsylvania being the latest. The aim of hiring these new assistants to work alongside AGs is to launch lawsuits to "protect" the environment—i.e., sue fossil fuel companies. It is a gross per-version of our legal system meant to challenge policies the very liberal NYU doesn't like. Our legal system is now, apparently, for sale—at least it is in PA and nine other blue Democrat-controlled states.[42]

A few months later, the nonprofit Natural Gas Now picked up the story and ran its own version, giving insights into where NYU School of Law was getting its funding and how that money was actually helping radical groups like the Natural Resources Defense Council ramrod through environmental regulations. "There's something nefarious going on with the supposedly non-political NYU Law School, which Mike Bloomberg seems to be using to buy AG offices for the NRDC," Natural Gas Now wrote.[43] Indeed. In August 2017, Philanthropy News Digest announced the forma-tion of a new center at NYU's School of Law, the State Energy and Environmental Impact Center, to "provide legal, analytics and com-munications support to state attorneys generals' office across the country; provide the services of ten NYU fellows as special assistant AGs for two years with the aim of strengthening the capacity of AG offices; [and] identify and coordinate pro bono representation."[44]

The Impact Center would also serve as an educational source for the attorneys general on environmental issues, and as a public relations mouth, so to speak, for whatever environmental controls and actions the attorneys general decided to take.[45]

As Philanthropy News Digest noted, the center was started with almost $6 million of Bloomberg-tied funds. And it was initially headed by David Hayes, the guy who served in leadership posts in the Department of the Interior during both Bill Clinton and Barack Obama administrations.[46] The underlying mission of the organization was to fight President Donald Trump's softening of Obama-era environmental regulations and provisions. "State attorneys general have a unique role in defending the citizens of their states from environmentally destructive actions and advancing the clean energy, climate change and environmental interests of their constituents," Hayes said. "We look forward to working in close cooperation with state attorneys general around the country to support their efforts to address complex energy and environmental matters."[47]

In 2018, the first round of approved attorneys general offices were selected for the program—all controlled by Democrats: Washington, DC, Illinois, Maryland, Massachusetts, New Mexico, New York, and Washington, and then later joined by Oregon, Virginia, and Pennsylvania. Fourteen NYU School of Law fellows, paid through the school's impact center, which was funded by Bloomberg, took up office in these 10 jurisdictions, and commenced doing battle on behalf of far-left environmentalists.[48] Some of their quasi-secretive campaigns?

These are examples of approved applications made by two states for Bloomberg's grant money:

- Halting natural gas pipeline developments through the state of New York that were opposed by his Green friends[49]
- Tying up the New York courts with petitions about efficiency standards for ceiling fans[50]

- Helping Pennsylvania pursue a "progressive environmental policy agenda"—whatever that means[51]

From *Natural News Now*:

This is what the very privileged Michael Bloomberg is funding in both Pennsylvania and New York—the implementation of the special interest agendas of other privileged families. Totally disgusting. Meanwhile, he lives here in Bermuda a good part of the time and flies fuel-guzzling jets and helicopters to go wherever he wants to go. Totally hypocritical. This is Michael Bloomberg and the fact he's buying attorneys general across the country, to tell the rest of us what we can have not have, ought to alarm every American.[52]

Yes—in much the same way the Soros purchase of local prosecutors should alarm every American.

It's not a matter so much of the First Amendment right to finance one's political candidates and appointments as one chooses—in the vein of freedom of speech. In both cases, in both the matter of Soros buying prosecutors and Bloomberg buying attorney general seats, it's the idea of wealthy elites trying to circumvent the Constitution, Congress, the White House, and the constituency with loads of cash—and in some cases, doing it through shadowy means that aren't exactly transparent and easy to trace. "How Bloomberg Pays to Prosecute the Trump EPA," the *Wall Street Journal* wrote in July 2019, in a piece exposing the billionaire's backroom dealings to strategically plant climate change warriors in the states' legal offices.[53]

It wasn't long before Bloomberg faced some backlash. "Massachusetts Attorney General Sued over Use of Bloomberg-Funded Attorneys," Energy in Depth reported in June 2019.[54] "Virginia Blocks Mike Bloomberg's Climate Lawyers," the *Associated Press* wrote in a headline in April 2019.[55] The AP story went on to

report, "Virginia has become the first state to crack down on billionaire Michael R. Bloomberg's effort to embed within the attorney general's office privately funded lawyers dedicated to pursuing
climate change litigation."[56]

Of course, that was when the General Assembly was controlled
by Republicans. In November of that year, Democrats won a clean
sweep of power across all the main state offices—the governor's
mansion, the House, and the Senate. Let the Bloomberg money
flow again. In fact, Bloomberg's first campaign stop on his presidential trail was in Virginia, a state where he spent big to usher
in Democrat control and where he expected big things in return.
"Southeastern Virginia," he said, from his opening Bloomberg
2020 campaign gathering, "proves that with the right candidate,
we can turn areas from red to blue."[57]

With the right amount of money is more like it. It's not the
Bloomberg and Soros don't have the constitutional rights to support whomever they wish for political offices, or to try to use their
billions of dollars to influence those in political offices to vote,
decide, legislate, or act a certain way. They do; they have the same
authority to express their speech by way of campaign donations as
the next guy or gal in America.

But Soros is a destroyer of all-things-American. Bloomberg
is a far leftist and elitist sneak bent on wreaking havoc with the
Second Amendment, through his Everytown for Gun Safety movement and on clamping the rights of private property owners and
businesses with his madcap climate change activism. If their purposes for their purchases of power and political influence were for
the furtherance of the Constitution, the protection of the democratic republic, the betterment of the citizenry—and by betterment,
it's meant the bolstering, not abridging, of individual rights and
natural law—then by all means, their efforts would have to be recognized as proper politicking. Their funding mechanisms would
have to be accepted as in line with the First Amendment.

But theirs are the behaviors of oligarchs, not freedom-loving American patriots. Moreover, they're hardly alone. The Democrats, much as they hate big business, denounce big money, and detest capitalism, happily take big money when it comes from far leftists who made their financial mark the good old-fashioned free market way—and who now want to spend to topple America and turn it toward socialism, or worse.

The Quiet Donors

The Intelligencer, in August 2019, ranked the top influential funders for the Democrats in 2020 as Bloomberg and Soros in the first and third spots, with their millions upon millions in donations; billionaire anti-Trumper Tom Steyer in second place, with roughly $240 million in campaign gifts; Facebook cofounder Dustin Moskovitz in fourth, with $30 million for Democrat candidates; and the largely unknown trio of Donald Sussman, Fred Eychaner, and Jim Simons tying for fifth, with a collective $250 million, give or take, in donations to leftist pols and causes over the past few years.[58]

The Democrats and their quiet donors. "You don't have any idea who these guys are, do you? They're mostly okay with that," the New York Intelligencer wrote, in reference to Sussman, Eychaner, and Simons. "Sussman (a hedge-fund manager who gave Democrats around $74 million from Obama's reelection through last year's midterms), Eychaner (a Chicago media don, $75 million), and Simons (a hedge-fund pioneer, $67 million) are hardly household names, and they've shown little interest in becoming Steyer- or Bloomberg-style celebrities. . . . But all three are at the top of practically every Dem fund-raiser's wish list after doling out huge amounts to both Obama and Clinton."[59]

There's something unsettling about realizing the donors with the biggest pockets to the Democrat Party are those who keep the lowest profiles. It's the snakes that slither unaware that often present the greatest danger.

Compare these Democrat donors to this, from the Heritage Foundation:

> The name that King George III is said to have called the "most damning name of all" on the Declaration of Independence was not that of Benjamin Franklin, John or Samuel Adams, or even John Hancock. Instead, it was businessman Robert Morris. . . . No other man single-handedly contributed more to funding the Revolutionary War. Morris truly lived out the words written in the declaration he signed, pledging his "life, fortune, and sacred honor" for the sake of his country.[60]

Now there's an American patriot. "Robert Morris, America's founding capitalist," is how NPR described him. "He was active in supplying Washington's army with gunpowder, which he smuggled in under the noses of British authorities in Europe and the Caribbean. [Journalist and author Charles] Rappleye argues that the Revolution couldn't have been won without Morris."[61]

What a different era we live in today. Neither Soros nor Bloomberg nor Steyer nor any of the liberal camp's big money donors would part with their precious money to fight for the God-given rights of the average American citizen. They're more intent on using what they earned under capitalism to kill capitalism. They're wanna-be overlords. But more than that, they're hypocrites—yet another characteristic of the socialists.

The fact these heavy-hitter Democrat funders often try to slip their money through back alley doorways via complicated redirects of political advocacy dollars and cents makes them snakes, as well. And warning to Americans: the Democrat Party's filled with such secretive slippery donations.

Republicans have their billionaires and millionaires, too. Sheldon Adelson, for instance, has contributed $300 million to

Republican candidates or organizations in just a few short years, according to Federal Election Commission data collected by the Center for Responsive Politics.[62] But the difference is this: At least conservatives aren't trying to use their finances to take down America, rip wide the borders, and outright kill capitalism.

At least Republicans aren't using their money to destroy the Constitution and all that for which it stands.

CHAPTER 9

CEDING THE CONSTITUTION TO TECHNOLOGY FOR CONVENIENCE'S SAKE

I n 2018, a Florida man named Raul Mas Canosa launched a lawsuit against his city of Coral Gables, the Florida Department of State, and the Florida Department of Law Enforcement, alleging local authorities violated his constitutional rights by installing automatic license plate readers (ALPR) on traffic lights, at various intersections, and near other hot-spot travel locations—including the heavily traveled nearby Interstate 95. "If I've done nothing wrong and have no criminal record, why is my city monitoring me?" Canosa asked, in one newspaper account of the suit, from 2019.[1]

That's a really good question. And it goes to the heart of the problems with much of the technological advances being made in recent years. The more data government collects, the less free Americans will be. There is a madcap tightrope being strung across the country right now, and it's being walked by government entities, police and security officials, constitutionalists and civil libertarians, and Average Joe and Jane Q. Citizens. Where the rope ends, nobody knows.

Back to Canosa. In late 2019, Florida's 11th Judicial Circuit Court ruled against the city's attempt to have the case dismissed, and instead gave Canosa and his attorneys at the New Civil Liberties Alliance the go-ahead to continue—so they did, entering a lengthy discovery phase of requesting, collecting, and disseminating scores of documents related to the surveillance system.[2] What they found was shocking. In a February 2020 sit-down interview for my "Bold and Blunt" podcast at the offices of the *Washington Times*, one of Canosa's attorneys, Caleb Kruckenberg, told me that in a three-year period, the city had collected a grand total of 101 million images.

Images of what? Vehicles. Drivers. Passengers. "These cameras," Kruckenberg said, "they take a picture of the car as it goes by, so they take a picture of the entire car. It's supposed to be just the license plate image but what happens is you get the car, you get the driver usually, and there's metadata associated with the image, so it says this time, this location, going this direction. And then because it's associated with the license plate, it's who[m]ever's the registered owner of the license plate, the person's name, their address, et cetera. And so what happens is, the city, we know in the last three years, they've accumulated more than 101 million of these unique images and they're just massing them in this huge data file."[3]

What's Wrong with ALPR

Coral Gables is hardly the only city using ALPR programs. The technology's spread far and wide—coming to a community near you, no doubt. And the data that's collected is not exactly kept private. In the Florida case, the data is all stored on a server in Virginia maintained by the private company Vigilant Solutions. Moreover, it's supposed to be destroyed after three years—but who really knows what happens.[4] "Once it's stored on the server, it's a little unclear [what happens to the data]," Kruckenberg said. "We know Vigilant Solutions has a commercial interest in the data. We don't know exactly what they do with it. But we also know that the city is allowed to share their data with other agencies. . . . They have all these agreements with other law enforcement agencies that they can share the data, and once they share it, the other law enforcement agency keeps it."[5] The other law-enforcement agencies keep it and do with it as they will. The other law-enforcement agencies use the data to bolster their own ALPR programs, or assist with their own surveillance and tracking activities.

So what? This is the part where someone generally weighs in or wonders, "Well, if you're not doing anything wrong, you have nothing to worry about"—as if government is to be trusted, at all times, with all things. That's a silly argument to make, though. History is filled with governments led by people who were supposedly trustworthy, only to find otherwise. Besides, in America, one of the basic guiding principles of freedom is the idea that individuals are innocent until proven guilty. It's an assumption that's backed by the Constitution's Fifth and Sixth Amendments guaranteeing due process and, in criminal cases, speedy, public, and impartial trials by jury as well as a right "to be confronted with the witnesses."[6] ALPR programs sort of speed walk right by these constitutional ideals. At the very least, ALPR surveillance flips the whole notion of innocent until proven guilty on its head, turning everybody into a possible suspect, and giving the government the power to decide who's innocent, who's suspicious, who's suspicious enough to red-flag and investigate. And all, mind you, without a warrant.

Police appreciate the tool because it gives them the ability to safely check for criminals and criminal activities without having to go through the sometimes time-consuming process of going to court to get a judge's permission to search or surveil. Police also say the program is great for finding stolen vehicles—and stolen children—and could prove crucial in cases involving escaped inmates or fleeing terrorists.

They have a point. Police have indeed been able to apprehend criminal suspects using the plate reading technology. In 2019, for instance, detectives in Kansas City, Missouri, credited the local ALPR system for helping locate and arrest a man they said shot and killed a 70-year-old woman as she drove on Interstate 70.[7] And in 2018, industry news source PoliceOne.com cited seven different instances in which license plate readers provided crucial assistance to law enforcement:

- In 2015, police in Doral, Florida, ran the license plate number of a vehicle parked at a local Walmart through their ALPR database and discovered a link between the registration number and a number of burglaries and auto thefts. That arrest led to the discovery of a local gang, the 400 Boys, which in turn led to several more arrests for other previously unsolved crimes.
- In 2014, police in Kansas City were able to piece together images collected from several ALPR images to identify a man wanted in connection with 18 felonies, including nine shootings, as Mohammed Pedro Whitaker—and to ultimately locate and arrest him.
- In 2013, police in Fayette County, Georgia, turned to historical data stored in several ALPR systems to arrest Christopher Bergeron, the "Pillowcase Bandit," and charge him with burglaries of several homes in seven different counties.
- In 2007, police in San Jose, California, acting on alerts and images from the cruiser's ALPR system of a stolen vehicle in the area, were able to tie the suspected thief to a child abduction and molestation case, and make the proper charges stick.
- In 2007, police in Roseville, California, were able to use ALPR to connect the dots between witness accounts and their reports of partial license plate numbers to locate and apprehend an individual charged with the fatal hit-and-run of a 76-year-old man.[8]

But the number of instances when police have relied on ALPR programs to root out crime and apprehend criminals is relatively low when compared to the amount of data that police, over the years, have scooped up from the surveillance system—and shared. Besides that, when it comes to stopping crime, the effect of ALPR is even more negligible. From CityLab:

> [In 2018], the Electronic Frontier Foundation (EFF), a digital rights organization, filed hundreds of Freedom of Information Act (FOIA) requests via Muckrock, a government transparency platform. The organization was looking for information on deals local and federal agencies have made with Vigilant Solutions, the largest private company selling ALPR technology and data. Recently, EFF released results from 200 responses.
>
> "We found a staggering amount of data that agencies are collecting on people—very little of which is of public interest," said Dave Maass, senior investigative researcher at EFF.
>
> "A total of 173 entities (largely police departments and sheriff's offices, but also some federal agencies) in 23 states scanned a total of 2.5 billion license plates in 2016 and 2017. On average, 99.5 percent of scans belonged to cars that weren't associated with crimes."[9]

That's in a two-year period. Billions upon billions of bits of data were scooped up by police in a two-year time frame from innocent Americans who weren't even suspected, never mind accused of, any crime.

"To put it another way," EFF wrote, "the overwhelming majority of the data is not relevant to crime."[10]

How's that for shocking? Whether or not you can make the argument that police won't misuse the data, or that law-enforcement officials truly need all this data to catch the 0.5 percent of criminal activity—do the EFF math—they otherwise, maybe, wouldn't catch, doesn't negate this larger point: That's a heck of a lot of data being amassed by government entities against private American citizens who've done nothing but drive the roads of their communities. The roads the citizens pay for, by the way.

Here's where the socialism comes in. If the Constitution is the standard, limited government the guiding principle, and the notion that individual rights come from God rather than bureaucrats the building block of the American way, then big data is a tool that gives big government the upper hand on determining who gets what freedoms, when and for how long. Police who spy without warrants are acting in counter to the Constitution. Law-enforcement officials who work with private business to amass and store the warrantless data are growing government's presence quietly, secretly behind closed doors. Individuals who don't know their privacies are being infringed, or who know but feel helpless to put a stop to the privacy infringements, are seeing their rights being chipped slowly but surely, slowly but daily, slowly—and just by driving down the road.

And all that, taken together, is causing a generational and societal shift of mindset that labels those who dare to even criticize such data collection as little more than conspiracy theorists. Think about that. It's putting those who oppose mass data grabs in the position of having to explain why they oppose, what their problem is—or worse, why they don't support police, why they care about their license plate numbers being captured on camera if they're not doing anything wrong, anyway. That's a flipped way of looking at the government-citizen relationship. It's backward.

In a free society, the government should be doing all the explaining, not the people. The government should be going out of its way to humbly, with an attitude of deference, explain to the people why a certain program is needed, why tax dollars are being spent on this versus that, why government should be granted this particular power, why feds ought to be trusted with that constitutional authority, why the bureaucracy should be ceded a portion of previously deemed individual rights in the name of the greater good. In a free society, the individuals are assumed to hold the authorities; the government, only those that are enumerated.

Calling something national security, citizen safety, or community protection, like with ALPR programs, doesn't give government a free pass to grab at God-given individual rights. Government is accountable to the people, not the other way around, and the people can't hold government accountable if they don't have access to the information—or worse, have to beg, plead, cajole, and sue for the information.

Socialism grows in secrecy. And any mindset that sets government first—collective first—and individual second is a danger to American freedoms. The ALPR program is an example of how government, for the greater good, has assumed for itself the power to bypass the Constitution—if not the letter of the Constitution, then certainly the spirit of the Constitution—and to gather data on innocent Americans, store that data, share that data, and to do so in a secretive enough manner that these same citizens can't hold government accountable on the necessity or value of gathering, storing, and sharing the data in the first place. Who's holding the reins of power here, anyway? If you said the people, you're wrong.

But the problem is not the ALPR system, per se. The problem is the ALPR system plus the change in power structure plus the flip in mindsets—multiplied by a million. That is to say: The ALPR program is just one very tiny spoke on the big data wheel that's all feeding a new American order putting government at the top and the individual at the bottom. Technology, at a rapidly evolving rate, is stripping American individuals of individualism and of individual freedoms. And youth, raised as they are on technology, are barely even noticing the loss of freedoms—the encroaching of big government—the insidious infiltration of outright socialism. Or maybe it's not that they're not noticing. Maybe it's they just don't care. Ignorance or apathy: Which is worse?

Anyway, look at where today's technology is leading:

- Facial recognition
- Mass microchipping
- Biometrics for identification purposes
- Predictive health care

- Cameras everywhere, watching all the time
- Police abuse—like parallel construction of crimes
- Predictive crime; predictive policing
- Social media surveillance
- Free speech censorship
- Bitcoin: something to watch
- Universal basic income

Facial Recognition

Matthew Feeney, director of the Cato Institute's Project on Emerging Technologies, wrote in a March 2020, opinion piece for Business Insider that "facial recognition technology is getting out of control"—and the point is valid.[11] Feeney focused on a company called Clearview AI to show how private tech companies are working with law enforcement to root out criminals on social media by using facial recognition software, and how, in the process, warrantless surveillance of innocent citizens is becoming a frequent red flag. But that's just one company; one privacy ding. What about facial recognition technology in drones? In cameras on the street corners? As extensions of the ALPR programs?

The National Institute of Standards and Technology reported in 2018 the technology for facial recognition is improving at a rapid pace.[12] That's due in large part to the massive amounts of data being collected by government and private companies in recent years. Data is the food of artificial intelligence (AI); data is what allows AI to test, recreate, test, grow, test, and fine-tune its theories. The more data, the more accurate the AI. Soon enough, instead of simply identifying faces by photos, AI-infused programs will be able to identify the emotions, feelings, and mental states of the faces in the photos—and draw conclusions, or allow for the human drawing of conclusions—as to the thoughts behind the faces. Thought crime, anyone? An excerpt from a 2020 news story in Gemalto:

[M]assive gains in accuracy have been made in the last five years (2013–2018) and exceed improvements achieved in the 2010–2013 period. Most of the face recognition algorithms in 2018 outperform the most accurate algorithm from late 2013. In its 2018 test, NIST found that 0.2% of searches, in a database of 26.6 million photos, failed to match the correct image, compared with a 4% failure rate in 2014. Yes, you read that right. It's a 20x improvement over four years.[13]

Imagine four more years of the same.

Not saying facial recognition doesn't have its place; certainly, it's fruitful for locating missing children and adults, tracking criminals as they flee, capturing terrorists—or even stopping acts of terrorism before they occur. But the potential for abuse is huge. A government with the power to surveil, identify, and track its citizens 24-7, wherever they roam, is unsettling at best.

Mass Microchipping and Biometrics

Once the stuff of science fiction, the idea of inserting a rice-grain-size electronic chip in a human's hand or wrist has moved a bit more into the mainstream, particularly in Sweden. Select private companies in America, meanwhile, have implemented voluntary programs allowing employees to insert chips that let them unlock office doors, store essential information, or even pay for certain products and services. It's not exactly common on US soil—yet. But the shock factor's fading. Patrick McMullan, chief operations officer of the River Falls, Wisconsin-based Three Square Market software company, for instance, said of his 2017 decision to offer microchipping to employees: "Why not us? Somebody's got to do it."[14]

Not really. In Indiana, for example, legislators made clear citizens hold the ultimate say in deciding whether or not they want a work-based microchip—and those bosses who try to force the technology into their employees' bodies can face punitive damages in court. Other states have passed similar commonsense laws.[15] Microchipping opens the doors for hacking of personal information, as well as for government—or business—tracking of individuals, absent their knowledge or permission.

It's the same for biometrics. Biometrics, which includes facial recognition, as well as voice recognition, iris scanning, and thumb printing, is being used widely for identification purposes on everything from personal cell phones to highly secretive government buildings and offices. Once again, it's not so much the single use technology that's problematic for privacy advocates, as it is the big data collection that goes along with the development and maintenance of the technology, and the fact that once one-piece surveillance becomes acceptable, it opens the floodgates for more. Facial recognition is everywhere in China. But London isn't that far behind.[16] America's airports regularly employ the technology; so, too, police departments from Detroit, Michigan, to Lincoln, Nebraska, to Albuquerque, New Mexico, and points all around and in between.[17]

And guess where iris scanning is making its biggest inroads? In the field of health care. At a hospital near you. "The increasing demand for precise patient identification and the need to reduce healthcare fraud are the significant factors driving the adoption of the iris recognition technology in the market," Mordor Intelligence reported.[18] Be prepared. A new medical era dawns.

Predictive Health Care

Speaking of technology and the health care industry—it's great for doctors to have at computerized hand the ability to determine the real risks of a patient to develop cancer, or of a patient to suffer bone loss, and to prescribe the necessary lifestyle change or medicines to stave off the problem before it occurs. It's great for doctors to have the AI to predict the health problems that might plague a patient by a certain age, so as to give the patient the tools to live a better life—and to be able to do it in a way that's cheaper and faster than most modern medical testing.

But how do you think the health care industry gets the information to make the computerized models that predict the individual health hazards? Big data. From the journal *Nature*, in November 2019:

> Google and one of the largest health-care networks in the United States are embroiled in a data-privacy controversy that researchers fear could jeopardize public trust in data-sharing practices and, potentially, academic studies. At issue is a project dubbed Nightingale that gives Google access to the health-care information, including names and other identifiable data, of tens of millions of people without their knowledge. The people were treated at facilities run by the health network Ascension, which is based in St. Louis, Missouri. . . . [T]he lack of patient knowledge—and the fact that identifiable data weren't scrubbed from the records—has caused U.S. lawmakers to cry foul.[19]

The US Department of Health and Human Services cried foul, too, and launched an investigation.[20] But honestly—so what? Once that cat's out of the bag, there's no putting it back.

Imagine your personal medical tests for sexually transmitted diseases, your in-patient clinic stay for alcoholism, or the notes from your psychotherapy sessions—in the hands of Google. In the hands of insurance companies. In the hands of government. In the hands of hackers. Would it matter, once that privacy's compromised, if they apologized?

Long gone are the days of in-home visits from doctors carrying little black bags. Long gone, too, are the days of expecting medical records to remain private.

Police Abuse, Predictive Policing

Even if courts were to reel in the powers of police to use ALPR and limit the program's use to specific localities where the suspects were known to frequent, and only in cases where law enforcement first went to court to obtain the proper warrants, chances are, the ALPR system wouldn't slip quietly into that good night. Chances are police would still use the program. Why? In a phrase: parallel construction. From *Wired*:

> Parallel construction is when law enforcement originally obtains evidence through a secret surveillance program, then tries to seek it out again, via normal procedure. In essence, law enforcement creates a parallel, alternative story for how it found information. That way, it can hide surveillance techniques from public scrutiny and would-be criminals.[21]

There has to be a certain amount of sympathy for police who work hard at keeping the community safe, only to see a suspect set free by a technicality, or worse, by the sleazy court maneuverings of a sleazebag defense attorney. There has to be a certain amount of understanding, even leeway, given to police who see a drug dealer daily, know what the drug dealer is doing daily, but can only capture and apprehend the drug dealer—and make a conviction stick—by using some sly tactics that butt right up against the line separating ethical from unethical. Police, particularly police walking their beats for years, know their neighborhoods, and more important, know the tricks of the defense court trade. But—that being said—however: Right is right, wrong is wrong, constitutional is constitutional.

Police who knowingly use unauthorized, unconstitutional, secret surveillance to get their guy, and then go back and retrace their investigative steps to try to construct some sort of legal story that will hold up in court and withstand the peppering of defense attorneys, are lying—there's no two ways about it. The lie, to some, might be justifiable; it might put an end to a greater evil that otherwise would cause injury, harm, death, and devastation. But it's still a lie.

And if police get the reputation of being liars, then it makes it even harder to accept and trust their use of technology like predictive crime analytics. Predictive policing comes when statistics of past criminal behaviors are fed into an AI-based system that then analyzes the data and spits out a prediction of when and where similar crimes will be committed in the coming days. Police can beef up staff or better utilize patrol units based on this predictive technology. What's more, this same sort of technology has been used in courts to help judges determine if defendants are more or less likely to become repeat offenders—and sentence and jail accordingly. On surface, it sounds terrific. In theory, it seems amazing.

But machinery that predicts human behavior is a best guess, at best. The pitfalls far outweigh the benefits. In 2016, for instance, Pro Publica found that the technology, when used in the court rooms, seemed biased against minorities.[22] And in 2019, police in California who had initially embraced the predictive policing software in 2010 as a potentially great tool to offset their manpower shortages later found too many inaccuracies and challenges. "We didn't find it effective," Palo Alto police spokeswoman Janine De la Vega told the *Los Angeles Times*. "We didn't get any value out of it. It didn't help us solve crime."[23] That's not to say the hundreds of other rapidly developing police tools in the technology world are going to go back in the box anytime soon.

The more cameras are mounted, the more data is collected and shared, the more the market for data mining and selling expands—the more technology will advance. The more policing will go high tech. The more civil rights will become murky. The more life, as free Americans know it, will mirror a George Orwell nightmare.

Social Media Surveillance and Censorship

In mid-2018, the Institute for Free Speech highlighted an emerging trend of state governments to consider bills that would regulate certain posts on the Internet, particularly those of political nature.[24] The pieces of legislation were all presented in the name of openness and transparency, as means of fighting off foreign meddling into US elections. But a regulation is a regulation is a regulation. And toward that thought, what gives government the right to determine the appropriateness of Internet posts—of an Internet poster's speech? As if the people were too stupid to determine, absent government's direction and intervention, the truthfulness or value of something online.

It's not just condescending. It's un-American. It's as the Institute for Free Speech wrote: "If successful, the end result [of these bills] will be a less vibrant democracy as Americans who fear for their privacy in these polarized times choose silence."[25] The Internet should be free from government controls. It's bad enough social media is owned by leftists who seek to boot conservatives from the platforms—to stomp out conservative thought in its entirety. It's bad enough social media's leading executives and administers play dumb when they're called to task for this anti-conservative censorship and for the bias of their staff. But setting government as the arbiter of appropriate Internet speech would be much worse. Simply put, it would mean the end of the First Amendment—the end of any semblance of free society.

Bitcoin and One-World Currency

If a one-world currency is a necessary step toward a one-world government—and a one-world government, obviously, the antithesis of a sovereign, constitutional, and limited government America—then Bitcoin certainly presents some scenarios worthy of watching. Bitcoin is digital money, created and stored on a computer, based on a complicated system of mathematics. Cryptocurrency is its formal name.[26] There's nothing tangible about it; no paper or metal or solid bit of material to hold—and that automatically makes it vulnerable to hackers, to currency manipulators, to those who would use money as a means to control.[27] It also makes it a viable go-to for the seedier sorts of the world: the drug dealers, the human traffickers, the dark underbellies who need secrecy for their wheelings and dealings.

But Bitcoin bypasses central banks and globally regulated markets.[28] It simply serves as a means by which anyone with access to a computer can buy or sell goods—from cars to pizza, from coffee to leather jackets—so long as the person at the other end of the transaction is willing to buy or sell in Bitcoin, too.[29] That makes it pure. That makes it simple. And that makes it a friend of limited-government types who don't like the feds coming in and mucking up simple, pure free market transactions with regulations, controls, and oversight. Socialism is centralized planning, remember.

Another Bitcoin plus? It's a fixed asset with a finite number of coins.[30] For those who wish America would return to the gold standard and jump off the print-as-you-wish, as-much-as-you-wish legal tender train of today's dollar, that's a tangible benefit that keeps the economy honest.

Another Bitcoin minus? Because Bitcoin is a mathematical system of currency—a commodity, really—it is divisible to infinity. Bitcoin actually specifies its product is divisible to eight decimal points, but with consensus of the network of traders, the division can go even farther.[31] That's infinity. That's good for growth, but it would seem to negate that whole fixed asset/finite feel, yes?

Fact of the matter is, it's hard to get a consensus on Bitcoin. "Twitter CEO Jack Dorsey says bitcoin will be the single global currency," CNBC reported in 2018.[32] Maybe not. "This is why a single global currency (like bitcoin) won't happen, says online payments company CEO," CNBC also reported that same year, 2018, citing Scott Galit, the chief executive of Payoneer.[33]

And which scenario is best for the fate of individual freedom is still up in the air. As the technology and cryptography news site Be In Crypto wrote:

Right from the start, Bitcoin has been associated with liberal left-wing ideology and as a result, it is a common understanding that many conservatives are against Bitcoin. It is also assumed that cryptocurrencies are considered a tool of anarchism that could potentially disrupt the establishment. . . .

In 2018, Coindesk conducted a survey aimed at creating a broader picture of the political biases of the crypto-community and their views regarding technology in general. The survey found that 52 percent of the crypto community had right-leaning political views while the people that aligned themselves with left-wing politics formed nearly 45 percent of the community.[34]

On top of all that, there's the whole mystery surrounding the creation of Bitcoin—namely, who did the creating? The story was Satoshi Nakamoto released a white paper in 2008 that was used as the basis of Bitcoin's creation, and shortly after, he disappeared. But that name is an alias. Dorian Nakamoto was named by *Newsweek* in 2014 as the real creator of Bitcoin; Dorian denied it. Australian tech consultant Craig Wright claimed he was the real inventor of Bitcoin—the real Nakamoto, so to speak.[35] There was even chatter that Tesla and SpaceX founder Elon Musk was the mad genius behind the Bitcoin mask, as well as cryptocurrency expert Nick Szabo. Both denied it.[36]

"The true identity of the creator of Bitcoin is one of the biggest mysteries in the modern world," the news section of Bitcoin.com reported.[37] Mysteries belong in the pages of books. They shouldn't plague a financial business. That in itself is unsettling. That in itself sets the system in direct opposition to free and open government and a free and open society.

Universal Basic Income

In an opinion piece published in the *Washington Post* in 2018, a Chinese scholar by the name of Feng Xiang wrote that AI would be the death knell for capitalism, the clanging gong welcome to worldwide socialism. His main idea was that the quickening of technology and the loss of human jobs to machinery, robotics, and AI would lead to a showdown between the two economies, and the world would have to choose: Let the rich get richer and the poor, poorer—or demand a governing structure that benefits all, equally. Feng's solution was for the governments of the world to take a page from China's "socialist market economy" and help usher in Option Two, a so-called fair-for-all system of technologically generated wealth redistribution. Socialism, on a global scale.

He wrote:

> If AI remains under the control of market forces, it will inexorably result in a super-rich oligopoly of data billionaires who reap the wealth created by robots that displace human labor, leaving massive unemployment in their wake. . . . But China's socialist market economy could provide a solution to this. If AI rationally allocates resources . . . a planned economy that actually works could be achievable.
>
> The more AI advances . . . the less sense it makes to allow it to remain in private hands that serve the interests of the few instead of the many. More than anything else, the inevitability of mass unemployment and the demand for universal welfare will drive the idea of socializing or nationalizing AI.[38]

He then finished by quoting Karl Marx—with a twist. "From the inability of an AI economy to provide jobs and a living wage for all," Feng wrote, "to each according to their needs."[39] Voilà, universal basic income is born.

Universal basic income, also called a citizen's income, is government's way of taking from Peter to pay Paul, when Paul has been put out of work by, say, a robot. It's a horrible system, it's a welfare program, and it's what the United Kingdom's leftists have been pushing for years. It doesn't belong in America, land of the free, land of the fiercely independent, land of capitalism and opportunity. "The idea," Inverse reported in 2019, on the Labour Party's push to bring a citizen's income to reality in the United Kingdom, "which would see every adult receive a fixed monthly sum regardless of their situation, has been lauded by campaigners as the key to reducing inequality in an increasingly-automated world where robots and A.I. take on more roles."[40] Reducing inequality, reallocating monies, redistributing tax dollars, and paying to not play—that is, payments for doing nothing, welfare, entitlement spending, these are all ideas of socialists; to each according to his needs. They stand in counter to a free market. They have little to do with the type of America founders envisioned. And they certainly don't stand up to the biblical test of reaping what one sows. One need only look at the pleas of out-of-work coronavirus employees to stay home a little longer and collect on the government dime as evidence of how a guaranteed basic income squashes human drive, creativity, and ambition. "Coronavirus Relief Often Pays Workers More Than Work," the *Wall Street Journal* reported.[41] And this, from ABC News: "Employers struggle to compete with $600 coronavirus unemployment payments."[42] Why work when it pays more to not work?

In a 2018 post on the World Socialist Web Site, writer Andre Damon laid out modern day's big battle as one that pits socialism against capitalism, where technological developments could either bring "human liberation" or "human enslavement."[43] The Socialist Party of the United Kingdom put it in even starker fashion:

In Marxist terms, the fight for our future is not dystopia or utopia, but one of capitalism [versus] socialism. . . . The real "third revolution" will be the socialist one which, linked to the internet of things can connect everything with everyone in an integrated planned global network . . . . People, machines, natural resources, production lines, logistic networks, consumption habits, recycling flows, and virtually every other aspect of economic and social life will be linked via sensors and software. . . . This is the outline for a socialist world, in which humankind will be transformed.[44]

If that doesn't set the hairs of the back of your neck on end, nothing will.

Technology is the dream of a socialist. It's a way to corral the people, control the people, curtail the individualism of the people, and usher in a brave new world of machine-mandated collectivism, where only a select few will be given the authority to program.

And here's the cold, dark, slimy reality of the situation: Because of America's need to compete with the likes of China—because of the irrefutable need to beat communist China at the AI game for security's sake, for freedom's sake, not just for the sake of America's sovereignty but also for the sovereignty of all America's allies—big tech is one genie that can't be put back in the bottle. At least, not easily. As China collects citizens' data that drives its technology development, so America must go forth with data dissemination and AI development, too.

We have no choice. We must win. We're in a race against technology and time to stay free. But that fight for freedom—that fight for technology dominance—against despotic nations like China doesn't come without a price for Americans.

The sad fact is that with AI, it's not really a matter of *if* America's freedoms will fall and socialism will rise. It's much more an issue of *when*. The only way to slow walk the constitutional demise is to make sure morals and ethics take the front seat of technology development, and at the same time, fight hard to keep countries with godless, secular despotism as their governing system from leading on the world stage. Even then, it's going to be an uphill climb. But with freedom as the goal, it's absolutely a climb worth making. It's absolutely a hill worth climbing.

CHAPTER 10

FORGETTING
OUR HISTORY

One of America's little-known facts is that more than 1,000 socialists held public office in select spots around the nation, as well as in Congress, in the early part of the twentieth century—specifically, in the couple of decades leading up to World War I.[1]

Representative Alexandria Ocasio-Cortez, splashy as her Democratic Socialist of America affiliation seems, is hardly the first. Between 1900 and 1920, open socialist Eugene Debs, a labor organizer from Terre Haute, Indiana, ran five times on the Socialist Party ticket for the White House.[2] He wasn't exactly an epic fail. In the 1912 race against Woodrow Wilson, Theodore Roosevelt, and William Howard Taft, Debs actually won 6 percent of the total votes cast.[3] In his last run, conducted behind prison walls and while serving a 10-year sentence for opposing the war, he received almost a million votes.[4] In America. In an America supposedly governed by a document that promises limited government and rights to the individual over the collective.

Meanwhile, in 1910, one of the Socialist Party's founding members, Victor Berger, was elected by his Milwaukee, Wisconsin, constituents to a seat in the US Congress. He lost reelection in 1912, but made a comeback to Congress—of sorts—in 1918, and again during a special election in 1919.[5] The caveat "of sorts" is affixed to his electoral wins because Berger's fellow congressional members refused to seat him. Twice. Why? Well, it had nothing to do with his socialism and everything to do with his refusal to support America's entry into World War I.

The official congressional House History recounts:

> [Berger] was indicted in various places in the federal courts, tried at Chicago, found guilty, and sentenced by Judge Kenesaw M. Landis in February 1919 to serve twenty years in the federal penitentiary; this judgment was reversed by the United States Supreme Court in 1921, whereupon the government withdrew all cases against him in 1922 . . . [and he was] elected as a Socialist to the Sixty-eighth, Sixty-ninth, and Seventieth Congresses (March 4, 1923–March 3, 1929).[6]

It's rather sobering to realize that Berger's congressional colleagues would go so far to take a stand against seating him for violating the Espionage Act, the then-recently passed law targeting war dissenters—but not take an equally strong if not stronger stand against his oh-so-obvious inability to simultaneously hail membership in the Socialist Party while declaring an oath of allegiance to the Constitution.[7] Socialists cannot uphold the Constitution; to try is to lie.

But Berger wasn't the only Socialist serving in Congress during that time. Meyer London, another founder of the Socialist Party who hailed from Lithuania, was first elected to Congress in 1914, again in 1916, and once more in 1920.[8] He was recognized for—get this—fighting against "the federal government's racist immigration quotas," as Jacobin reported in a March 2019 story.[9] That's the same sort of nonsense the left likes to sell for its open borders' visions in modern-day politics, too.

With socialists, border controls aren't common sense laws and controls; they're racist. As socialists see it, trying to keep track of who enters America is an offense to those entering—an untoward, undeserved sign of suspicion. The socialist sneers, "Of course migrants are only coming to the United States to find jobs to help feed their 16 children and grandchildren who live in squalor—why else would they come here?" The socialist sneers that while turning blind eyes to the likes of this, a headline from Homeland Security Today in April 2019: "ISIS Fighter Claims Attack Plot Via Mexico, Underscoring Border Vulnerability."[10] Or while pooh-poohing the likes of this, a March 2020 headline from the Daily Wire at the height of the spread of the coronavirus from China to America and other worldly points: "328 Chinese Nationals Caught Trying to Illegally Enter U.S. at Southern Border."[11]

To socialists, terrorists are simply frustrated workers, fatigued at their failed job search. And they're certainly not carriers of any diseases that could harm American citizens. It's a cute spin on words that gives the leftists the high perch from which to gaze scornfully at the opposition—and to shut down sane debate from the opposition by tossing out accusatory words like "racist," "xenophobe," "heartless," and "cruel." But it works. When the societal conditions are right, it works.

Exploiting the Downtrodden

When the majority of people are downtrodden, or when the downtrodden few can be exploited far and wide enough to create an impression of mass dissatisfaction and unease, the societal conditions give the leftists the wedge they need. So it was in the early part of the twentieth century, when more than 15 million immigrants came to America in the years between 1900 and 1915.[12] As the Library of Congress wrote, that "was about equal to the number of immigrants who had arrived in the previous 40 years combined."[13]

It wasn't just hard for these mostly non-English-speaking newcomers to adapt to their new home. Their new home had trouble absorbing the swell. The immigrants settled mostly in cities, seeking jobs. But there weren't enough jobs; there wasn't enough infrastructure to provide adequate shelter and services for all. Conditions were oftentimes desperate. Messages from politicians promising equality and economic opportunity resonated—particularly when it was so easy to put a face to the enemy of equality and opportunity: the fat-cat capitalist. It's a blame game that stands the test of time. "President Barack Obama complained about 'fat-cat bankers' and sharply criticized Wall Street banks for paying out big bonuses to executives . . . [after] supporting a Wall Street bailout . . . under the government's Troubled Asset Relief Program," Reuters reported in 2009.[14] That's essentially the song Berger and London sung as they infiltrated America's hallowed halls of Congress. That's the same tune their comrades in red whistled as they busily set up camp in hundreds of state and local political offices in the early 1900s. They played up the populism, played down truths.

Socialists always sell their ugly visions of government control by pretending they're all in it to help the little guy. From a University of Maine historian, published in 2017:

Created in 1901, the Socialist Party of America unsurprisingly declared its primary goal to be the collectivization of the means of production. Yet the party's highly decentralized and democratic structure enabled it to adapt to the needs and cultures of diverse constituencies in different regions of the country. Among those attracted to the movement in its heyday were immigrant and native-born workers and their families, tenant farmers, middle-class intellectuals, socially conscious millionaires, urban reformers, and feminists. Party platforms regularly included the reform interest of these groups as well as the long-term goal of eradicating capitalism.[15]

Sound familiar? That's the same rhetoric being put out by today's socialists, today's democratic socialists, today's progressives, today's

Democrats. It's all about the special interest, the poor downtrodden minority, the left-behind migrant—it's all about dividing the population into as many tiny groups as possible, exploiting their sufferings, promising to provide for their specific needs, then rallying their anger into one big pot of protest against the free market, against the Constitution, against any and all aspects of a limited government system that allows for individualism, that threatens collectivism.

They disguise their un-American proposals by twisting words and meanings of words and telling tall tales and half-truths. They rely on the undereducated, the uneducated, the angry and bitter, the jealous and envious, the hate-filled and secular, to storm their ideas into being. They use misery to grab power. They lie.

Lies and Twisting the Truth

In 1912, the Socialist Party managed to win more than a million votes around the nation for candidates running for president, governor, and Congress. Party membership between 1904 and 1940 varied, but at the high in 1912, there were 113,000 who paid dues—untold numbers of others who believed in the socialist platform, but didn't back that belief with money. That may not sound like a huge following. In fact, when considered through the vein of a share of the population, the state-by-state percentage of card-carrying Socialist Party members in America, even in the early 1900s, didn't rise above half a percent.[16] As records best reflect, anyway. Researchers with the University of Washington's "Mapping American Social Movements" project found, "reliable data" from the Socialist Party on the number of dues-paying members "has not been located for 1920-1922, 1931, 1938-1939."[17]

But it really doesn't matter. It really doesn't matter if there were 113,000 dues-paying Socialist Party members in America in 1912 versus an even higher number in another year. The standard is zero. Socialists do not belong in political office in a country such as America, where rights come from God, not government. Allowing even a little bit of cancer into a body can still prove fatal.

In a February 2020 "Savage Exposes Bernie the Bolshevik" podcast episode, the brilliant talk radio host Michael Savage said:

> A guy like Bernie Sanders is a con man from the get-go . . . But having said that, millions of people are gulled by him. Millions of people are deceived by him. . . . [W]hat does democratic socialism really mean? . . . There's no such thing. Either it's socialism or it's not socialism. It's like it's either cancer or it's not cancer. Now there are varieties of cancer. And there are stages of cancer. Let's put it to you that way. As you well know, there're stages One, Two, Three and Four in cancer. . . . Bernie Sanders is a Stage Two cancer on the political landscape. He is a clear Bolshevik . . . [a grouping of revolutionaries who first organized into] the Russian social-democratic party, which renamed itself the communist party after seizing power.[18]

Sanders, the Bolsheviks—potato, potahto. The common denominator is the placating promises that disguise the takeover intents. Sanders counts on lulling Americans into following him with calls for equality and justice and fairness. It's only after his sheep are herded and the gates shut and locked that the real evil is revealed: Socialism/communism/collectivism/tyranny—it's one and the same. It leads to the same killing field—to stage IV fatal cancer, Savage might say.

Between 1904 and 1912, according to researchers with the University of Washington, the number of members counted by the Socialist Party in America soared from 19,932 to 113,371.[19] Other sources reported the surge capped at 150,000.[20] But through 1919, the level of dues-paying members hovered between 77,647 and 95,106.[21] The majority of the Socialists lived in Pennsylvania, New York, Massachusetts, and New Jersey, though there were other large populations scattered about the nation. Then in 1923, the next year after 1919 for which records were available, dues-paying membership numbers dropped precipitously.

Here's a look, again from the University of Washington's social movement report, which pulled from information reported by the Socialist Party:

In 1912:

- 12,689 dues-paying Socialist Party members lived in Pennsylvania, less than 1 percent of the state's total population; 9,801 lived in New York, 4,519 lived in Massachusetts, 3,486 in New Jersey, 7,090 in Ohio, 6,727 in Illinois, 5,514 in Minnesota, 4,775 in Oklahoma, 4,583 in Texas, 5,962 in California, and 6,326 in Washington.[22]

In 1923, membership dropped to 10,642:

- 1,936 dues-paying members lived in New York, 1,787 in Wisconsin, 1,544 in Massachusetts, 1,440 in Pennsylvania, 723 in Illinois, 646 in Ohio, and 424 in California, with the remaining few spread among almost all the other states.[23]

Between 1932 and 1935, the party saw a resurgence in dues-paying members:

- In 1932, the 14,188 members lived predominantly in New York (3,026), Wisconsin (2,458), Pennsylvania (2,388), Massachusetts (890), Ohio (706), and Illinois (689).
- In 1933, the party's 16,670 members lived primarily in New York (2,888), Pennsylvania (1,986), New Jersey (1,139), Wisconsin (1,586), Illinois (1,141), California (1,334), Ohio (817), and Michigan (743).
- In 1935, dues-paying Socialists lived mostly in New York (3,817), Pennsylvania (3,044), Wisconsin (2,599), Connecticut (939), Massachusetts (1,049), Illinois (1,104), New Jersey (639), and Michigan (686).[24]

After 1935, dues-paying memberships fell again, to 11,287 in 1936, to 5,747 in 1937, and finally, to 2,103 in 1940, the next year after 1937 for which statistics were available. Why the huge drop? Both drops in membership—the one in 1923 and the one between 1936 and 1937—can be attributed to a resurgence in patriotism tied to America's involvement in World War I and World War II, as well as to a Red Scare that history paints as occurring in the 1917–1920 time frame, followed by a second one, dubbed McCarthyism, running in the late 1940s and through the 1950s.

On the first Red Scare, Ohio History Central wrote:

> As World War I was ending, a fear-driven, anti-communist movement known as the First Red Scare began to spread across the United States of America. In 1917, Russia had undergone the Bolshevik Revolution. The Bolsheviks established a communist government that withdrew Russian troops from the war effort. Americans believed that Russia had let down its allies, including the United States, by pulling out of the war. In addition, communism was, in theory, an expansionist ideology spread through revolution. It suggested that the working class would overthrow the middle class. Once the United States no longer had to concentrate its efforts on winning World War I, many Americans became afraid that communism might spread to the United States and threaten the nation's democratic values.[25]

Such fears are well placed. Socialism starts with a whisper, but ends with a fist.

Vladimir Lenin, born Vladimir Ilich Ulyanov, established the Russian Social-Democratic Workers' Party with a grouping of Marxists in 1903, promising better working conditions for the middle class. It wasn't long before the soft-sounding social-democratic name of the party lost any semblance of softness. Lenin's Bolsheviks favored a militant approach to protest; the others in the RSDWP, the Mensheviks, favored a more democratic walk toward outright socialism.[26] Guess who won? Years later, Lenin would go on to become dictator of "the first Marxist state in the world," as History wrote.[27] In so doing, he defied the very principles of the supposed equality-for-all social-democracy he pretended to cherish, the very principles of "peace, land and bread" he promised to deliver the peasants.[28] He's a perfect example of how socialists, both then and now, use whatever words that work to align the necessary political and societal stars to meet their personal power-grabbing crusades. So in Russia, so in America.

Between 1901 and 1960, more than 130 mayors and dozens of state legislators served the citizens of the United States as card-carrying, dues-paying members of the Socialist Party.[29] Hundreds more socialists held local level offices: trustees, aldermen, councilmen, supervisors, and the like.[30] They obtained these positions by promising, just like Lenin, a fairer, more equitable, more profitable opportunity for the downtrodden; they obtained these positions, in some cases, by downplaying their socialism—by even outright discarding their socialist labels, when politically pragmatic.

Take Irving C. Freese, for example.[31] Between 1947 and 1959, Freese served five terms as mayor of Norwalk, Connecticut.[32] He served three terms as a Socialist, lost to Democrat George R. Brunjes in 1955, then ran again, and won, under the umbrella of the Independent Party he formed.[33] It's rather like Bernie Sanders' run for the Senate as an Independent, while claiming to be a democratic socialist, while running for the Democrat Party's nomination for president, all the while harboring communist views. Socialists will twist words to mean whatever they want them to mean. Socialists will toss labels to the left, labels to the right, and even adopt whole new labels if need be. The confusion that generates plays to their benefit. It allows them to twist this way in one wind; that way, in another. "What is socialism?" Business Insider asked, in a February 2020 article. "It depends on who[m] you're talking to."[34]

Quite right. How very clever of them. There's the academic definition of socialism; there's the historical look at socialism; there's the political shop talk of socialism—with all its meanderings and misdirects, some purposeful, some inadvertent; then there's the campaign presentation of socialism, which morphs in direct relation to the candidates' audiences; there's the leftist's clever disguising of socialism, based on abject lies and empty promises; and finally, most important, there's the common sense, layman American's understanding of socialism, which goes simply like this: It's government force. That's the go-to definition.

If government is forcing something on the people that's in violation of the Constitution, any ensuing discussion about socialism versus democratic socialism seems moot. It's either American, or not. It's either freedom, or not. Since socialists like to use words as tools to confuse and hide, then the only way to beat socialists with their constant redirects and attempts to redefine history and truth is to remind everyone: Hey, here in America, it's all about the God-given.

That's called keeping it simple. Keeping it simple shows the utter travesty of so many socialists, through time, serving so openly in American office. "For much of the 20th century," the far-left *Nation* magazine reported in 2019, "Milwaukee was run by socialists."[35] In Davenport, Iowa, too. A clipping from the *San Bernardino County Sun* in California, published April 4, 1920, read: "DAVENPORT, Iowa, April 3.—Socialists elected their entire city ticket today and five out of eight aldermen. Dr. C.L. Barewald will be Davenport's first Socialist mayor."[36]

Elsewhere, it was more of the same—oftentimes, with the approval of those who should know better: the conservatives. "Between 1916 and 1931," the Vermont Historical Society wrote, "Barre, Vermont, elected two socialist mayors, Robert Gordon and Fred Suitor. Future Republican governor Deane Davis worked in both administrations and declared both men 'good mayors' and pronounced them 'conservative.' Did it matter that Gordon and Suitor were socialists?"[37]

Yes, It Matters

It should matter. Of course it should matter. This is America, a nation where rights come from God, not government. But far too frequently, that core aspect of American exceptionalism has been forgotten. It's been violated. How else to explain the election of, gulp, open socialists to serve as stewards of our Constitution?

- Between 1906 and 1908, Ray Austin served as mayor of Red Lodge, Montana, as a member of the Socialist Party of America.[38]
- In 1912, Peter Stewart, a Socialist, was elected mayor of Hartford, Arkansas, beating out Democrat and Independent opponents for the position.[39]
- Between 1912 and 1914, J. F. Johnston served as the Socialist mayor for Fairhope, Alabama.[40]
- Between 1909 and 1917, Charles F. Stauffer was the Socialist mayor for the community of Winslow, Arkansas.[41]
- In 1905 in Wisconsin, socialists W. J. Alldridge, E. J. Berner, Fred Brockhausen, and August Strehlow were all elected to the state legislature, and Jacob Rummel to the Senate.[42]
- In 1911, Herbert Merrill was elected as a Socialist to the New York State Assembly.[43]
- In 1913, C. W. Kingsley was elected to California's state assembly as an open Socialist; meanwhile, H. W. Harris, C. M. Madsen, Joseph Mason, and Seymour Stedman were all elected to the state assembly for Illinois; Charles H. Morrill was elected as a Socialist to the Massachusetts assembly; Everett Miller and Benjamin Wilson were socialists elected to serve in the Kansas state legislature; Charles Conner, to the Montana legislature; Nels Hillman, to Minnesota's; I. F. Davis, to Nevada's; W. H. Kingery, to Washington's; and all these socialists, to Wisconsin's: Martin Gorecki, E. H. Kiefer, Carl Minkley, William L. Smith, J. H. Vint, and E. H. Zinn.[44]

There are more—so, so, so many more. Specifically: "Some 1,200 socialists were elected to various political offices in 340 American cities between 1912 and the 1919 Red Scare," wrote one history teacher, for the Vermont Historical Society.[45]

And it's not like, once elected, these socialists sat idle. From the Socialist Party's own Legislative Program, published in 1914:

In the Massachusetts legislature, Charles H. Morrill introduced 28 measures . . . Mr. Morrill secured the passage of a bill, permitting cities or towns to provide meals or lunches for school children . . . [In Illinois] over 900 bills were introduced in the house, and about 700 in the senate. The socialists took an active part in the discussions and voted as a unit on every measure. They often found it comparatively easy to defeat vicious or obnoxious bills. . . . In the state of Washington, William H. Kingery introduced six bills, all bearing directly on the demands of the socialist program, and although none of them passed, he was successful in securing the passage of a few measures directly benefiting his own district. . . . In Wisconsin, the six socialists in the assembly had the deciding votes on many important measures in the legislature of 1913.[46]

The pamphlet of socialist legislative wins and losses spans more than 40 pages. But in summary, between 1907 and 1913, the Socialist Party touted its state policy wins this way: Of 895 socialist-promoted, socialist-supported pieces of legislation that were introduced, 141 passed.[47]

At least these socialists serving in US offices were open about their Socialist Party affiliations. They wore their *S* buttons openly—proudly even. It's the socialism with the small *s* that's more worrisome. It's the socialism that comes by a different name, a different political party, by rhetoric that plays down the socialism and, in some cases, outright denies the socialism, that is the biggest danger.

This cannot be emphasized enough: Just because politicians don't use the *S* doesn't mean they're not socialists at heart, pressing forward socialist policies, working in cahoots with other Socialists and socialist-minded. As the *Nation* noted in 2019:

> [In] the 1932 elections, [t]he Socialist ticket did well, securing almost 900,000 votes nationwide and registering its highest percentage of the total vote in Wisconsin. The winner of that year's [presidential] race, Democrat Franklin Delano Roosevelt, took notice: He met with [the 1932 Socialist Party's presidential candidate, Norman] Thomas after the election and borrowed liberally from proposals that had long been championed by the Socialists—for a Social Security system, unemployment compensation, strengthened labor unions, and public-works programs.[48]

That FDR worked hand-in-hand with socialists is hardly a surprise. If socialists are known for their "government knows best" attitudes, FDR was elitism personified. He was the guy who bucked the eight-year White House leadership limits laid in place by George Washington, and rather than leaving after two terms, FDR ran for another—and won. Justifying his actions as due to the need for American stability at the outbreak of World War II, Roosevelt stayed as commander-in-chief for 12 years, ultimately serving as the key reason for the 22nd Amendment that limited a US president's service to two terms.[49] And when FDR worried he wouldn't be able to get his famous New Deal legislation past Supreme Court muster, he simply proposed a "court-packing" plan to add more justices.

"Roosevelt's motive was clear—to shape the ideological balance of the Court so that it would cease striking down his New Deal legislation," the Federal Judicial Center reported.[50] All that—while wearing a button that says Democrat. This is how today's socialists stretch their influences, too. Bit by bit, any which way that works, using any which words that work best.

The clear warning for America is this, from German socialist and Social Democratic Party of German cofounder Wilhelm Liebknecht, whose words were printed on the cover of the 1914

"Legislative Program of the Socialist Party" in America: "We are not going to attain Socialism at one bound. The transition is going on all the time ... "[51] In other words: *Socialists ... don't ... sleep.* Take a look at today's political landscape, and it's easy to see that truth. Those who don't learn from history are doomed to repeat it.

CHAPTER 11

MISSING THE LINKS, BUYING THE LIES

For the Democratic Socialists of America, 2018 was a pretty good year. There were the congressional wins of New York's Alexandria Ocasio-Cortez and Michigan's Rashida Tlaib. There was the state senate victory of New York's Julia Salazar, the Maryland delegates' victories of Gabriel Acevero and Vaughn Stewart, and the Pennsylvania state representatives' wins of Summer Lee, Sara Innamorato, and Elizabeth Fiedler.[1] There was the win of Lee Carter to Virginia's House of Delegates—a win the Democrat Socialists of America (DSA) considered all the more impressive as it meant the unseating of strong, outspoken conservative Jackson Miller, who served as House Majority Whip.[2] There was the reelection of Maine's Mike Sylvester as a state representative.[3] There were even the primary wins of Kristin Seale for Pennsylvania state representative and James Thompson of Kansas for US Congress[4]—both of whom lost in the general elections, but not without drawing much attention to the socialist cause in the process.[5]

All in all, a good year—a good era for the DSA. "The Democratic Socialists of America (DSA) has grown from 7,000 members to 50,000 since President Trump was elected," Axios reported in

2018. "At least 46 Democratic socialist candidates and two DSA-backed ballot measures . . . won their primaries in 2018. . . . Of those, 14 were endorsed by the national DSA chapter (but the other were endorsed by their local chapter). . . . The bottom line: The Democratic socialist movement is growing at every level of government."[6] That's a warning. It's a warning that requires a bit of context. In 2017, by comparison, the Libertarian Party recorded 511,277 newly registered voters; the Constitution Party, 97,893; the Republican Party, 32.8 million; and the Democrat Party, 44.6 million. Fifty thousand DSA members seem barely a blip among the more mainstream parties.[7] But the warning is still real.

First Socialism, Then Communism

Not only are the DSA membership rolls on an upswing, but also democratic socialists have plenty of friends in the other political parties. Reflecting on the 15 DSA members who served in 2019 as aldermen in Chicago under the umbrella of a "progressive bloc" or "progressive reform caucus," Independent Institute president Jon Caldara told Governing that "it's different flavors of the same ice cream."[8] That is, democrat is progressive is socialist. "In a lot of places," Caldara went on, "if you go to Aspen or Boulder [for example], you're going to find city councilmen who are not socialist, but they are elitist progressives . . . [who] want to make decisions for you."[9]

Discernment is key. In America, it's not the socialist label that's the biggest problem. It's the socialist influence. The farther left the nation swings, the more radical America's core governing concepts seem, and then the easier it becomes to paint conservatives, constitutionalists, limited government types, and just plain old Republicans as out of touch with the people, too ideologically adrift to elect. And the easier it becomes to slide even farther-leftist nuts into America's political offices.

"'A leftward shift': Communist Party USA sees chance as progressives surge," the *Guardian* wrote in mid-2019.[10] Right. Because once socialism is admitted as a viable economic and political structure, well then, communism is right around the corner. It's been said socialism is communism's quieter sister. There's truth in those words. One historian wrote, of the lulls and surges of socialism in America in the early 1900s:

> The Socialist Party [in America] was particularly weakened by government repression during World War I, by the postwar Red Scare, and by a communist insurgency within its ranks in the aftermath of the war. By the onset of the Great Depression, the Communist Party would displace the Socialist Party as the leading voice of radical change in the United States![11]

Communism is socialism is democratic socialism is social-democracy—is un-Americanism.

In the end, the degrees of separation between governing structures that take by military force versus those that take by government-imposed redistribution, versus those that take by regulatory controls disguised as societal goods to promote a fairness for all—in the end, these degrees of differences are few and irrelevant. In America, individual freedoms come first. God-given freedoms, to be precise. Why degrade that principle by accepting another, no matter how deviously harmonized with American ideals it sounds? "The truth is the communist party isn't out to hurt you," Jarvis Tyner, the vice chair of the Communist Party USA and its candidate for vice president for the United States in 1972 and 1976, said at the CPUSA 100-year anniversary celebration in Chicago in 2019. "It will set you free." It's just that kind of rhetoric that has lulled so many into following the far left in the first place.

In a March 2020 man-on-the-street type of video, Will Witt for PragerU interviewed a few college-age students about socialism, asking first for their definitions of the system.

"I think it's like equality for all," said one.

"Isn't it like sharing—like everything's evenly distributed, throughout everybody," said another.

"It's more like a helping everybody else," said the first one again. "So like if you have enough, why not give to those who haven't got it."

And capitalism? What do you guys think of capitalism?

"Capitalism is evil," said the one who saw socialism as "equality" and "helping everybody." She went on: "I think it gives like a running start to most people who have money for it, but it gives a really a big disadvantage for people who are like in the lower class, middle class."[12]

Voilà. There's where socialism gets it wings. From the uneducated, the undereducated, the poorly or wrongly educated, and by way of messages about equality, justice, fairness, and helping others. Socialism's noble; capitalism's selfish. You don't want to be a selfish capitalist, do you?

Socialism used to be commonly understood as the government's control of society's means of production. But socialism's gone ambiguous. It's become soft and squishy. And that makes it all the more dangerous. In 1949, Gallup found 34 percent of Americans defined socialism as "government ownership or control, government ownership of utilities, everything controlled by the government, state control of business." In 2018, only 17 percent saw it that way. In 1949, just at 12 percent saw socialism as a system of "equality"—one that provided "equal standing for everybody, all equal in rights, equal in distribution." In 2018, the number of Americans who defined socialism in those terms soared to 23 percent.[13] Some say these numbers show socialism in America is not a threat because Americans, particularly the emerging youthful Americans, don't even know the true definition of socialism. But really, that makes socialism more of a threat, not less. It just makes it easier for socialists to sell their socialist message, but under the cover of feel-good populism and utopianism. It just makes it easier for socialists to paint the freedoms of capitalism as oppression.

Take a look at this list of quotes:

- "History calls those men the greatest who have ennobled themselves by working for the common good; experience acclaims as happiest the man who has made the greatest number of people happy."[14]
- "Democratic socialism means that our government does everything that it can to create a full employment economy."[15]
- "To me, what socialism means is to guarantee a basic level of dignity. It's asserting the value of saying that the America we want and the America that we are proud of is one in which all children can access a dignified education. It's one in which no person is too poor to have the medicines they need to live."[16]
- "At times, I've referred to Christ's miracles and have said, 'Well Christ multiplied the fish and the loaves to feed the people.' That is precisely what we want to do with the revolution and with socialism."[17]
- "[C]apitalist relations of production, wage labor, competitiveness, the ideology of 'possessive individualism'—all must be regarded as fundamentally antihuman. Libertarian socialism is properly to be regarded as the inheritor of the liberal ideas of the Enlightenment."[18]
- "I don't think *socialism*, and I don't think *warmness* and *respect* are necessarily bad words."[19]
- "Socialism is a sacred cause for realizing the demand and desire of the masses of the people for independence."[20]
- "I'm tired of this discussion of capitalism and socialism. We live in the 21st century; we need an economic system that has democracy as its underpinnings and an ethical code."[21]

- "The only way to save the world is through socialism, but a socialism that exists within a democracy; there's no dictatorship here."[22]

The common denominator is socialism is good, capitalism bad—that socialism saves, capitalism destroys. And no matter what the era, that message never changes. In order, these quotes come from Karl Marx, Senator Bernie Sanders, Representative Alexandria Ocasio-Cortez, Fidel Castro, American political activist and philosopher Noam Chomsky, singer/songwriter Dave Matthews, North Korea's despotic Kim Jong Il, Hollywood's Michael Moore, and Venezuela's Hugo Chavez.

A Kim Jong Il is a Michael Moore is a Senator Bernie Sanders. They've all peddled the same impossible promise of a government that can bring equality for all, economic prosperity for all, fair opportunities for all—while denying the truth that capitalism and individualism are the means by which societies stay the freest. They've all peddled collectivism—"working for the common good," as Marx put it—as the key to a successful society. They've all tried to disguise the evils of socialism by making socialism mean whatever sounds most pleasing to the ears of the day. Be not fooled.

Subtleties of "socialism" with a Small s

A paper on socialism published at a Stanford online source offers a concise look at the subtleties of the system, and how its principles weave into politics and economies over the decades:

> Socialism is a rich tradition of political thought and practice, the history of which contains a vast number of views and theories, often differing in many of their conceptual, empirical, and normative commitments. In his 1924 "Dictionary of Socialism," Angelo Rappoport canvassed no fewer than forty definitions of socialism, telling his readers in the book's preface that 'there are many mansions in the House of Socialism.'. . . Socialists have condemned

capitalism by alleging that it typically features exploitation, dom-
ination, alienation, and inefficiency. . . . Socialists have deployed
ideals and principles of equality, democracy, individual freedom,
self-realization, and community or solidarity.[23]

In other words, the labels change, the definitions change, but
the argument always remains the same. Socialists may be clever,
adapting their messaging to fit the modern-day struggles, but in
the end, they're really quite unimaginative. They simply repeat
time-worn, tired mantras based on drumming up envy, anger,
and hate. Keeping that in mind is crucial to warding off today's
socialists—and that's socialist with a small *s*—from spreading their
un-American views throughout the country. Some examples?

- From Speaker of the House Nancy Pelosi, D-California,
  in context of advocating on her congressional website for
  her Women's Economic Agenda, this bit: "Workers in 145
  countries around the world have earned paid sick days—but
  there is no policy to ensure earned paid sick days in the
  U.S. The United States has no mandatory paid family leave
  policy—making it one of just three countries in the world
  and the only country among industrialized countries to not
  mandate paid maternity leave for new mothers."[24] Question:
  What right does the US government have to require private
  businesses to pay for employees' time away from work? The
  reason America is one of the few countries in the world without a mandatory paid family leave policy is that America is,
  by design, separate and different from the other countries of
  the world.
- From Senator Chuck Schumer, D-New York, in context
  of advocating for tax breaks for a special segment of the
  population because college was a "necessity"—this quote:
  "In today's globally competitive job market, a college education is a necessity that is being priced as a luxury—and

it is breaking the bank for students and families all across upstate York. . . . I will continue to urge my colleagues in Congress to make the American Opportunity Tax Credit a permanent fixture in the tax code."[25] Question: Since when is college education a necessity—and since when is it the US government's job to pick winners and losers, via special tax credits, in the arena of education?

- From Senator Elizabeth Warren, D-Massachusetts, in context of introducing a plan that would, in part, put government in charge of private businesses' scheduling of workers' hours, this line: "My aim as president will be to return power to working families and to pursue an agenda of economic patriotism that puts the interests of American workers ahead of the interests of multinational corporations."[26] Question: In what world is it the authority of a US president to tell private companies how to schedule employee shifts—and what the heck is economic patriotism, anyway?

- From Democrat Barack Obama, in context of explaining to Joe Wurzelbacher, otherwise known as "Joe the Plumber," that his tax plan wouldn't "punish success" and harm the economy—this: "I just want to make sure that everybody who is behind you, that they've got a chance at success, too. My attitude is that if the economy's good for folks from the bottom up, it's going to be good for everybody. If you've got a plumbing business, you're going to be better off if you've got a whole bunch of customers who can afford to hire you . . . and I think when you spread the wealth around, it's good for everybody."[27] Question: What right does the federal government in general, and the executive in particular, have to use the tax code to spread wealth?

- From Obama again, this time in context of talking to voters in Illinois, this quote: "We're not trying to push financial reform because we begrudge success that's fairly earned. Now I do think at a certain point you've made enough money."[28]

Question: Why would an American president think it a
White House duty to determine which successes are "fairly
earned" versus unfairly earned—and since when does government get to determine a suitable level of personal, private
market earnings?

- From Republican George W. Bush, in context of signing
  his American Dream Downpayment Act to help 5.5 million
  minorities purchase, rather than rent—this quote: "Many
  people are able to afford a monthly mortgage payment,
  but are unable to make the down payment. So this legislation will authorize $200 million per year in down payment
  assistance to at least 40,000 low-income families."[29] Question: Why is the federal government involved in the private
  housing market at all—why is the federal government using
  tax dollars to help special interests?

- From Tony Fratto, Republican White House spokesman, in
  context of issuing a statement about then-President Bush's
  quiet, closed-door signing of a multibillion dollar bailout
  bill for homeowners who couldn't pay their mortgages and
  were facing foreclosures, this line: "We look forward to put
  in place new authorities to improve confidence and stability
  in markets . . . intended to keep more deserving American
  families in their homes."[30] Comment: This is what happens
  when the government gets involved in spread-the-wealth,
  equality-for-all schemes that take from the never-ending
  pool of taxpayer dollars: failure, coupled with repeat failures,
  leading to widespread economic chaos.

- From Senator Kamala Harris, D-California, in context of
  explaining from the presidential campaign trail her plan for
  college students, this bit: "I am running to declare education
  is a fundamental right, and we will guarantee that right with
  universal pre-K and debt-free college."[31] Question: In what
  world is it constitutional to believe American citizens must
  cough up money for all to attend college?

- From Democrat Joe Biden, on the presidential campaign trail, at a town hall in Illinois, in context of explaining why he thinks college students should be given a right to skip on repaying their loans: "I've endorsed Elizabeth Warren's bankruptcy proposal, which . . . allows for student debt to be relieved in bankruptcy and provides for a whole range of other issues."[32] Question: How is it capitalism for the government to require taxpayers to pick up the tab for those who skirt their contracted debts; how is it free market for government to order that colleges and courts must forgive loans?

The answer to all these questions can be found in a phrase: seeds of socialism. It's only by planting the seeds of socialism that these policies are able to see the light of day in America.

Today's socialist-minded are tomorrow's openly democratic socialists and progressives, are next week's trendy socialists, are next year's angry communists. Yanking the seeds of socialism before they root is imperative to securing the long-term freedoms of America. And the primary way to do that is to bring the topic back 'round to the standard: that in this country, it's the Constitution and the notion of individual rights from God, not government, that guide. If it doesn't stand that smell test, it doesn't belong.

The Media's Influence

There's an entire Congressional Progressive Caucus, filled with dozens of duly elected members of the House, simply screaming for a testing of that sorts. But there's also an entire fourth branch of government that can't be forgotten—or forgiven—its pro-socialist push into American politics and culture, either.

When it comes to the media, socialists have enjoyed a long and illustrious partnership. So important was the link between socialism and the media—or, more to point, between the growth of socialism and the media—that Vladimir Lenin, in a 1901 essay called

"Where to Begin," wrote of the need to properly lasso the power of the press for maximum revolutionary potential. From Lenin:

> [T]he starting point of our activities, the first step toward creating the desired organisation, or, let us say, the main thread which, if followed, would enable us steadily to develop, deepen, and extend that organisation, should be the founding of an All-Russian political newspaper. A newspaper is what we most of all need; without it we cannot conduct that systematic, all-round propaganda and agitation, consistent in principle, which is the chief and permanent task of Social-Democracy in general and, in particular, the pressing task of the moment, when interest in politics and in questions of socialism has been aroused among the broadest strata of the population.[33]

America's socialists, circa early twentieth century, tore a page from that playbook. Between 1900 and 1920, at least 380 newspapers tied to socialists and the Socialist Party were in print—some of them, with impressive circulations.[34] Much of the socialist press came by way of dissatisfied and exploited workers during and after the age of industrialization. In just the few years leading up to 1919, for example, the Industrial Workers of the World was responsible for putting out more than 70 papers and periodicals.[35] And these were hardly slapstick papers. The publications frequently prided on the pedigrees of their writers. One publication, the socialist weekly *Appeal to Reason*, touted a circulation of 760,000 in 1913.[36] Another, the radical, revolutionary magazine *The Masses*, was considered by one account to be alternately "beautiful, intelligent, surprising, deadly serious, laugh-out-loud funny, hard-edged and frivolous"—the "Socialist movement's greatest tangible gift to American culture."[37]

Other socialist newspapers dotted the American landscape, from California to Maine, from Minnesota to Florida. Among them:

- The *Iconoclast* of North Dakota, initially named the *Socialist Advocate* and published from 1912–1916 by J. M. Near.[38]
- The *Rebel* of Hallettsville, Texas, published in 1912 by the Ireland-born Thomas Hickey. Hickey sold his fiery brand of socialism on the wings of evangelism, both in print and verbally. In one of his many political speeches to like-minded Texas radicals, Hickey said: "Be Ye of Good cheer, ye disinherited of the earth, for the day is coming when, with the spirit of the Lord in your hearts and with your footsteps lighted with the lamp of Socialism . . . we will, with that old prophet Nehemiah, say to the rulers of the nation: 'Restore, I pray you, even to this day, their land, their vineyards, and their houses.' And they shall be restored."[39]
- The *Citizen*, a weekly founded in Schenectady, New York, in 1910 by George R. Lunn, the same year he joined the local Socialist Party chapter. Prior to publishing, Lunn had been a preacher. But the congregants at the Dutch Reformed Church he founded in 1904 became so uncomfortable with his take-no-prisoners approach to naming names of corrupt politicians from the high-and-mighty heights of his pulpit, they asked him to leave.[40]
- The *American Socialist*, published from 1914–1917 out of Chicago, as an official outreach effort of the Socialist Party National Office.[41]
- The *Miami Valley Socialist*, published and edited in Dayton, Ohio, in 1912 by Joseph W. Sharts, who also served in his lifetime as an author and attorney.[42] Sharts wasn't just a committed socialist; he was a three-time Socialist Party candidate for governor and a Socialist Party national executive committee member between 1925 and 1932.[43] Interestingly enough, in his own *Miami Valley Socialist*, Sharts was attributed as writing a story on the outcome of the July 1919 Ohio State Convention, which underscores the dangers of letting socialism go unchecked in America. The headline—an

inherent warning, though no doubt completely unwit-
ting—stated this: "Left Wingers Capture the Ohio Socialist
Convention: Resolve to Rule or Wreck National Party—
'Communist Party' to Be Formed." The piece, when origi-
nally published, was unsigned, but according to
MarxistHistory.org, it was later credited to Sharts.[44]

● The *Liberator* was a monthly socialist magazine published
out of New York by Max Eastman and his sister, Crystal, as a
sort of successor to the culturally iconic *The Masses* that was
shuttered, post–Red Scare, on the heels of a Department of
Justice investigation. As one avid supporter of the socialist
Liberator rag wrote: "The *Liberator*, arguably the greatest radical magazine ever produced in America, began in the spring
of 1918" and included filings from the likes of "Communist
Labor Party founder John Reed . . . on the ongoing situation
in Soviet Russia," as well as from other writers covering post-
war Europe and from "intelligent participants" of political
conventions and union gatherings.[45]

It could prove eye-opening to look at the full list—the dozens
upon dozens, the hundreds and hundreds—of newspapers, magazines, periodicals, and pamphlets put out by socialists on American
soil in the early 1900s. But the bigger issue is the here and now.

The bigger concern is modern media. Many of today's corre-
spondents, talking heads, television hosts, newspaper reporters,
media members self-identify as independents—meaning, unaffiliated when it comes to political party.[46] That's hogwash. As with
liberals in the Democrat Party who mask their outright socialism
as something else, so too, left-leaners in the press. In a widely cited
set of surveys of 1,080 members of the media and 1,230 US citizens
conducted in 2013 and 2014, to be updated every 10 years, Indiana
University professors Lars Willnat and David Weaver found that the
number of full-time US journalists who identified as Republican
dropped from almost 26 percent in 1971 to 18 percent in 2002

to just over 7 percent in 2013.[47] At the same time, the number of US journalists identifying as Democrat or Independent surged. In 2013, just over 50 percent of members of the media, in fact, said they were Independent—the highest percentage ever recorded in the history of the survey.[48] Another 28 percent said they were Democrat; almost 15 percent said "other."[49]

Politico summed the findings this way: "That means nearly 65 percent of journalists polled don't identify with either of the major parties."[50] A better way to sum it would be to say: That means nearly 65 percent of liberal-leaning journalists pretend as if they're unbiased. How do we know this to be true? By paying attention to how journalists frame the news—how they act.

"News outlets show significant bias in favor of same-sex marriage," *Pacific Standard* wrote in a headline for a 2013 story that was updated in 2017.[51] "Media bias at the border," the *Washington Examiner* wrote in a headline for a 2019 story showing all the subtle and not-so-subtle ways the modern press tore into the Donald Trump administration for enacting some of the same border controls from Barack Obama White House days that had then, at that time, been reported favorably—or not at all.[52] A pertinent line? "Only Democrats fighting a Republican administration benefit when 'fences' are suddenly called 'cages' and 'detainment facilities' are rebranded 'internment camps' or 'concentration camps,'" the *Examiner* wrote.[53] It'd be almost a yawner at this point to go through the myriad ways the mainstream media leans left and pushes its far left views. Secret's out; everybody knows.

It's time to drop all the pretenses, though. Just as with calling out the Democrats for what they are—socialists—it's time to slap a more fitting label on all the journalists in today's media who pretend to be Independent, or unaffiliated, or "other." Let's be real; many in today's modern media are little more than socialists, too. They're cut from the same cloth as the writers and reporters of the *Iconoclast*, or the *Liberator*, or the *Rebel*, or the *Citizen*, of early twentieth-century times. They're just not as honest about it.

In March of 2019, *New Yorker* staff writer Osita Nwanevu joined in a panel discussion with *Jacobin* editor and Democratic Socialist Micah Uetricht and Democratic Socialists of American organizer Marianela D'Aprile to chat about the future of socialism. Here's an excerpt of the *Chicago Maroon*'s write-up on the gathering:

> Nwanevu noted that he does not call himself a socialist—though he often writes about the socialist left—and suggested that DSA proposals, while frequently consistent with his own policy preferences, might be better described as social democracy.
>
> "If you tell people that a vision far short of socialism is socialism, you're foreshortening their political horizons, limiting their sense of the range of political and societal possibilities," he said.
>
> While many socialists would be thrilled to get behind proposals such as expropriating billionaires and tearing up golf courses, Nwanevu argued, those policies aren't what is meant by socialism. Rather, socialist politics is specifically directed at the means of production—at physical and financial capital, or the parts of the economy that aren't labor. Socialism, correctly understood, would expropriate capital and put the means of production under worker control.[54]

Look. There's freedom. And there's not freedom. It's actually fairly simple. Particularly when there's an easy-peasy, short and breezy reference point for comparison called the Constitution; when in doubt, read this document.

But as with Nwanevu's duck and dodge, see how the socialist lies spread? In 2015, the DSA's national director, Maria Svart, was a guest on *Washington Journal* on C-SPAN and fielded calls from around the nation about her political ideology, the fate of socialism in America, and her organization's push for relevancy in US politics. One caller asked, "Socialism requires that you take from some and give to the others. What is your philosophical basis for being able to do that?"[55] Svart's response: "I would just say that

that's what's happening right now under capitalism, from the bank bailouts to Walmart. Anybody that works really hard for a boss who pays them very little and takes a lot of money in, knows that that's taking from some to give to others."[56]

Except, of course, the two—capitalism and socialism—aren't anything alike. Capitalism allows for consumer choice, for employee choice, for individual choice, for voluntary choices and decisions and actions. Socialism is force, no matter how gently the government presents it. Svart's lie is aimed at confusing and, ultimately, conflating freedom with bondage, so that one day, America's light will be extinguished. Lies, lies, lies. This is the energy that fuels the socialist machine. Fending off socialism depends in large part on discerning the lies, and then bringing to forefront those who can effectively fight for the American dream. This is why Christians are so crucial to today's political battleground.

CHAPTER 12

SCOFFING THOSE
MOST EQUIPPED TO
SAVE THE DREAM

I n 2020, amid coronavirus chaos, America got a little taste of how the other communist side lives.

That's not a comment on the medical aspects of coronavirus. That's a blunt assessment of the outcomes of responding to the medical aspects of coronavirus. We as a people, we as a free people, saw firsthand, and for many, for the first time, what happens when a government is given power to rule by fear—to shutter businesses, shut down schools, shut up citizens in their.homes, impose curfews, and even, unbelievably enough for a country that grew primarily and mightily from a dream of religious freedom, close church doors and order congregants out of the pews.[1] That's right; for the first time in American history, the churches, by government command, were closed.[2]

It was a time of empty-store-shelf socialism; of "I am zee law!" police state finings of churchgoers,[3] of totalitarian-style governors with their flurried issuance of executive orders defying the rights of free assembly, crushing the free market, curtailing even free speech.[4]

Government-Mandated Face Masks

It was a collectivist's dream come true—and one only had to look to the number of face masks, both medical and makeshift, paraded by coronavirus-fearing American citizens in public to see the physical manifestation of the change in national spirit. If America stands for individual rights, bestowed by God, not government, and countries like China, where face masks have been normal outerwear for decades, epitomize everything that America is not—communist, collectivist, atheist, real chokeholds on freedom—well then, coronavirus proved a real turning point for US identity.[5]

Coronavirus provided a real opportunity for the un-American globalists, socialists, and collectivists of the left to turn America's identity. From bold to cowed, practically overnight. Oh, but the face masks were only to protect others against the spread of the virus—and after all, you don't want to be selfish, do you? There's the subtly genius and satanic slippery slope argument, 99 percent truth, 1 percent lie.

It's one thing for citizens concerned about catching coronavirus, or any virus or disease, for that matter, to choose to wear masks. It's another thing for a government to first recommend, then strongly advise, then in some cases, outright order citizens to wear face masks, all for the good of the people. "People say it's a personal intrusion on them but again, remember, it is not just about you," said New York governor Andrew Cuomo, in defense of the executive order he issued in April 2020, mandating face masks for all people in public when they could not maintain six-foot social distance buffers, NY1.com reported. "And my kids have rights and your kids have rights. And you have a right for another person to take reasonable safeguards so you are not infected."[6] That's a dangerous determination for government to be allowed to make. Especially when the determination does not seem rooted in any sort of absolute or universal truth. From the BBC:

US President Donald Trump has said he will not wear a face mask despite new medical guidance [from his own Centers for Disease Control and Prevention] advising Americans to do so.

He could not see himself greeting "presidents, prime ministers, dictators, kings, queens" in the Oval Office wearing one, he said.[7]

He had a point. Meanwhile, a face-mask-wearing American public missed the larger point—and it's not just one of hypocrisy, where government can confusingly choose which rules apply to all, which rules can exempt some, which advisements are simply advisements versus which are more like orders or dictates. It's not just about public servants telling people to wear masks, while excusing themselves from the same standards.

That is a point to note. But the larger point is freedom and the true source of that freedom. In America, where individual rights are inherent, the government doesn't have the right to require or even recommend citizens to cover up their faces for the good of others and for the protection of others' health, any more than government has the right to order citizens to take cough medicine as a protection of others. Are we to believe citizens can't determine for themselves how best to protect their own health? Are we to believe that Americans are truly that stupid?

Consider these questions:

- Once it's admitted that government can indeed dictate to one based on the health protection needs for all, where does it end?
- Can government then order citizens to wear winter coats during cold weather—so as to prevent illness that can then infect others?
- Can government demand citizens stop smoking, swear off sweets, drink more water, and eat three or more servings of

vegetables per day—so as to boost immunity levels and help lower sicknesses that can infect others?

- Can government impose daily exercise classes—so as to keep health care costs for the obese from spiraling out of control and unfairly burdening the fit? How about meditation for mental health—so as to calm and soothe the would-be nut-cases who could harm others? Mandatory vaccines, anyone?

Just because the government says it's good for the society at-large doesn't mean the government has the right to demand the people do it. That's the communist way; that's the collectivist way.

In 2010, the city of Beijing, after a three-year hiatus, "resumed mandatory daily workplace calisthenics" for the region's four million or so workers. The exercises were broadcast over the radio every day at 10 a.m. and 3 p.m., lasting about eight minutes each segment.[8] How nice. Forced exercise for citizens. For the good of the country. That's communism for you. That's not America. But that's where the logic of a government imposing face masks on citizens for some greater good—for some greater good that's not even based in fact—can lead.

These coronavirus masks in America were not simply masks. They were symbols of socialism, signs of America's cultural and political downfall. They were signs of the changes in heart and spirit that have stolen into America's people for some time now, ultimately manifesting in a government takeover of what used to be God's domain.

Fact is, citizens who take their moral direction and exercise their civil duties based on godly principles don't need government to tell them what to do, how to act, what to wear—either in sickness or in health. They are self-guided, self-governed. And a government that's run by people who are similarly guided by God—or that are at least aware that the people they are governing are morally com-passed by God—don't take on leadership duties of nannies and nurses. They are held in check by a people who insist on government sticking to its limited role, subservient to God's omniscience. That's what America's founders knew. That's what America's framers believed.

Amid coronavirus, the only Americans who wore face masks should have been those who truly believed in the power of the face masks to prevent spread of disease, and who made the choice to don mask completely free of government recommendation, coercion, or order. All the rest were simply signs of the growth of government powers and simultaneous loss of US identity. In America, medical professionals wear masks. Coal miners wear masks. Chemical manufacturers wear masks. But McDonald's employees? McDonald's employees who then also hand over the food in a plastic tub, proffered by gloved hands? This level of public isolation—of public fear—is new for the West.

From *Time* magazine:

[According to] Mitsutoshi Horii, a sociology professor at Japan's Shumei University, who works in the United Kingdom. . . . The difference in perception of the mask comes down, in part, to cultural norms about covering your face, he says. "In social interactions in the West, you need to show your identity and make eye contact. Facial expression is very important . . ."

The shadow of SARS 17 years ago also helps to explain the prevalence of masks, especially in Hong Kong . . .

[As] Ria Sinha, a senior research fellow at the University of Hong Kong's Center for the Humanities and Medicine, tells TIME . . . "Although the younger generation do not remember SARS, their parents and grandparents [do]. . . ." Wearing a mask, she explains, has become a "symbol and a tool of protection and solidarity"—even if research proving their efficacy is lacking. "Mask wearing is not always a medical decision for many people, but bound up in sociocultural practice," she adds."[9]

Dismissing the deeper significance of this "sociocultural practice" as it comes to America would be folly. Why? Americans, circa coronavirus, weren't predominantly wearing face masks because of science-based, sound medical reasons. Look, common sense says that either masks work, or they don't. They either stop transmission of the virus, or they don't. The fact bureaucrats couldn't settle on a single, simple message on masks, and in many cases, actually flip-flopped on their original messages, only shows the whole logic behind the masks wasn't so much medical but political—or "sociocultural," as Sinha might put it.

- On January 30, 2020, Nancy Messonnier, director of the National Center for Immunization and Respiratory Diseases, said: "We don't routinely recommend the use of face masks by the public to prevent respiratory illness."[10]
- A month later, on February 29, Surgeon General Jerome Adams tweeted, "Seriously people: STOP BUYING MASKS! They are NOT effective in preventing general public from catching #coronavirus."[11]
- On April 3, the Centers for Disease Control and Prevention reversed its own earlier issued guidance against the wearing of masks and instead said members of the public should indeed wear cloth facial coverings so as not to pass on the virus to others.[12] Also that day, the Trump administration recommended the same—even as the president said he wouldn't wear one.[13]
- Just hours later, the surgeon general reversed course on his earlier "STOP BUYING MASKS!" tweet and, in a video tutorial, showed how to make masks from "items you can find around the house, like an old scarf, a bandana or a hand towel, or [even] . . . an old T-shirt."[14]

Make up your mind, will you?

Americans should have scoffed the government on this back-and-forth, busted the government on its ever-changing recommendations. At the least, Americans should have come back at the mask-insisting politicians, medical wonks, and media talking heads with a collective "you first" roar. The *New York Post*, for instance, in an April 21 pictorial, splashed the elitism of perennial leftist and Democrat apologist George Stephanopoulos, of Bill Clinton White House and ABC *Good Morning America* fame, with this front-page headline: "Virus-positive Stephanopoulos steps out with no covering on his face."[15] But one of the casualties of fear is critical thinking. Coronavirus was certainly a time of citizen fear and of governing by fear. So off to the masks, Americans willingly went.

But fact is, they were wearing them either out of ignorance—hoping against science-based, sound medical hope that the flimsy, makeshift cloth or bandana coverings they banded about their faces would keep the coronavirus microbes from seeping into their mouths, or escaping out their noses into someone's six-foot buffer of air space. Or they were wearing them out of societal and government pressures, out of shame-based or guilt-induced concern for others—despite the fact most science and medical evidence pointed to the nonsensical nature of wearing one. They were wearing the masks to make others feel better, even while knowing most of the available science and medical data showed the protective abilities of facial coverings as negligible, at best. Either way, fear was the undercurrent.

But it's that unthinking quality of the face mask craze of coronavirus that's most concerning. It suggests a willingness to obey and a reluctance to buck authority—even when authority is pushing for something that doesn't make sense. It suggests a stifling of the self for the greater good—even when the stated greater good, by all facts and logic, is an impossibility to achieve. It suggests a choking of reason and sound thinking to give others feelings of security and comfort—no matter how false the premise upon which those warm and fuzzy feelings are built.

But at root, and most grossly, it shows a tilting of rugged American individualism toward a collectivist way of thinking. Do not shrug off the significance of this mask-wearing moment in American history.

It's just the sort of symbolism Saul Alinsky, one of communism's most influential teachers, would have seen as a checkmark on a list of to-do items to win a people's heart and bind a nation's soul—as a waymark toward the enslavement of a once-soaring American spirit. Alinsky, in his 1971 *Rules for Radicals: A Practical Primer for Realistic Radicals*, wrote: "Remember: once you organize people around something as commonly agreed upon as pollution, then an organized people is on the move. From there it's a short and natural step to political pollution, to Pentagon pollution."[16] Alinsky's pollution is America's face masks.

Once it's accepted in American culture that others come before self—that the concern for the collective is more important than the comfort, concern, or condition of self and not as a biblical command but rather governmental and political duty—it's a short and natural step to socialist takeover, to collectivist win, to communist smashing of the Constitution. If logic is tossed to the side during the takeover, all the better. As coronavirus showed, it's easy to influence a nation of people driven by fear. It's easy to squash freedoms when a fearful population willingly cedes those freedoms based on false promises of security to come. It's easier and longer-lasting than, say, using the military or the police to physically conquer the country. It's easier and faster than, say, going the duly elected route where politicians have to, gasp, answer questions and account for their actions to the people. The left—the committed, hard-core, communist-like left—doesn't want simple obedience, anyway.

The end game is worship. The end game is a population that swoons over government, the provider and protector of all that's good. Like North Korea with its dear leaders, and the public shows of gasping, choking mourning that occurred when the despotic

Kim Jong Il died, today's collectivists working busily against America's interests don't want votes so much as they want pure adoration.[17] Yes, they'll take the votes for now. But in the end, they want the transformation of this country to be so complete, that citizens' hearts and minds are captured in their propaganda cages, never to again be freed. Never again to even want to be freed. Never again to question the socialist, collectivist, communist order. That's a fearful scenario. But there's a saving grace—and it's the same one that brought the amazing grace and greatness of America in the first place: Judeo-Christian teachings. If America is to be saved from socialism and rescued from the globalist-minded bureaucrats who'd collect the world's citizens and arrange them within nice, tight corrals to be easily ruled, rather than let them roam free, it's the biblically based ideals that founded this country that must be reignited. It's the churchgoers and believers and followers of Christ who must take up reins and fight.

It's Up to the Believers

Why the Christians? Why the Bible-readers, why the biblically focused, why the Bible-centered individuals more than any other segment of society—more so than the scholars, the intellectuals, the hard workers, the patriotic Republicans, the hard-charging conservatives? More than the Tea Party types, the America First types, and Make America Great Again types of definite, irrefutable sovereign nation fame?

First, because we need wins that last the long term. It's Judeo-Christianity that served as the founding principles of our country—not politicians tied to one specific party versus another. That's to say: voting in a new Republican or Democrat is only a short-term win.

Second, because we need warriors who won't grow weary. It's Judeo-Christians who know all of earthly living is a struggle—that this life is only a blink in preparatory time for the next, permanent, everlasting life. So the conditioning of mind, body, spirit, and soul for political and cultural battles is to stay the course, stay in the fight, 'til death comes to part.

And third, because we need to fight for the right things. We need motivations that are pure so that the end results might be clean—or at least, as untainted as earthly possible. We need men and women of good character and solid moral compass who unceasingly, unreservedly, unashamedly push forward a godly vision of America, as close to what was conceived in the Mayflower Compact, in the Declaration of Independence, in the Articles of Confederation, in the Constitution, in the writings and opinions and essays of framers and founders—as close to these brilliant and just ideals as modernly possible. And that means insisting on a government of people who are rooted in those very documents, along with the Bible, the Ten Commandments, and the Judeo-Christian system of beliefs and values.

Anything less and it's just playing whack-a-mole with the socialists. Anything less and it's just fighting an endless number of battles, but never winning the war. That's not to say only Christians can serve in public office—or only Christians can be solid, upstanding, fine patriotic American citizens. But it is to say that if the greatness of America came by way of a founding that was steeped deep in the philosophy and biblical beliefs of Judeo-Christianity—if the exceptionalism that became America's reputation around the world, the exceptionalism that enticed the poor, the weary, the downtrodden to look with hope at the freedom and opportunity this country offered, above and beyond any others—well then, the solution to socialism that's rotting our nation is not to go left, not to head farther into communist territory. It's to circle back to what made us great in the first place. It's to retrace the steps that worked and readopt the ideals that worked. Then it's to boldly insist on a culture and a political world that recognizes and abides these same ideals.

If America's churches were filled, America's prisons would be empty. That's overly simplistic—but the general idea is this:

individuals who believe in a higher power don't need man-made laws to keep them in line. They are already constrained by the higher power. They are self-governed. They are able to govern themselves. And because they're able to govern themselves, they aren't willing to accept a government that wants to run their lives—so they insist on a government that stays in check. Limited. Subservient, even.

That's why founders knew this democratic republic called America would only survive so long as the people were moral and virtuous. "Only a virtuous people are capable of freedom," Benjamin Franklin is quoted as saying. "As nations become corrupt and vicious, they have more need of masters."[18] An out-of-hand, chaotic people requires a heavy-handed, controlling government. A self-disciplined, self-controlled people only needs the lightest of government touch.

Do we truly need government to tell us to stay home if we're sick? Or is that simply an excuse for government to crack its already considerable whip over the backs of free Americans and drive them to their homes, away from their businesses, to cower in a corner awaiting a health-related fate that may or may not even come?

In 2020, Americans took government at face value when coronavirus struck, and out of concern for the health and welfare of themselves, their families, and their neighbors, bucked up and abided the stay-at-home requirements, the social distancing and face mask recommendations, the costly out-of-work, out-of-school sacrifices. Then things got stupid—really stupid. The numbers on coronavirus fatalities weren't matching the predictions.[19] The numbers of case counts became suspect because the very medical professionals in charge of reporting coronavirus patients to the federal authorities were dependent on these same federal authorities for their livelihoods. How so? In March, Surgeon General Jerome Adams advised medical providers to only perform those procedures that were lifesaving, and to postpone elective surgeries and any other services deemed nonessential.[20] The Centers for Medicare and Medicaid followed suit.[21] States then took those advisements and issued outright orders to hospitals and clinics to close down shop, save for the most urgent of medical circumstances, and make room for the coronavirus surge.[22] In practical terms, that meant hospitals and clinics in most states lost their sources of usual revenue.

Enter the feds. Enter Congress and the White House and the political beast with $100 billion in stimulus dollars for the medical community to treat coronavirus cases.[23] The first wave was disbursed based on hospitals' previous year's Medicare revenues—leading to an unbalanced and disproportionate allotment of about $8,300 per coronavirus patient to New York, versus $88,300 per coronavirus patient to Idaho, versus $230,000 per coronavirus patient to North Dakota.[24] That set the stage for hospitals around the nation to demand a fairer formula, as well as more money. That set the stage for hospitals to aggressively lobby Capitol Hill for more taxpayer money.

The obvious red flag is this: If hospitals were ordered to close down services so that they became primarily dependent on federal handouts to treat coronavirus patients to stay financially afloat—isn't it just common sense to say their coronavirus counts might be artificially inflated? Even just a little? Minnesota State Senator Scott Jensen, in an April interview with Laura Ingraham on Fox News, suggested as much. From Fox:

> Dr. Scott Jensen, a Minnesota family physician who is also a Republican state senator, told "The Ingraham Angle" . . . that the Centers for Disease Control and Prevention's guidelines for doctors to certify whether a patient had died of coronavirus are "ridiculous" and could be misleading. . . .
>
> Jensen gave a hypothetical example of a patient who died while suffering from influenza. If the patient was elderly and had symptoms like fever and cough a few days before passing away, the doctor explained, he would have listed "respiratory arrest" as the primary cause of death.

"I've never been encouraged to [notate 'influenza']," he said. . . . "I would never put influenza down as the underlying cause of death and yet [with coronavirus] that's what we are being asked to do."[25]

Jensen was soon after attacked for furthering the conspiracy theory crowd.[26] But to the larger point, it really didn't matter if he was to be believed or not. It only mattered that the hospitals indeed had a conflict of interest with the reporting of coronavirus—and that so long as the government kept the shutdown in place, it was in the financial interest of the hospitals to have more, not fewer, cases of coronavirus.

There's a cyclical nature to this hospital conflict of interest, as well, and it's one that goes like this: The more coronavirus cases were reported, the longer the government wanted to keep citizens at home, away from work; the longer the US economy stayed closed, the more the hospitals relied on coronavirus dollars to stay afloat; the more hospitals reported cases of coronavirus, the more financially incentivized the government would be to disburse more money the hospitals' way; the more the coronavirus numbers came from the hospitals, the longer the government wanted to keep citizens at home, away from work.

And always, always, always, the message from those at the bureaucratic top was the only reason coronavirus numbers were dropping was due to the stay-at-home, stay-away-from-work provisions the government had taken in the first place. 'Round and 'round and 'round she goes, and where she stops, nobody knows.

Enter Christians. Enter Judeo-Christians. Enter those with biblical wisdom. One of the key traits Christians bring to the political fold is discernment. And not just discernment using earthly data, such as the kinds that come from prospectus documents and that help identify which companies might make good investment opportunities, versus which seemed poised for crises of leadership and corporate collapse, but discernment by using data from above—spiritual discernment.

Spiritual discernment relies on God for guidance. And it's more than wisdom; it's deeper than knowledge. It's the application of wisdom, yes—but without the fleshly, worldly snares that entrap, fool, and deceive. It's a gift of the Holy Spirit, and it allows the receiver to see beyond the façade and separate the good from the evil, as through the eyes of God.

Discernment doesn't concern itself with the billionaire-size wallets of self-professed philanthropists so much as the godly—or ungodly—motives of the billionaire philanthropist. Discernment doesn't look at the medical degrees and education status of a bureaucratic spokesperson so much as the conflicts of interest carried by the scholarly spokesperson and whether they're in line with the rhetoric that comes from his or her mouth. Discernment doesn't waffle, discernment isn't wishy-washy, and discernment doesn't bend or break with the political or popular culture winds, because discernment comes from above, through the Holy Spirit, like a blazing beacon toward truth. It clears a path, it cuts through clutter.

It's curiosity that looks at coronavirus and wonders "why"; it's discernment that shows the lies and deceptions and fills in the blanks of the spiritual battle. "Beloved," 1 John 4:1 states, "do not believe every spirit, but test the spirits to see whether they are from God, for many false prophets have gone out into the world."

More spiritually discerning people—that's who America needs. Not simply more Republicans or conservatives or libertarians or constitutionalists. More spiritual discerners who can truly see the seeds of socialism before they root and spread. America needs more biblically based spiritual discernment at work in politics and culture, the kind that takes a worldview of Judeo-Christianity first, Constitution second—and then checkmarks what takes place in the modern times as either fitting or falling outside those admittedly narrow boxes.

This is wildly out of context—but Alexander Hamilton, in *Federalist Paper* No. 26 about the constitutional justification for funding and maintaining standing armies during times of peace, even specifically mentions the need for discernment. "The citizens of America have too much discernment to be argued into anarchy," he wrote.[27] That's both debatable and a hope; in any case, the latter rests with Judeo-Christians seizing the day, so to speak, by seizing on discernment from above and applying the revelations to the physical plane, in the here and now.

Christians are also well-equipped to fight the evils of socialism and collectivism for a variety of other reasons.

- Christians have a realistic, proper view of humankind as fallen—as sin-filled, as born into sin. And that causes a dependency on God, not government.
- Christians are trained on freedom from the get-go—that Jesus saves, that Jesus frees from bondage, that Jesus is the healer and protector and savior, that through Jesus, even death cannot constrain. The concept of freedom is inextricably woven into Christianity.
- Christians are taught early on that God grants free will— meaning, individuals are at liberty to choose their own paths in life. In other words, freedom, to Christians, is ingrained as a natural human trait bestowed at birth.
- Christians are cautioned against judging others—"Do not judge by appearances, but judge with right judgment," John 7:24 states—so that tolerance of others is part and parcel of the faith; love of others is the Golden Rule. Acts of tolerance and love, taken together and in proper form, with discernment as the guide, are actually examples of freedom- in-Christ at work. They allow for differences of opinion, differences of speech, differences of dress, differences in personalities, all without the oft heavy-handed demands of a burdensome government that puts the body above the indi- vidual—that presses for collectivism, not individualism.
- Christianity is filled with standards of behavior-type teach- ings that encourage followers to practice self-discipline,

compassion, charity, humility, self-control, and the like, and to be honest, be steadfast, be industrious, be purposeful and poised, and be partakers of good—and true enemies of evil.

- Christianity recognizes the special and specific gifts, talents, spiritual endowments of each and every of God's humanly creations—meaning, individualism, not collectivism, is a core facet of the Bible. Jesus wants individual relationships.
- Christianity accepts the idea of absolutes—even while recognizing the simultaneous existence of some shades of gray—and never wavers from the fundamental idea: Jesus is the way, the truth and the life. Not government.
- Christianity points the way to living for something higher, something intangible and spiritual, not of this earth—which makes the acceptance and recognition of America as a spirit, not a simple piece of property, so much the easier. And that makes the striving to live for something greater than oneself, and to honor the sacrifices of those who went before, those who gave blood and sweat and tears so that today's Americans can live free—that makes that striving all the more natural.

Philip Vander Elst wrote in *The Christian Roots of Freedom and Tolerance*:

[I]f nothing is objectively right or wrong, tolerance becomes an arbitrary prejudice rather than a moral virtue, and its rejection by others cannot be logically condemned . . . . The historical case for linking the growth of freedom with the development of Judaism and Christianity begins with the observation that the world of classical pagan antiquity was almost entirely hostile to the idea of liberty. With the rare exception of some Stoic philosophers, it had no conception of human rights, let alone respected them in practice. Not only was despotism practically universal, with political power concentrated in the hands of absolute monarchs, but slavery was an omnipresent institution whose raison d'être was not even questioned . . .[28]

It's no wonder communist nations seek to drive out God. Collectivism and Christianity can't coexist—at least, not for long. Socialism and America can't coexist, either—at least, not for much longer.

If America is to be free, America needs Christians to get louder. It's that simple. It's the Judeo-Christian belief set that brought America to such great heights; it's the turning from Judeo-Christian beliefs—the turning from God, the secularization of the nation, the refusal to uphold biblical standards and morals and values—that opened the door to big, bigger, biggest, even socialist government to enter. It's only by turning to what worked in the first place that America can recapture and hold for the long term its cherished freedoms.

That starts with the churches. That starts with national confession and repentance. That starts with the hearts and souls of the people. From Alinsky's *Rules for Radicals* again—a most interesting citation of John Adams: 'The Revolution was effected before the war commenced,' John Adams wrote. 'The Revolution was in the hearts and minds of the people . . . . This radical change in the principles, opinions, sentiments and affections of the people was the real American Revolution.' A revolution without a prior reformation would collapse or become a totalitarian tyranny."[29] Yes. Grab the heart of the people—and it's not long before the soul of the nation will follow. Face mask, anyone? "For God has not given us a spirit of fear," 2 Timothy 1:7 states, "but of power and of love and of a sound mind."[30]

Socialists in America aren't sleeping—they're advancing. And they're coming not just for the country, but for the soul of the country. Let us awaken, fall to knees in confession, repentance, and prayer, don spiritual armor, and stop the advance. Before it's too late. Even as others mock—save the dream of America before it's too late.

Onward, Christian soldiers.

EPILOGUE

AND THE
8 O'CLOCK CLUB

At the time of this book's writing, a *National Review* headline blared this: "Facebook Removes Coronavirus Protest Pages at Request of States."[1] At the time of this book's finishing, a CNS headline blared this: "LinkedIn Targets Conservative Journalist with Infantile Censorship"—about the booting of yours truly from LinkedIn for one of my *Washington Times*' postings.[2] That's to say: Social media cannot be trusted. Social media cannot be counted upon as a tool for Americans to spread liberty views. Soon enough, there could come a day when freedom focused patriots have nowhere to turn, nowhere to gather, nowhere to see they are not alone, nowhere to assemble to wage mass fights against the socialists, the globalists, the collectivists, the communists who seek to tear down America's pride and rip out America's greatness.

We had a taste of what that world would look like in mid-2020, when the streets filled with Black Lives Matter protesters and Antifa rioters and outright anarchist thugs, bent on destroying any semblance of law and order by defunding and abolishing police. We had a shocking, glaring example of how our nation would be without respect for patriotism, respect for freedom, respect for constitutional standards and societal standards in the summer of 2020,

219

when looters and rage-filled radicals and Marxist-like militants took over sections of Seattle, Washington, and set up a Capital Hill Autonomous Zone where armed guards patrolled to keep out police, and lunatic fringe insurrection leaders sent out lists of demands to local government that included everything from an end to youth incarceration to the hiring of black doctors to the infusion of "social equality" into budget matters.[3] Do we want such uprisings to become the norm? We can't rely on government to be the solution—particularly when government simply stands by and watches or worse, stands behind the podium and politically preaches, as the thugs dance in our streets. We need real solutions. We need for Christians and those of faith to grow bolder, louder, and more organized in their appeals on America's behalf.

Join me. Every day at 8 a.m. Eastern Time and again, at 8 p.m. Eastern Time, take a time-out and pray for the saving of this exceptional nation and its people. Take two seconds, 10 seconds, 30 seconds, 30 minutes, whatever is practical and possible—to pray. Do it as often as possible, as often as you can, as frequently as you remember, for as many years as you're able. Make it generational. Matthew 18:20 promises God will listen. "For where two or three are gathered together in my name," it reads, "there am I in the midst of them."[4] Strength in numbers. Social media, God's way.

If *Socialists Don't Sleep* can be summed in a single word, it would be this one: Repent. And that means the solution for all that *Socialists Don't Sleep* pointed out as problematic in this country can be summed up in a single word: Jesus. That's not trite. That's truth. The 8 O'Clock Club is a way for all Americans to unite, with a single forceful voice, in a manner that recognizes this truth and that simultaneously sets God, not government, as the leader of this nation. Once we reestablish who's really in charge, the seeds of socialism will naturally wither and die. It's our only hope. Malachi 3.

Respectfully yours,
Cheryl Chumley

Notes

CHAPTER 1

1. U.S. Department of the State, Office of the Historian, "Continental Congress, 1774–1781," https://history.state.gov/milestones/1776-1783/continental-congress.

2. Evan Andrews, "Patrick Henry's 'Liberty or Death' Speech," History, August 22, 2018, https://www.history.com/news/patrick-henrys-liberty-or-death-speech-240-years-ago.

3. USHistory.org, Pre-Columbian to the New Millennium, "The Revolution on the Home Front," https://www.ushistory.org/us/11e.asp.

4. Library of Congress, "Documents from the Continental Congress and the Constitutional Convention, 1774–1789," https://www.loc.gov/collections/continental-congress-and-constitutional-convention-from-1774-to-1789/articles-and-essays/timeline/1773-to-1774/.

5. HistoricStJohnsChurch.org, "Patrick Henry and the Second Convention," https://www.historicstjohnschurch.org/convention.

6. The Gilder Lehrman Institute of American History, AP US History Study Guide, "The American Revolution, 1763–1783," https://ap.gilderlehrman.org/essay/american-revolution-1763%C3%A2%E2%82%AC%E2%80%9C1783.

7. Colonial Williamsburg, "Dunmore's Proclamation: A Time to Choose," https://www.history.org/almanack/people/african/aadunpro.cfm.

8. Yale Law School, Lillian Goldman Law Library, The Avalon Project: Documents in Law, History and Diplomacy, "Patrick Henry—Give Me Liberty or Give Me Death," March 23, 1775, https://avalon.law.yale.edu/18th_century/patrick.asp.

9. Bartleby.com, "Respectfully Quoted: A Dictionary of Quotations, 1989," Number 1061, Patrick Henry, https://www.bartleby.com/73/1061.html.

10. University of Pennsylvania, Law Review, "Patrick Henry and St. George Tucker," https://scholarship.law.upenn.edu/cgi/viewcontent.cgi?article=7679&context=penn_law_review.

11. McCants, David A. "The Authenticity of William Wirt's Version of Patrick Henry's 'Liberty or Death' Speech." *The Virginia Magazine of History and Biography*, vol. 87, no. 4, 1979, pp. 387–402. *JSTOR*, www.jstor.org/stable/4248338.

12. Evan Andrews, "Patrick Henry's 'Liberty or Death' Speech," *History*, August 22, 2018, https://www.history.com/news/patrick-henrys-liberty-or-death-speech-240-years-ago.

13. *The Layman's Magazine of the Living Church*, Issues 1–20, edited by Cliff Phelps Morehouse, https://books.google.com/books?id=t7HSAAAAMAAJ&pg=RA13-PA11&lpg=RA13-PA11&dq=colonel+edward+carrington

+buried+st+john%27s+church&source=bl&ots=kLk0ChU1SC&sig
=ACfU3U2k4Zbuh6SBrymfy5ztiu4hJT1wdg&hl=en&sa=X&ved
=2ahUKEwjHrOfXs7vmAhUOZd8KHc2eBLUQ6AEwA3oECAgQAQ#v
=onepage&q=colonel%20edward%20carrington%20buried%20st%20
john's%20church&f=false, p. 11.

14. Biographical Directory of the United States Congress, "Carrington, Edward, 1748–1810," http://bioguide.congress.gov/scripts/biodisplay.pl ?index=c000183.

15. HistoricStJohnsChurch.org, "Patrick Henry and the Second Convention," https://www.historicstjohnschurch.org/convention.

16. USHistory.org, "Signers of the Declaration of Independence: Thomas Nelson Jr.," https://www.ushistory.org/declaration/signers/nelson.html.

17. History.com, "This Day in History: Parliament Passes the Boston Port Act," By History.com Editors, November 13, 2009, updated July 27, 2019, https://www.history.com/this-day-in-history/parliament-passes-the -boston-port-act.

18. AmRevMuseum.org, "Read the Revolution: Williamsburg Gunpowder Incident," September 15, 2015, https://www.amrevmuseum.org/ read-the-revolution/history/williamsburg-gunpowder-incident.

19. The Society of the Descendants of the Signers of the Declaration of Independence, "Thomas Nelson Jr.," by DSDI Staff, December 11, 2011, https://www.dsdi1776.com/signers-by-state/thomas-nelson-jr/.

20. Ibid.

21. The Society of the Descendants of the Signers of the Declaration of Independence, "Thomas Nelson Jr.," by DSDI Staff, December 11, 2011, https://www.dsdi1776.com/signers-by-state/thomas-nelson-jr/.

22. National Park Service, "Brigadier General Thomas Nelson Jr.," https:// www.nps.gov/york/learn/historyculture/nelsonjrbio.htm.

23. The Institute on the Constitution, "Thomas Nelson Jr.—Patriot Above Profit," July 10, 2014, https://www.theamericanview.com/thomas-nelson -jr-patriot-above-profit/.

24. National Park Service, "Brigadier General Thomas Nelson Jr.," https:// www.nps.gov/york/learn/historyculture/nelsonjrbio.htm.

25. The Institute on the Constitution, "Thomas Nelson Jr.—Patriot Above Profit," July 10, 2014, https://www.theamericanview.com/thomas-nelson -jr-patriot-above-profit/.

26. National Philanthropic Trust, "Charitable Giving Statistics," https:// www.nptrust.org/philanthropic-resources/charitable-giving-statistics/.

27. Giving USA, "Giving USA 2019: Americans Gave $427.71 Billion to Charity in 2018 Amid Complex Year for Charitable Giving," by Giving USA writers, July 18, 2019, https://givingusa.org/giving-usa-2019 -americans-gave-427-71-billion-to-charity-in-2018-amid-complex-year-for -charitable-giving/.

28. Giving USA, "See the Numbers—Giving USA Infographic," by Giving USA writers, June 12, 2017, https://givingusa.org/see-the-numbers-giving -usa-2017-infographic/.

29. Giving USA, "Giving USA: 2015 Was America's Most-Generous Year Ever," by Giving USA writers, June 13, 2016, https://givingusa.org/giving -usa-2016/.

30. Charity Navigator, Your Guide to Intelligent Giving, "Giving Statistics," https://www.charitynavigator.org/index.cfm?bay=content.view&cpid=42.

31. Ibid.

32. Daniel J. Mitchell, "Americans Are More Charitable than 'Socially Conscious' Europeans," Foundation for Economic Freedom, February 3, 2017, https://fee.org/articles/americans-are-more-charitable-than-socially -conscious-europeans/.

33. Leslie Albrecht, "The U.S. Is the Number 1 Most Generous Country in the World in the Last Decade," MarketWatch, December 7, 2017, https:// www.marketwatch.com/story/the-us-is-the-most-generous-country -but-americans-say-debt-is-keeping-them-from-giving-more-to-charity -2019-10-18.

34. Charities Aid Foundation, "CAF World Giving Index 10th Edition: Ten Years of Giving Trends," October 2019, https://www.cafonline.org/docs/ default-source/about-us-publications/caf_wgi_10th_edition_report_2712a _web_101019.pdf, p. 4.

35. Charities Aid Foundation, "CAF World Giving Index 10th Edition: Ten years of giving trends," October, 2019, https://www.cafonline.org/docs/ default-source/about-us-publications/caf_wgi_10th_edition_report_2712a _web_101019.pdf, pp. 7–8.

36. Indiana University–Purdue University Indianapolis, IUPUI Lilly Family School of Philanthropy, "Religiously Affiliated People More Likely to Donate, Whether to Place of Worship or Other Charitable Organizations," October 24, 2017, https://philanthropy.iupui.edu/news-events/news-item/ religiously-affiliated-people-more-likely-to-donate,-whether-to-place-of -worship-or-other-charitable-organizations.html?id=241.

37. Beeman, Richard R. "The Democratic Faith of Patrick Henry." *The Virginia Magazine of History and Biography*, vol. 95, no. 3, 1987, pp. 301–316. *JSTOR*, www.jstor.org/stable/4248954, pp. 305–306.

38. Beeman, Richard R. "The Democratic Faith of Patrick Henry," from *The Virginia Magazine of History and Biography*, vol. 95, no. 3, 1987, pp. 301–316, JSTOR, www.jstor.org/stable/4248954, pp. 305–306.

39. CarolsHouse.com, Grace Church Cemetery, Yorktown, Virginia, Grace Episcopal Church, Entry for Gen. Thomas Nelson Jr., http://www .carolshouse.com/cemeteryrecords/grace/.

40. The Institute on the Constitution, "Thomas Nelson Jr.—Patriot Above Profit," July 10, 2014, https://www.theamericanview.com/thomas-nelson -jr-patriot-above-profit/.

41. Doug Stanglin, "'How We Can Show Love for the Most Vulnerable': Churches Cancel In-Person Easter Services," USA Today, March 20, 2020, updated March 28, 2020, https://www.usatoday.com/story/news/ nation/2020/03/20/coronavirus-church-services-how-outbreak-affecting -easter-services/2864084001/.

42. Luke Barr, "To Enforce Coronavirus Distancing, Police Say Arrests Are Last Resort," ABC News, March 31, 2020, https://abcnews.go.com/Health/enforce-coronavirus-distancing-police-arrests-resort/story?id=69885017.

43. Rebecca Panico, "Cops in 4 N.J. Cities Set up Border Patrols to Enforce Coronavirus Restrictions," NJ Advance Media, April 1, 2020, https://www.nj.com/coronavirus/2020/04/cops-in-4-nj-cities-are-pulling-over-drivers-to-enforce-coronavirus-restrictions.html.

44. Josh Michaud and Kellie Moss, "The U.S. Military and the Domestic Coronavirus Response: Key Questions," Global Health Policy, March 20, 2020, https://www.kff.org/global-health-policy/issue-brief/the-u-s-military-and-the-domestic-coronavirus-response-key-questions/.

45. Laura Seligman, "Trump Authorizes Call-Ups of Military Reservists to Fight Coronavirus," Politico, March 28, 2020, https://www.politico.com/news/2020/03/27/trump-dod-dhs-reserves-coronavirus-152513.

46. Reuters, "Trump Says Thousands of Military to Be Sent to Help States Battle Coronavirus," Reuters, via *U.S. News & World Report*, April 4, 2020, https://www.usnews.com/news/top-news/articles/2020-04-04/trump-says-thousands-of-military-to-be-sent-to-help-states-battle-coronavirus.

47. Lyndsey Matthews, "Yosemite, Yellowstone, and Other National Parks Close Due to Coronavirus," *Good Housekeeping*, March 25, 2020, https://www.goodhousekeeping.com/life/a31919987/national-parks-closed-coronavirus/.

48. Irina Ivanova and Thom Craver, "Closed Due to Coronavirus: List of Activities and State Shutdowns over COVID-19 Outbreak Concerns," CBS News, March 18, 2020, https://www.cbsnews.com/news/closed-due-to-coronavirus-list-of-activities-and-state-shutdowns-over-covid-19-outbreak-concerns/.

49. Terry Nguyen, "The Toilet Paper Shortage Is More Complicated Than You Think," Vox, April 3, 2020, https://www.vox.com/the-goods/2020/4/3/21206942/toilet-paper-coronavirus-shortage-supply-chain.

50. Lev Facher, "President Trump Just Declared the Coronavirus Pandemic a National Emergency. Here's What That Means," *Stat Reports*, March 13, 2020, https://www.statnews.com/2020/03/13/national-emergency-coronavirus/.

51. Noam M. Levey, "Hospitals Say Feds Are Seizing Masks and Other Coronavirus Supplies Without a Word," *LA Times*, via Yahoo! Sports, April 7, 2020, https://sports.yahoo.com/hospitals-feds-seizing-masks-other-210748808.html.

52. Marty Johnson and Jessie Hellmann, "Cuomo Signs Order for New York to Commandeer Ventilators, Protective Gear," The Hill, April 3, 2020, https://thehill.com/homenews/state-watch/491009-cuomo-order-new-york-commandeer-ventilators-protective-gear.

53. Adam Cancryn, "Kushner's Team Seeks National Coronavirus Surveillance System," Politico, April 7, 2020, updated April 8, 2020, https://www.politico.com/news/2020/04/07/kushner-coronavirus-surveillance-174165.

54. Barack Obama, Twitter, April 8, 2020, https://twitter.com/BarackObama/status/1247890918440448003.

55. Jon Cohen, "'I'm Going to Keep Pushing.' Anthony Fauci Tries to Make the White House Listen to Facts of the Pandemic," *Science Magazine*, March 22, 2020, https://www.sciencemag.org/news/2020/03/i-m-going-keep-pushing-anthony-fauci-tries-make-white-house-listen-facts-pandemic.

56. Daniel Villarreal, "Fauci Says All States Should Enforce Coronavirus Stay-At-Home Orders as Trump Resists Issuing Nationwide Mandate," *Newsweek*, April 3, 2020, https://www.newsweek.com/fauci-says-all-states-should-enforce-coronavirus-stay-home-orders-trump-resists-issuing-1495906.

57. Ibid.

58. Ibid.

59. Paul LeBlanc, "Fauci: 'I Don't Understand Why' Every State Hasn't Issued Stay-at-Home Orders," CNN, April 3, 2020, https://www.cnn.com/2020/04/02/politics/fauci-stay-home-coronavirus-states-cnntv/index.html.

60. Ibid.

61. Matthew Impelli, "Coronavirus Guidelines Sent by Mail Should Be Considered a National Stay-at-Home Order, Says US Surgeon General," *Newsweek*, April 1, 2020, https://www.newsweek.com/coronavirus-guidelines-sent-mail-should-considered-national-stay-home-order-says-us-surgeon-1495546.

62. Aaron Holmes, "Bill Gates Says We Need a Nationwide Shutdown for at Least 10 More Weeks to Fight Coronavirus: 'The Window for Making Important Decisions Hasn't Closed,'" *Business Insider*, April 2, 2020, https://www.businessinsider.com/bill-gates-coronavirus-10-weeks-nationwide-shutdown-required-2020-4.

63. Eric Bangeman, "Bill Gates Steps Down from Microsoft Board," *Ars Technica*, March 13, 2020, https://arstechnica.com/information-technology/2020/03/bill-gates-steps-down-from-microsoft-board/.

64. Jennifer Calfas, "Bill Gates Says He'll Spend Billions on Coronavirus Vaccine Development," MarketWatch, April 6, 2020, https://www.marketwatch.com/story/bill-gates-says-hell-spend-billions-on-coronavirus-vaccine-development-2020-04-06.

65. Natalie Huet and Carmen Paun, "Meet the World's Most Powerful Doctor: Bill Gates," Politico, May 4, 2017, updated May 8, 2017, https://www.politico.eu/article/bill-gates-who-most-powerful-doctor/.

66. Lydia Ramsey, "Bill Gates Says the Novel Coronavirus Is a 'Once-in-a-Century-Pathogen.' The Gates Foundation Just Joined Wellcome and Mastercard in Committing $125 Million to Find New Treatments for It," Business Insider, March 10, 2020, https://www.businessinsider.com/gates-foundation-wellcome-mastercard-commit-125-million-to-covid-19-drugs-2020-3.

67. Ibid.

68. Bill & Melinda Gates Foundation, Press Room, "Bill & Melinda Gates Foundation, Wellcome, and Mastercard Launch Initiative to Speed

Development and Access to Therapies for Covid-19," Bill & Melinda Gates Foundation, March 10, 2020, https://www.gatesfoundation.org/Media -Center/Press-Releases/2020/03/COVID-19-Therapeutics-Accelerator.

69. World Health Organization, "WHO Director-General's Opening Remarks at the Media Briefing on COVID-19—11 March 2020," WHO, March 11, 2020, https://www.who.int/dg/speeches/detail/who-director-general-s -opening-remarks-at-the-media-briefing-on-covid-19---11-march-2020.

70. Ed Lin, "Bill & Melinda Gates Trust Invests Big in Mexico Fund," Barron's, March 31, 2020, https://www.barrons.com/articles/bill-gates -trust-invests-big-in-mexico-fund-amid-coronavirus-51585652435.

71. Bill & Melinda Gates Foundation, Press Room, "Global Health Leaders Launch Decade of Vaccines Collaboration," The Gates Foundation, 2010, https://www.gatesfoundation.org/Media-Center/Press-Releases/2010/12/ Global-Health-Leaders-Launch-Decade-of-Vaccines-Collaboration.

72. Ibid.

73. Charles Creitz, "Franklin Graham on New York City Field Hospital: 'We're Going to Give the Best Health Care We Can to All New Yorkers," Fox News, March 30, 2020, https://www.foxnews.com/media/ franklin-graham-nyc-field-hospital-coronavirus.

74. Bob McManus, "Mayor Bill de Blasio's Despicable Baiting of Samaritan's Purse," *New York Post*, April 3, 2020, https://nypost.com/2020/04/03/ mayor-bill-de-blasios-despicable-baiting-of-samaritans-purse/.

75. Tim Haines, "CDC Director Robert Redfield: Because American Public Did Social Distancing, Coronavirus Death Toll Will Be 'Much, Much, Much Lower,'" RealClearPolitics.com, April 7, 2020, https://www .realclearpolitics.com/video/2020/04/07/cdc_director_robert_redfield _because_american_public_did_social_distancing_coronavirus_death _toll_will_be_much_much_much_lower.html.

76. Johns Hopkins University & Medicine, "Coronavirus Resource Center," updated June 15, 2020, https://coronavirus.jhu.edu/data/mortality.

77. Johns Hopkins University of Medicine, Coronavirus Resource Center, "COVID-19 Dashboard by the Center for Systems Science and Engineering (CSSE) at Johns Hopkins University," Johns Hopkins University of Medicine, real-time global statistics on coronavirus, updated April 12, 2020, https://coronavirus.jhu.edu/map.html.

78. WorldoMeter, "United States Population (Live)," 1950–2020, WorldoMeters.info, https://www.worldometers.info/world-population/ us-population/.

79. Johns Hopkins University of Medicine, Coronavirus Resource Center, "COVID-19 Dashboard by the Center for Systems Science and Engineering (CSSE) at Johns Hopkins University," Johns Hopkins University of Medicine, real-time global statistics on coronavirus, updated April 12, 2020, https://coronavirus.jhu.edu/map.html.

80. Emil W. Henry Jr., "Will Coronavirus Launch the Second Wave of Socialism?" The Hill, March 26, 2020, https://thehill.com/opinion/ campaign/489612-will-coronavirus-launch-the-second-wave-of-socialism.

81. Eric Levitz, "Covid-19 Creates an Opening for Socialism (Also Barbarism)," and alternate headline, "Coronavirus Creates an Opening for Progressivism (Also Barbarism)," *New York Magazine*, The Intelligencer, April 1, 2020, https://nymag.com/intelligencer/2020/04/coronavirus -undocumented-nationalism-socialism-climate-progressives.html.

82. Yale Law School, Lillian Goldman Law Library, The Avalon Project: Documents in Law, History and Diplomacy, "Patrick Henry—Give Me Liberty or Give Me Death," March 23, 1775, https://avalon.law.yale.edu/ 18th_century/patrick.asp.

CHAPTER 2

1. Patricia Heaton, Twitter, February 12, 2020, https://twitter.com/ PatriciaHeaton/status/1227643710646566914.

2. Sarah D., "'At least I'm not a communist': James Carville has some colorful thoughts on Bernie Sanders calling him a 'political hack,'" Twitchy.com, February 13, 2020, https://twitchy.com/sarahd-313035/2020/02/13/at -least-im-not-a-communist-james-carville-has-some-colorful-thoughts-on -bernie-sanders-calling-him-a-political-hack/.

3. C-SPAN, "Senator Bernie Sanders Remarks on Democratic Socialism," June 12, 2019, https://www.c-span.org/video/?461581-1/senator-bernie-sanders -delivers-remarks-democratic-socialism&start=1913.

4. Ibid.

5. Ibid.

6. Ian Schwartz, "Trump: 'America Will Never Be a Socialist Country'; 'We Were Born Free, and We Will Stay Free,'" RealClearPolitics.com, February 5, 2019, https://www.realclearpolitics.com/video/2019/02/05/trump _america_will_never_be_a_socialist_country_we_were_born_free_and_we _shall_stay_free.html.

7. Dominic Rushe, "Trump Vows America 'Will Never Be a Socialist Country' During Wisconsin Rally," *The Guardian*, April 28, 2019, https:// www.theguardian.com/us-news/2019/apr/28/trump-wisconsin-rally-touts -economy.

8. WhiteHouse.gov, "Remarks by President Donald Trump to the 74th Session of the United Nations of the General Assembly," September 24, 2019, https://www.whitehouse.gov/briefings-statements/ remarks-president-trump-74th-session-united-nations-general-assembly/.

9. Democratic Socialists of America, NPC Statement on 2018 Elections, November 7, 2018, https://www.dsausa.org/statements/npc-statement -on-2018-elections/.

10. George H. Smith, "Ayn Rand on Fascism," Libertarianism.org, January 8, 2016, https://www.libertarianism.org/columns/ayn-rand-fascism.

11. ARI, "Conservatism: An Obituary," https://courses.aynrand.org/works/ conservatism-an-obituary/.

12. Lydia Saad, "Gallup Vault: Americans' Views of Socialism, 1949–1965," Gallup Vault, August 10, 2018, https://news.gallup.com/vault/240749/gallup-vault-americans-views-socialism-1949-1965.aspx.

13. Ibid.

14. Cathy J. Cohen, Matthew Fowler, Vladimir E. Medenica, and Jon C. Rogowski, "Political Polarization and Trust Among Millennials," for GenForward survey, May, 2018, file:///C:/Users/cheryl/Downloads/GenForward%20May%202018%20Final%20Report_1531083570.pdf.

15. Frank Newport, "Democrats More Positive About Socialism Than Capitalism," Gallup, August 13, 2018, https://news.gallup.com/poll/240725/democrats-positive-socialism-capitalism.aspx.

16. Ibid.

17. Olivia B. Waxman, "Socialism Was Once America's Political Taboo. Now, Democratic Socialism Is a Viable Platform. Here's What to Know," *Time*, October 24, 2018, https://time.com/5422714/what-is-democratic-socialism/.

18. Ibid.

19. Helen Raleigh, "Here's How to Successfully Debate a Democratic Socialist," *The Federalist*, September 28, 2018, https://thefederalist.com/2018/09/28/heres-successfully-debate-democratic-socialist/.

20. Jeff Stein, "9 Questions About the Democratic Socialists of America You Were Too Embarrassed to Ask," *Vox*, August 5, 2017, https://www.vox.com/policy-and-politics/2017/8/5/15930786/dsa-socialists-convention-national.

21. https://democrats.org/, "2016 Democratic Party Platform," as approved by the Democratic Platform Committee July 8–9, 2016, file:///C:/Users/cheryl/Downloads/2016_DNC_Platform.pdf.

22. Democrats.org, "Where We Stand," https://democrats.org/where-we-stand/.

23. Democrats.org, "Party Platform: The 2016 Democratic Platform," https://democrats.org/where-we-stand/party-platform/.

24. ProgressivePartyUSA.com, "Progressives Believe" list, https://progressivepartyusa.com/home/.

25. Democratic Socialists of America, "About Us," https://www.dsausa.org/about-us/.

26. Democratic Socialists of America, "Political Platform Update," https://www.dsausa.org/national-convention/update-on-the-preliminary-political-platform/.

27. Steve Lehto, "The Shocking Incompetence of the USPS," Oppositelock.com, June 20, 2015, https://oppositelock.kinja.com/the-shocking-incompetence-of-the-usps-1712755126.

28. Pinzler.com, "Populist Party Platform, 1892 (July 4, 1892)," http://www.pinzler.com/ushistory/popparplatsupp.html.

29. Communist Party USA, "About CPUSA," https://www.cpusa.org/about-us/.

30. Communist Party USA, "The Road to Socialism USA: Unity for Peace, Democracy, Jobs and Equality," May 19, 2006, https://www.cpusa.org/party_info/party-program/.

31. Ibid.

32. Democratic Socialists of America, "What Is Democratic Socialism?" https://www.dsausa.org/about-us/what-is-democratic-socialism/.

33. GOP Convention 2016, "Republican Platform 2016," from the preamble, https://prod-cdn-static.gop.com/media/documents/DRAFT_12_FINAL%5B1%5D-ben_1468872234.pdf.

34. Lauren Markoej, from Religion News Service in the *Washington Post*, "Democrats Under Fire for Removing 'God' from Party Platform," September 5, 2012, https://www.washingtonpost.com/national/on-faith/democrats-under-fire-for-removing-god-from-party-platform/2012/09/05/61b3459a-f79e-11e1-a93b-7185e3f88849_story.html.

CHAPTER 3

1. President Donald Trump, "Proclamation on Declaring a National Emergency Concerning the Novel Coronavirus Disease (COVID-19) Outbreak," The White House, March 13, 2020, https://www.whitehouse.gov/presidential-actions/proclamation-declaring-national-emergency-concerning-novel-coronavirus-disease-covid-19-outbreak/.

2. Rosie Perper, Ellen Cranley, and Sarah Al-Arshani, "Almost All US States Have Declared States of Emergency to Fight Coronavirus—Here's What It Means for Them," *Business Insider*, March 17, 2020, https://www.businessinsider.com/california-washington-state-of-emergency-coronavirus-what-it-means-2020-3.

3. Paul Davidson, Josh Peter, and Charisse Jones, "A Record 3.3M Americans File for Unemployment Benefits as the Coronavirus Takes a Big Toll on the Economy," *USA Today*, March 26, 2020, updated March 27, 2020, https://www.usatoday.com/story/money/2020/03/26/coronavirus-jobless-claims-surge-3-3-m-coronavirus-spreads/5084277002/.

4. Jacob M. Schlesinger and Joshua Jamerson, "After Three Coronavirus Stimulus Packages, Congress Is Already Prepping Phase Four," *Wall Street Journal*, March 29, 2020, https://www.wsj.com/articles/after-three-corona-virus-stimulus-packages-congress-is-already-prepping-phase-four-11585483203.

5. Miranda Devine, "In the Midst of Coronavirus Crisis, Pelosi Goes for Woke: Devine," *New York Post*, March 25, 2020, https://nypost.com/2020/03/25/in-the-midst-of-coronavirus-crisis-pelosi-goes-for-woke-devine/.

6. Charles Creitz, "Pelosi 'Jiu-Jitsu' Claim on Coronavirus Relief All Wrong, Mccarthy Says: 'She Held the Bill Up,'" Fox News, March 27, 2020, https://www.foxnews.com/media/pelosi-jiu-jitsu-claim-on-coronavirus-relief-all-wrong-mccarthy-says-she-held-the-bill-up.

7. Lauren Hirsch, "Trump Pushes Back Against Congressional Oversight for $500 Billion Bailout Fund," CNBC, March 28, 2020, https://www.cnbc.com/2020/03/28/trump-pushes-back-against-congressional-oversight-for-500-billion-bailout-fund.html.

8. Michael Collins, "Q&A: How Could the Historic $2 Trillion Coronavirus Economic Recovery Package Benefit You?" *USA Today*, March 27, 2020, updated March 29, 2020, https://www.usatoday.com/story/news/politics/2020/03/27/coronavirus-stimulus-package-questions-answers/2930656001/.

9. Andrew Keshner, "The $2 Trillion Stimulus Deal Will Help People Filing for Unemployment Benefits—Here's How," MarketWatch, March 27, 2020, https://www.marketwatch.com/story/the-2-trillion-stimulus-deal-will-help-those-filing-unemployment-claims-heres-how-2020-03-26.

10. Anya van Wagtendonk, "Trump Says He Won't Comply with Key Transparency Measure in the Coronavirus Stimulus Bill," Vox, March 28, 2020, https://www.vox.com/policy-and-politics/2020/3/28/21197995/coronavirus-stimulus-trump-inspector-general-wont-comply.

11. Tim Hepher and Sarah Young, "Airlines Beg for Rescue as Coronavirus Hit Soars to $250 Billion," Reuters, March 24, 2020, https://www.reuters.com/article/us-health-coronavirus-iata-airlines/airlines-beg-for-rescue-as-coronavirus-hit-soars-to-250-billion-idUSKBN21B1VK.

12. Anya van Wagtendonk, "Trump Says He Won't Comply with Key Transparency Measure in the Coronavirus Stimulus Bill," Vox, March 28, 2020, https://www.vox.com/policy-and-politics/2020/3/28/21197995/coronavirus-stimulus-trump-inspector-general-wont-comply.

13. Nicholas Wu, Maureen Groppe, and Ledyard King, "As Trump Acknowledges U.S. 'May Be' Headed for Recession, House Passes Coronavirus Aid Package," *USA Today*, March 16, 2020, https://www.usatoday.com/story/news/politics/2020/03/16/coronavirus-task-force-hold-briefing-live-updates/5057442002/.

14. Alan Levin and Ari Natter, "Airlines Are No. 1 Priority for Virus Relief, Trump Says," Bloomberg, March 18, 2020, https://www.bloomberg.com/news/articles/2020-03-18/airlines-are-no-1-priority-for-coronavirus-relief-trump-says.

15. Lauren Hirsch, "Trump Pushes Back Against Congressional Oversight for $500 Billion Bailout Fund," CNBC, March 28, 2020, https://www.cnbc.com/2020/03/28/trump-pushes-back-against-congressional-oversight-for-500-billion-bailout-fund.html.

16. Joseph Zeballos-Roig, "Airlines are begging for a bailout, but they've used 96% of their cash flow on buybacks over the past ten years. It highlights an ongoing controversy over how companies have been spending their money," *Markets Insider*, March 17, 2020, https://markets.businessinsider.com/news/stocks/airline-bailout-coronavirus-share-buyback-debate-trump-economy-aoc-2020-3-1029006175.

17. Ibid.

18. Fox News, "Kudlow: No Stock Buybacks, Extra Executive Compensation for Large Businesses Who Receive Funds," Fox News, March 29, https://www.foxnews.com/transcript/kudlow-no-stock-buybacks-extra-executive-compensation-for-large-businesses-who-receive-funds.

19. Alexandria Ocasio-Cortez, "Coronavirus: Alexandria Ocasio-Cortez Blasts 'Shameful' Corporate Bailout," Guardian News, via YouTube, March 28, 2020, https://www.youtube.com/watch?v=spVHLx3YMKk.

20. Fox News, "Kudlow: No Stock Buybacks, Extra Executive Compensation for Large Businesses Who Receive Funds," Fox News, March 29, https://www.foxnews.com/transcript/kudlow-no-stock-buybacks-extra-executive-compensation-for-large-businesses-who-receive-funds.

21. John Cassidy, "An Inconvenient Truth: It Was George W. Bush Who Bailed out the Automakers," *New Yorker*, March 16, 2012, https://www.newyorker.com/news/john-cassidy/an-inconvenient-truth-it-was-george-w-bush-who-bailed-out-the-automakers.

22. Pew Research Center, "Was TARP Passed Under Bush or Obama?" Pew Research Center, FactTank News in the Numbers, October 10, 2010, https://www.pewresearch.org/fact-tank/2010/08/10/was-tarp-passed-under-bush-or-obama/.

23. ProPublica, "Bailout Tracker: General Motors," Pro Publica, https://projects.propublica.org/bailout/entities/233-general-motors.

24. ProPublica, "Bailout Tracker: Preferred Stock Investments, Fannie and Freddie Bailout," Pro Publica, https://projects.propublica.org/bailout/programs/10-preferred-stock-investments.

25. Harvard Law Review, "Fifth Amendment—Illegal Exaction—Court of Federal Claims Holds That Government Acquisition of Equity Share in AIG Effected an Illegal Exaction," *Harvard Law Review*, 2015, http://cdn.harvardlawreview.org/wp-content/uploads/2016/01/859-866-Online.pdf.

26. ProPublica, "Bailout Tracker: Targeted Investment Program, More Money for Citi and BofA," Pro Publica, https://projects.propublica.org/bailout/programs/4-targeted-investment-program.

27. US Department of the Treasury, "Programs to Invest in Banking Institutes," Department of Treasury, https://www.treasury.gov/initiatives/financial-stability/programs/Pages/default.aspx.

28. Peter Grier, "Has John Boehner Surrendered on Debt Ceiling?" *Christian Science Monitor*, October 4, 2013, https://www.csmonitor.com/USA/Politics/Decoder/2013/1004/Has-John-Boehner-surrendered-on-debt-ceiling.

29. Lori Montgomery and Paul Kane, "Boehner Offers Debt Ceiling Increase in Cliff Compromise," *Washington Post*, December 16, 2012, https://www.washingtonpost.com/business/economy/boehner-offers-to-take-debt-limit-off-the-table/2012/12/16/8b369b7e-47c6-11e2-b6f0-e851e741d196_story.html.

30. Zachary Roth, "GOP Caves on Debt Ceiling Fight—for Now," MSNBC, January 18, 2013, updated October 2, 2013, http://www.msnbc.com/the-last-word/gop-caves-debt-ceiling-fight-now.

31. The Associated Press, "House Passes Debt-Ceiling Increase with No Add-ons," CNBC, February 11, 2014, https://www.cnbc.com/2014/02/11/us-house-republican-leaders-set-wednesday-debate-on-clean-debt-limit-bill.html.

32. Lisa Mascaro, "Speaker John Boehner Seeks Compromise with Democrats over Raising the Debt Limit," with Google search headline, "Boehner Considers Raising Debt Limit Without a Fight," *Los Angeles Times*, October 20, 2015, https://www.latimes.com/nation/politics/la-na-congress-debt-ceiling-20151020-story.html.

33. Dave Ramsey, "The Truth About Debt," https://www.daveramsey.com/blog/the-truth-about-debt.

34. Jake Sherman and John Bresnahan, "Conservatives Rebel Against Boehner," Politico, January 3, 2013, https://www.politico.com/story/2013/01/conservatives-rebel-against-boehner-085749.

35. Ibid.

36. Leigh Ann Caldwell, "Obamacare Repeal Fails: Three GOP Senators Rebel in 49–51 Vote," Politico, July 28, 2017, https://www.nbcnews.com/politics/congress/senate-gop-effort-repeal-obamacare-fails-n787311.

37. Molly E. Reynolds, "Republicans Learn the Limits of Reconciliation with Failed ACA Repeal," Brookings.edu, July 28, 2017, https://www.brookings.edu/blog/fixgov/2017/07/28/limits-of-reconciliation-and-failed-aca-repeal/.

38. Burgess Everett and Seung Min Kim, "Why McCain Screwed the GOP on Obamacare Repeal—Again," Politico, September 22, 2017, https://www.politico.com/story/2017/09/22/john-mccain-obamacare-repeal-opposition-243036.

39. Emmarie Huetteman, "McCain Hated Obamacare. He Also Saved It," Kaiser Health News reporting in NBC News, August 27, 2018, https://www.nbcnews.com/health/obamacare/mccain-hated-obamacare-he-also-saved-it-n904106.

40. History, Art & Archives of the US House of Representatives, "Party Divisions of the House of Representatives, 1789 to Present," https://history.house.gov/Institution/Party-Divisions/Party-Divisions/.

41. US Senate, "Party Division," https://www.senate.gov/history/partydiv.htm.

42. Donald J. Trump, Twitter, July 18, 2017, from CBS News, "Why is a simple majority usually not enough to pass a bill in the Senate?" Posted July 18, 2017, https://www.cbsnews.com/news/why-is-a-simple-majority-usually-not-enough-to-pass-a-bill-in-the-senate/.

43. Lisa Mascaro, "GOP Tax Bill Is Latest Example of Senate Leader Mitch Mcconnell Breaking the Norms He Often Espouses," *Los Angeles Times*, December 3, 2017, https://www.latimes.com/politics/la-na-pol-mcconnell-trump-taxplan-20171203-story.html.

44. Sabrina Siddiqui, "GOP Senator Jeff Flake Attacks 'Reckless, Outrageous and Undignified' Trump," *Guardian*, October 25, 2017, https://www.theguardian.com/us-news/2017/oct/24/jeff-flake-retire-republican-senate-trump.

45. "Trump Administration Unable to Separate 'Truth From Lies,' Says McCain," *Irish Times*, February 18, 2017, https://www.irishtimes.com/news/world/us/trump-administration-unable-to-separate-truth-from-lies-says-mccain-1.2980788.

46. Justin Amash, Twitter post @justinamash, https://twitter.com/justinamash/status/1165018079908237312?lang=en. Also accessed *USA Today*, "Justin Amash on Trump: 'We Must Elect Someone Who Will Restore Respect for Our Constitution," by Savannah Behrmann, August 23, 2019, https://www.usatoday.com/story/news/politics/2019/08/23/justin-amash-tweets-trump-we-must-elect-2020-threat-to-liberty-america-unstable/2101562001/.

47. Annie Karnie, "No One Attacked Trump More Than Republicans in 2016. It Didn't Work," *New York Times*, August 13, 2019, https://www.nytimes.com/2019/08/13/us/politics/trump-attacks-republicans-democrats.html.

48. Arthur Nelsen, "Donald Trump 'Taking Steps to Abolish Environmental Protection Agency,'" *Guardian*, February 1, 2017, https://www.theguardian.com/us-news/2017/feb/02/donald-trump-plans-to-abolish-environmental-protection-agency.

49. US Housing and Urban Development, "HUD: Environmental Justice Strategy 2016–2020," https://files.hudexchange.info/resources/documents/HUD-Environmental-Justice-Strategy.pdf.

50. Environmental Protection Agency, "Partnership for Sustainable Communities: A Year of Progress for African Communities," October 2010, https://www.epa.gov/sites/production/files/2014-06/documents/partnership_year1.pdf, p. 2.

51. Stephanie Akin, "Some GOP Lawmakers Push Back Against EPA Cuts," *Roll Call*, April 4, 2017, https://www.rollcall.com/2017/04/04/some-gop-lawmakers-push-back-against-epa-cuts/.

52. Freedom Works, "Key voting record, Scott Taylor," http://congress.freedomworks.org/legislators/scott-taylor.

53. Stephanie Akin, "Some GOP Lawmakers Push Back Against EPA Cuts," *Roll Call*, April 4, 2017, https://www.rollcall.com/news/gop-lawmakers-environmental-protection-agency.

54. US Environmental Protection Agency, "EPA History: The Origins of the EPA," https://www.epa.gov/history/origins-epa.

55. OpenSecrets.org, Center for Responsive Politics, "Client Profile: U.S. Chamber of Commerce," Hired Firms, https://www.opensecrets.org/federal-lobbying/clients/hired-firms?cycle=2019&id=D000019798.

56. OpenSecrets.org, Center for Responsive Politics, "U.S. Chamber of Commerce, Outside Spending Summary 2018," https://www.opensecrets.org/outsidespending/detail.php?cycle=2018&cmte=US+Chamber+of+Commerce.

57. OpenSecrets.org, Center for Responsive Politics, "U.S. Chamber of Commerce," Summary and various linked options, https://www.opensecrets.org/pacs/lookup2.php?strID=C00082040&cycle=2020.

58. Lou Dobbs, "Lou Dobbs Tonight," Facebook post of *Lou Dobbs Tonight* television segment on Fox Business Network, https://www.facebook.com/LouDobbsTonight/videos/10153750842242951/?v=10153750842242951.

59. Kate Ackley, "Chamber's Donohue: 'Loud Voices' in 2016 'Politically Stupid,'" *Roll Call*, January 14, 2016, http://www.rollcall.com/news/chambers_donohue_loud_voices_in_2016_politically_stupid-245455-1.html.

60. Julie Creswell, "Trump and U.S. Chamber of Commerce Pull No Punches on Trade Policy," *New York Times*, July 11, 2016, https://www.nytimes.com/2016/07/12/business/us-chamber-of-commerce-donald-trump.html.

61. US Chamber of Commerce Twitter feed, @USChamber, embedded tweet, https://twitter.com/uschamber/status/747862410267136000?lang=en.

62. Brooks Jackson, "Trump's Numbers October 2019 Update," FactCheck.org, October 11, 2019, https://www.factcheck.org/2019/10/trumps-numbers-october-2019-update/.

63. Sean Higgins, "Chamber President Warns U.S. Is 'Out of People,' Needs More Immigration," *Washington Examiner*, October 30, 2018, https://www.washingtonexaminer.com/policy/economy/chamber-president-warns-us-is-out-of-people-needs-more-immigration.

64. Ibid.

65. US Chamber of Commerce, "U.S. Chamber Statement on Closing the U.S.–Mexican Border," April 1, 2019, https://www.uschamber.com/press-release/us-chamber-statement-closing-the-us-mexico-border.

66. "Trump Says He Will Delay Closing the Border with Mexico for One Year," *The Yucatan Times*, April 4, 2019, https://www.theyucatantimes.com/2019/04/trump-says-he-will-delay-closing-the-border-with-mexico-for-one-year/.

67. US Chamber of Commerce, "U.S. Chamber's Statement on the President's Decision Not to Close the Borders," April 4, 2019, https://www.uschamber.com/press-release/us-chamber-statement-the-presidents-decision-not-close-the-border.

68. Adam J. White, "The Many Virtues of Scalia's Speeches," *Washington Examiner*, October 4, 2017, https://www.washingtonexaminer.com/weekly-standard/the-many-virtues-of-scalias-speeches.

CHAPTER 4

1. Brad Knickerbocker, "Gov. Scott Walker Not Backing Down on Wisconsin Union Fight," *The Christian Science Monitor*, February 27, 2011, https://www.csmonitor.com/USA/Politics/2011/0227/Gov.-Scott-Walker-not-backing-down-on-Wisconsin-union-fight.

2. Scott Bauer, "Thousands Protest Anti-Union Bill in Wisconsin," Associated Press via MPR News, February 16, 2011, https://www.mprnews.org/story/2011/02/16/wisconsin-unions.

3. Ibid.

4. Mike "Mish" Medlock, "40% of Madison teachers Call in Sick to Join Austerity Protest at the Wisconsin State Building," Business Insider, February 17, 2011, https://www.businessinsider.com/wisconsin-teacher -strike-2011-2.

5. Ibid.

6. Tyler Bond, "An Ominous Future: A United States Without Pensions," National Public Pension Coalition, January 2, 2018, https:// protectpensions.org/2018/01/02/united-states-without-pensions/.

7. Ballotpedia, "Party Control of Wisconsin State Government," https:// ballotpedia.org/Party_control_of_Wisconsin_state_government.

8. Tom Kertscher, "U.S. Sen. Rand Paul Says the Average Public School Teacher In Wisconsin Makes $89,000 in Salary and Benefits," PolitiFact Wisconsin, March 4, 2011, https://www.politifact.com/wisconsin/ statements/2011/mar/04/rand-paul/us-sen-rand-paul-says-average-public -school-teache/.

9. Best Places, "Cost of Living in Wisconsin," https://www.bestplaces.net/ cost_of_living/state/wisconsin.

10. Mike "Mish" Medlock, "40% of Madison Teachers Call in Sick to Join Austerity Protest at the Wisconsin State Building," *Business Insider*, February 17, 2011.

11. Scott Bauer, "Thousands Protest Anti-Union Bill in Wisconsin," Associated Press via MPR News, February 16, 2011, https://www.mprnews.org/story/ 2011/02/16/wisconsin-unions.

12. Ed Lavandera, "Wisconsin Assembly Passes Bill to Curb Collective Bargaining," CNN Politics, March 10, 2011, https://www.cnn.com/2011/ POLITICS/03/10/wisconsin.budget/index.html.

13. NPR Staff and Wires, "Wis. Democrats Flee to Prevent Vote on Union Bill," NPR, February 17, 2011, https://www.npr.org/2011/02/17/ 133847336/wis-democratic-lawmakers-flee-to-prevent-vote.

14. Monica Davev and Steven Greenhouse, "Wisconsin May Take an Ax to State Workers' Benefits and Their Unions," *New York Times*, February 11, 2011, https://www.nytimes.com/2011/02/12/us/12unions.html.

15. Ed Lavandera, "Wisconsin Assembly Passes Bill to Curb Collective Bargaining," CNN Politics, March 10, 2011, https://www.cnn.com/2011/ POLITICS/03/10/wisconsin.budget/index.html.

16. David Madland and Eric Powell, "Attacks on Public-Sector Unions Harm States: How Act 10 Has Affected Education in Wisconsin," Center for American Progress Action Fund, November 15, 2017, https://www. americanprogressaction.org/issues/economy/reports/2017/11/15/ 169146/attacks-public-sector-unions-harm-states-act-10-affected -education-wisconsin/.

17. Emily Stewart, "All of West Virginia's Teachers Have Been on Strike for over a Week," Vox, updated March 4, 2018, https://www.vox.com/ policy-and-politics/2018/3/3/17074824/west-virginia-teachers-strike -justice-union.

18. Office of the Governor, Jim Justice, "Gov. Justice Signs Pay Raise Bill," February 21, 2018, https://governor.wv.gov/News/press-releases/2018/Pages/Gov.-Justice-signs-pay-raise-bill.aspx.

19. Matt Pearce, "West Virginia Teachers Win 5% Pay Raise as Massive Strike Comes to an End," *Los Angeles Times*, March 6, 2018, https://www.latimes.com/nation/la-na-teacher-funding-20180306-story.html.

20. Ron Allen and Daniel Arkin, "West Virginia Governor Announces Deal to End Teachers' Strike," NBC News, "February 27, 2018, https://www.nbcnews.com/news/education/west-virginia-teachers-strike-enters-fourth-day-n851671.

21. Facebook post from Dedicated Teachers, West Virginia Education Association, February 27, 2018, https://www.facebook.com/dedicatedteachers/posts/1790593410972078.

22. Madeline Will, "Which States Have the Highest and Lowest Teachers' Salaries?" *Education Week Teacher*, April 30, 2019, http://blogs.edweek.org/teachers/teaching_now/2019/04/which_states_have_the_highest_and_lowest_teacher_salaries.html.

23. BestPlaces.net, "Cost of Living in West Virginia," https://www.bestplaces.net/cost_of_living/state/west-virginia.

24. Charles Young, "Local Experts: Despite Rising Cost of Living, W.Va. Remains Among Most Affordable States to Live," WVNews.com, August 19, 2018, https://www.wvnews.com/news/wvnews/local-experts-despite-rising-cost-of-living-w-va-remains/article_4d8d7307-743b-566a-b34d-9eefa4687863.html.

25. Alan Woods, "Cost of Living in West Virginia: How Does It Stack Up Against the Average Salary?" Movoto.com, https://www.movoto.com/guide/wv/cost-of-living-in-west-virginia-how-does-it-stack-up-against-the-average-salary/.

26. Charles Young, "Local Experts: Despite Rising Cost of Living, W.Va. Remains Among Most Affordable States to Live," WVNews.com, August 19, 2018, https://www.wvnews.com/news/wvnews/local-experts-despite-rising-cost-of-living-w-va-remains/article_4d8d7307-743b-566a-b34d-9eefa4687863.html.

27. DSA teachers of West Virginia, "Why Socialists Should Become Teachers," Democratic Socialists of America, https://teachers.dsausa.org/.

28. Ibid.

29. Ibid.

30. 270toWin, West Virginia, https://www.270towin.com/states/West_Virginia.

31. Lydia Saad, "Trump's Approval Highest in West Virginia; Lowest in Vermont," Gallup, January 30, 2018, https://news.gallup.com/poll/226454/trump-approval-highest-west-virginia-lowest-vermont.aspx.

32. Ibid.

33. DSA teachers of West Virginia, "Why Socialists Should Become Teachers," Democratic Socialists of America, https://teachers.dsausa.org/.

34. Ibid.

35. Alexia Fernandez Campbell, "West Virginia Teachers Are on Strike Again. Here's Why," Vox, February 19, 2019, https://www.vox.com/2019/2/19/18231486/west-virginia-teacher-strike-2019.

36. Ibid.

37. Associated Press, "West Virginia Teachers Going on Strike. Again," NBC News, February 19, 2019, https://www.nbcnews.com/news/us-news/west-virginia-teachers-going-strike-again-n972986.

38. Ibid.

39. Katie Endicott, @Katie_Endicott, Twitter post from February 19, 2019, https://twitter.com/Katie_Endicott/status/1097907959995265025?ref_src=twsrc%5Etfw%7Ctwcamp%5Etweetembed%7Ctwterm%5E10979079 59995265025&ref_url=https%3A%2F%2Fwww.vox.com%2F2019 %2F2%2F19%2F18231486%2Fwest-virginia-teacher-strike-2019.

40. Socialist Alternative, "2019 Introduction," https://www.socialistalternative .org/the-battle-of-wisconsin/2019-introduction/.

41. Rebecca Friedrichs, "Rebecca Friedrichs: I'm a Veteran Public School Teacher, Here's What I Told Trump About School Choice," Fox News, December 17, 2019, https://www.foxnews.com/opinion/veteran-public -school-teacher-trump-school-choice-rebecca-friedrichs.

42. Brian Miller, "Unpacking the Janus Decision," Forbes, June 27, 2018, https://www.forbes.com/sites/briankmiller/2018/06/27/unpacking-the -janus-decision/#6b195c941a42.

43. Rebecca Friedrichs, "Rebecca Friedrichs: I'm a Veteran Public School Teacher, Here's What I Told Trump About School Choice," Fox News, December 17, 2019, https://www.foxnews.com/opinion/veteran-public -school-teacher-trump-school-choice-rebecca-friedrichs.

44. Rebecca Garelli, "Inspired by West Virginia, Teachers Spread Red for Ed Movement Across Arizona," Labor Notes, March 15, 2018, https://labor-notes.org/2018/03/inspired-west-virginia-teachers-spread-red-ed -movement-across-arizona.

45. ADI staff reporter, "#Redfored Leader Korvalis Boasts at Socialism 2018 Conference," Arizona Daily Independent News Network, July 10, 2018, https://arizonadailyindependent.com/2018/07/10/redfored-leader -karvelis-boasts-at-socialism-2018-conference/.

46. Facebook page, @WearRed4PublicEd, Wear Red to Support Public Ed, https://www.facebook.com/WearRed4PublicEd/.

47. Facebook page from "Red for Ed" search, https://www.facebook.com/search/top/?q=red%20for%20ed.

48. Elementary Educators, Twitter post from @ETFOeducators, https://twitter.com/ETFOeducators/status/1218155436181987333.

49. National Education Association, "Red For Ed," http://neatoday.org/redfored/#our-fight.

CHAPTER 5

1. Obery M. Hendricks Jr., "The Biblical Values of Ocasio-Cortez's Democratic Socialism," Sojourners, Jan. 30, 2019, https://sojo.net/articles/biblical-values-ocasio-cortezs-democratic-socialism.
2. Ibid.
3. Robert Freeman, "Teaching Democrats to Talk About Socialism," Common Dreams, September 15, 2019, https://www.commondreams.org/views/2019/09/15/teaching-democrats-talk-about-socialism.
4. Ibid.
5. Real Clear Politics Video, "Obama: 'If You've Been Successful, You Didn't Get There on Your Own,'" July 15, 2012, https://www.realclearpolitics.com/video/2012/07/15/obama_if_youve_got_a_business_you_didnt_build_that_someone_else_made_that_happen.html.
6. Jack Schwartz, "How Socialism Made America Great," Daily Beast, June 21, 2019, updated July 1, 2019, https://www.thedailybeast.com/how-socialism-made-america-great.
7. NBC News, "Clinton Still Believes 'It Takes a Village,'" NBC News video, July 28, 2016, https://www.nbcnews.com/video/clinton-still-believes-it-takes-a-village-734433859888.
8. Ibid.
9. Sam Hodges, "North Texas Conference Ordains Openly Gay Pastor," UM News, June 4, 2019, https://www.umnews.org/en/news/north-texas-conference-ordains-openly-gay-pastor.
10. Cynthia B. Astle, "First Openly LGBTQ Pastor Ordained in Southern Conferences," United Methodist Insights, June 5, 2019, https://um-insight.net/in-the-church/ordained-ministry/first-lgbtq-clergywoman-ordained-in-southern-conference/.
11. Amelia Thomson-DeVeaux, "Presbyterian Church Ordains First Openly Gay Pastor," PRRI, October 12, 2011, https://www.prri.org/spotlight/presbyterian-church-ordains-first-openly-gay-pastor/.
12. Libby Solomon, "One Year in, Young Pastor Breathes Fresh Life into Progressive Towson Church," Baltimore Sun, August 20, 2018, https://www.baltimoresun.com/maryland/baltimore-county/towson/ph-tt-md-presbyterian-0822-story.html.
13. Adelle M. Banks, "Married Lesbian Baptist Co-pastors Say All Are 'Beloved,'" Religion News Service, March 2, 2017, https://religionnews.com/2017/03/02/married-lesbian-baptist-co-pastors-say-all-are-beloved/.
14. Laurie Goodstein, "Lutherans Offer Warm Welcome to Gay Pastors," New York Times, July 25, 2010, https://www.nytimes.com/2010/07/26/us/26lutheran.html.
15. CBS/AP, "Church Unveils Nativity Scene Depicting Holy Family as Caged Refugees," CBS News, December 9, 2019, https://www.cbsnews.com/news/nativity-scene-claremont-united-methodist-church-shows-holy-family-as-caged-refugees/.
16. Karen Clark Ristine, Facebook post, December 7, 2019, https://www.facebook.com/karen.clark.ristine.

17. Miriam Valverde, "Fact-checking Biden on Use of Cages for Immigrants During Obama Administration," PolitiFact, September 13, 2019, https://www.politifact.com/truth-o-meter/statements/2019/sep/13/joe-biden/fact-checking-biden-use-cages-during-obama-adminis/.

18. Pius XI, "Divini Redemptoris: Encyclical of Pope Pius XI on Atheistic Communism to the Patriarchs, Primates, Archbishops, Bishops and Other Ordinaries in Peace and Communion with the Apostolic See," March 19, 1937, https://w2.vatican.va/content/pius-xi/en/encyclicals/documents/hf_p-xi_enc_19370319_divini-redemptoris.html.

19. Ibid.

20. Ibid.

21. Ibid.

22. Papal Encyclicals Online, "Relevant Documents from the Past," https://www.papalencyclicals.net/.

23. Pius XI, "Non Abbiamo Bisogmo: Encyclical of Pope Pius XI on Catholic Action in Italy to Our Venerable Brethren the Patriarchs, Primates, Archbishops, Bishops and Other Ordinaries in Peace and Communions with the Apostolic See," June 29, 1931, http://www.vatican.va/content/pius-xi/en/encyclicals/documents/hf_p-xi_enc_29061931_non-abbiamo-bisogno.html.

24. Pius XI, "Mit Brennender Sorge: Encyclical of Pope Pius XI on the Church and the German Reich to the Venerable Brethren the Archbishops and Bishops of Germany and Other Ordinaries in Peace and Communion with the Apostolic See," March 14, 1937, http://www.vatican.va/content/pius-xi/en/encyclicals/documents/hf_p-xi_enc_14031937_mit-brennender-sorge.html.

25. History.com Editors, "Benito Mussolini," History.com, October 29, 2009, updated September 3, 2019, https://www.history.com/topics/world-war-ii/benito-mussolini.

26. GlobalSecurity.org, "Lateran Treaty—1929," https://www.globalsecurity.org/military/world/europe/va-lateran-treaties.htm.

27. Pope Francis, "Letter Sent by the Holy Father for the Event 'Economy of Francesco,'" May 1, 2019, http://www.vatican.va/content/francesco/en/letters/2019/documents/papa-francesco_20190501_giovani-imprenditori.html.

28. Ibid.

29. Ibid.

30. Ibid.

31. Elise Harris, "Top Vatican Officials Says Americans Misunderstand Pope's Social Agenda," Crux, May 15, 2019, https://cruxnow.com/vatican/2019/05/top-vatican-official-says-americans-misunderstand-popes-social-agenda/.

32. Ibid.

33. Ibid.

34. Biography, "Adam Smith," https://www.biography.com/scholar/adam-smith.

35. Jose Mena, "The Catholic Turn to Socialism Is Something to Celebrate," Catholic Herald, May 30, 2019, https://catholicherald.co.uk/commentandblogs/2019/05/30/the-catholic-turn-to-socialism-is-something-to-celebrate/.

36. Chris Agoranos and John Thornton, Jr., "Why a Southern Church Is Hosting Socialist Meetings," Sojourners, April 22, 2018, https://sojo.net/articles/why-southern-church-hosting-socialist-meetings.

37. Sarah Ngu, "Why These Young American Christians Embraced Socialism," Religion & Politics, January 28, 2020, https://religionand politics.org/2020/01/28/why-these-young-american-christians-embraced-socialism/.

38. Editors of Encyclopaedia Britannica, "Walter Rauschenbusch, American Minister," https://www.britannica.com/biography/Walter-Rauschenbusch.

39. Christianity Today, "Walter Rauschenbusch: Champion of the Social Gospel," *Christianity Today*, https://www.christianitytoday.com/history/people/activists/walter-rauschenbusch.html.

40. Jacob Dorn, "The Social Gospel and Socialism: A Comparison of the Thought of Francis Greenwood Peabody, Washington Gladden, and Walter Rauschenbusch," Wright State University CORE Scholar History Faculty Publications, 1993, https://corescholar.libraries.wright.edu/cgi/viewcontent.cgi?article=1026&context=history, p. 91.

41. Walter Rauschenbusch, *Christianity and the Social Crisis of the 21st Century*, HarperOne, 2007.

42. Lyman Abbott, "Christianity Versus Socialism," *North American Review*, vol. 148, no. 389, 1889, pp. 447–453, JSTOR, https://www.jstor.org/stable/25101760?seq=1#metadata_info_tab_contents.

43. Jane Addams Project, "Abbott, Lyman 1835–1922," https://digital.janeaddams.ramapo.edu/items/show/3710.

44. National Archives, "Washington Gladden Collection," National Historical Publications & Records Commission, https://www.archives.gov/nhprc/projects/catalog/washington-gladden.

45. The Conversation authors, "How a 1905 Debate About 'Tainted' Rockefeller Money Is a Reminder of Ethical Dilemmas Today," The Conversation, October 2, 2019, https://theconversation.com/how-a-1905-debate-about-tainted-rockefeller-money-is-a-reminder-of-ethical-dilemmas-today-124068.

46. Jacob Dorn, "The Social Gospel and Socialism: A Comparison of the Thought of Francis Greenwood Peabody, Washington Gladden, and Walter Rauschenbusch," Wright State University CORE Scholar History Faculty Publications, 1993, https://corescholar.libraries.wright.edu/cgi/viewcontent.cgi?article=1026&context=history, pp. 82–91.

47. Justus Anglican writers, "Biographical Sketches of Memorable Christians of the Past: Frederick Denison Maurice," http://justus.anglican.org/resources/bio/134.html.

48. Cambridge University Press, "John Malcolm Ludlow: The Builder of Christian Socialism," book by N.C. Masterman, published September, 2008, from description from Cambridge University Press website promoting book, https://www.cambridge.org/us/academic/subjects/history/british-history-general-interest/john-malcolm-ludlow-builder-christian-socialism?format=PB.

49. John Spargo, "Christian Socialism in America," *American Journal of Sociology*, vol. 15, no. 1, 1909, JSTOR, https://www.jstor.org/stable/2762617?seq=1#metadata_info_tab_contents, pp. 16–20.

CHAPTER 6

1. Cal Thomas, "It's the Spoiled Children of America Who Are Drawn to Socialism," *Chicago Tribune*, June 26, 2018, https://www.chicagotribune.com/opinion/commentary/ct-perspec-thomas-socialism-spoiled-children-0727-20180726-story.html.

2. Jill Russo, "'We Will Not Forgive You': Greta Thunberg's Speech to Leaders at UN—Video," Climate Home News, September 23, 2019, https://www.climatechangenews.com/2019/09/23/dare-greta-thunbergs-tearful-speech-leaders-un-video/.

3. Sharon Hendry, "Females with Autism: What It's Like to Live with Greta Thunberg's 'Superpower,'" *The Times*, February 2, 2020, https://www.thetimes.co.uk/article/women-with-autism-what-it-s-like-to-live-with-greta-thunberg-s-superpower-8jd79csr2.

4. Autism Society, "DSM-5," https://www.autism-society.org/what-is/diagnosis/diagnostic-classifications/.

5. Heavy, "Greta Thunberg's Family: 5 Fast Facts You Need to Know," Heavy.com, September 2019, https://heavy.com/news/2019/09/greta-thunbergs-family-parents/.

6. Greta Thunberg, compiled by NPR Staff, "Transcript: Greta Thunberg's Speech at the U.N. Climate Action Summit," NPR, September 23, 2019, https://www.npr.org/2019/09/23/763452863/transcript-greta-thunbergs-speech-at-the-u-n-climate-action-summit.

7. IPCC, "Special Report: Global Warming of 1.5 Degrees Celsius," 2018, https://www.ipcc.ch/sr15/.

8. IPCC, "2018: Summary for Policymakers: Global Warming of 1.5 Degrees Celsius," IPCC Special Report, 2018, https://www.ipcc.ch/site/assets/uploads/sites/2/2019/05/SR15_SPM_version_report_HR.pdf, pp. 3–4.

9. Kayla Epstein, "Greta Thunberg Wants You to Listen to the Scientists, Not Her," *Washington Post*, via Science Alert, September 19, 2019, https://www.sciencealert.com/greta-thunberg-wants-you-to-listen-to-scientists-not-her.

10. Earth Talk editors, "Bad Hair Day: Are Aerosols Still Bad for the Ozone Layer?" *Scientific American*, Earth Talk, September 4, 2008, https://www.scientificamerican.com/article/are-aerosols-still-bad/.

11. The Petition Project, "Global Warming Petition Project," PetitionProject.org, http://www.petitionproject.org/index.php.

12. The Petition Project, "Global Warming Petition Project: Qualifications of Signers," PetitionProject.org, http://www.petitionproject.org/qualifications_of_signers.php.

13. Michael Shellenberger, "Why Apocalyptic Claims About Climate Change Are Wrong," *Forbes*, November 25, 2019, https://www.forbes.com/sites/michaelshellenberger/2019/11/25/why-everything-they-say-about-climate-change-is-wrong/#2f6b76ab12d6.

14. Ibid.

15. Sarah Pike, "Uprooted," Aeon, May 7, 2013, https://aeon.co/essays/eco-activists-speak-about-their-conversion-experiences.

16. Paulina Neuding, "Self-Harm Versus the Greater Good: Greta Thunberg and Child Activism," Quillette, April 23, 2019, https://quillette.com/2019/04/23/self-harm-versus-the-greater-good-greta-thunberg-and-child-activism/.

17. Petra Lambeck, "'Scenes from the Heart': Backstory of 16-Year-Old Climate Activist Greta Thunberg," *LiveWire*, May 16, 2019, https://livewire.thewire.in/politics/greta-thunberg-film-childhood8491/.

18. Paulina Neuding, "Self-Harm Versus the Greater Good: Greta Thunberg and Child Activism," Quillette, April 23, 2019, https://quillette.com/2019/04/23/self-harm-versus-the-greater-good-greta-thunberg-and-child-activism/.

19. Joanna Williams, "Stop Scaring Children Witless About Climate Change," Spiked, April 25, 2019, https://www.spiked-online.com/2019/04/25/stop-scaring-children-witless-about-climate-change/.

20. Benjamin Fearnow, "Psychologists Warn Parents, Climate Change Alarmists Against Causing 'Eco-Anxiety' in Children," *Newsweek*, September 17, 2019, https://www.newsweek.com/eco-anxiety-climate-change-parent-fear-discussion-children-global-warming-depression-effects-1459731.

21. Laura M. Holson, "Climate Change Is Scaring Kids. Here's How to Talk to Them," *New York Times*, June 27, 2019, https://www.nytimes.com/2019/06/27/science/climate-change-children-education.html.

22. Henry Bodkin, "Parents Told Not to Terrify Children over Climate Change as Rising Numbers Treated for 'Eco-Anxiety,'" *Telegraph*, September 15, 2019, https://www.telegraph.co.uk/news/2019/09/15/parents-told-not-terrify-children-climate-change-rising-numbers/.

23. "The Environmental Burden of Generation Z," *Washington Post Magazine*, https://www.washingtonpost.com/magazine/2020/02/03/eco-anxiety-is-overwhelming-kids-wheres-line-between-education-alarmism/.

24. Deborah Fleischer and Ana Toepel, "Feeling Stressed About Climate Change? You Might Have Eco-Anxiety," UCSF Office of Sustainability, September 2019, https://sustainability.ucsf.edu/1.830.

25. Medical News Today editors, "What to Know about Eco-Anxiety," Medical News Today, undated, https://www.medicalnewstoday.com/articles/327354.php.

26. American Psychological Association, "Ecopsychology," https://www
.apadivisions.org/division-34/interests/ecopsychology/.

27. Susan Clayton et al., "Mental Health and Our Changing Climate: Impacts,
Implications and Guidance," American Psychological Association, March
2017, https://www.apa.org/news/press/releases/2017/03/mental-health
-climate.pdf, pp. 14–16.

28. Benjamin Fearnow, "Psychologists Warn Parents, Climate Change
Alarmists Against Causing 'Eco-Anxiety' in Children," Newsweek,
September 17, 2019, https://www.newsweek.com/eco-anxiety-climate
-change-parent-fear-discussion-children-global-warming-depression
-effects-1459731.

29. National Fatherhood Initiative, "The Proof Is in: Father Absence Harms
Children," https://www.fatherhood.org/father-absence-statistic.

30. The Annie E. Casey Foundation, Kids Count Data Center, "Child
Population by Household Type in the United States," Years: 2012–2016,
https://datacenter.kidscount.org/data/tables/105-child-population
-by-household-type?loc=1&loct=1#detailed/1/any/false/870,573,869,36,
868/4290,4291,4292/427,428.

31. Centers for Disease Control and Prevention, "About Teen Pregnancy,"
https://www.cdc.gov/teenpregnancy/about/index.htm.

32. DoSomething.org, "11 Facts About Teen Dads," https://www
.dosomething.org/us/facts/11-facts-about-teen-dads.

33. National Fatherhood Initiative, "The Proof Is in: Father Absence Harms
Children," https://www.fatherhood.org/father-absence-statistic.

34. Fathers.com, "The Consequences of Fatherlessness," http://fathers.com/
statistics-and-research/the-consequences-of-fatherlessness/.

35. Wayne Parker, "Statistics on Fatherless Children in America," LiveAbout
.com, May 24, 2019, https://www.liveabout.com/fatherless-children-in
-america-statistics-1270392.

36. Fathers.com, "The Consequences of Fatherlessness," http://fathers.com/
statistics-and-research/the-consequences-of-fatherlessness/.

37. Minnesota Psychological Association, "Father-Absent Homes:
Implications for Criminal Justice and Mental Health Professionals,"
abstract, MPA, August, 2004, https://www.mnpsych.org/index.php%3
Foption%3Dcom_dailyplanetblog%26view%3Dentry%26category%3
Dindustry%2520news%26id%3D54.

38. Kathryn Kost, Isaac Maddow-Zimet, and Alex Arpaia, "Pregnancies,
Births and Abortions Among Adolescents and Young Women in the
United States, 2013: National and State Trends by Age, Race and
Ethnicity," Guttmacher.org, 2013, https://www.guttmacher.org/report/
us-adolescent-pregnancy-trends-2013.

39. Guttmacher Institute, "Unintended Pregnancy in the United States,"
Guttmacher.org, January 2019, https://www.guttmacher.org/fact-sheet/
unintended-pregnancy-united-states.

40. Marilynn Marchione, "Blurred Lines: A Pregnant Man's Tragedy Tests Gender Notions," Associated Press, May 15, 2019, https://apnews.com/b5e7bb73c6134d58a0df9e1cee2fb8ad.

41. MFI News, "The Lie of Transgenderism and Its Victims," Massachusetts Family News, May 16, 2019, https://www.mafamily.org/abortion/the-lie-of-transgenderism-and-its-victims/10252/.

42. Lizette Borelli, "Transgender Surgery: Regret Rates Highest in Male-to-Female Reassignment Operations," *Newsweek*, October 3, 2017, https://www.newsweek.com/transgender-women-transgender-men-sex-change-sex-reassignment-surgery-676777.

43. Jody L. Herman, Taylor N.T. Brown and Ann P. Haas, "Suicide Thoughts and Attempts Among Transgender Adults: Findings from the 2015 U.S. Transgender Survey," UCLA School of Law Williams Institute, September 2019, https://williamsinstitute.law.ucla.edu/wp-content/uploads/Transgender-Suicide-Sept-2019.pdf, pp. 1–2.

44. Pat Eaton-Robb, "Girls Sue to Block Participation of Transgender Athletes," Associated Press, February 12, 2020, https://apnews.com/8fd300537131153cc44e0cf2ade3244b.

45. Georgi Boorman, "Trans Athletes Destroy the Meaning of Women, Then Ask 'What Is a Woman?'" The Federalist, October 31, 2019, https://thefederalist.com/2019/10/31/trans-athletes-destroy-the-meaning-of-women-then-ask-what-is-a-woman/.

46. AP, "Sex-Change Treatment for Kids on the Rise," CBS News, February 20, 2012, https://www.cbsnews.com/news/sex-change-treatment-for-kids-on-the-rise/.

47. Bruce Ashford, "The Ugly Truth About Sex Reassignment the Transgender Lobby Doesn't Want You to Know," Daily Signal, October 30, 2017, https://www.dailysignal.com/2017/10/30/ugly-truth-sex-reassignment-transgender-lobby-doesnt-want-know/.

CHAPTER 7

1. Article One, Sections 9 and 10, Constitution, Cornell Law School, Legal Information Institute, https://www.law.cornell.edu/constitution/articlei.

2. Colum Lynch, "Trump Turns U.N. Visas, Travel Restrictions into Foreign Policy Cudgel," *Foreign Policy*, November 5, 2019, https://foreignpolicy.com/2019/11/05/trump-administration-un-diplomats-united-nations-makes-life-difficult/.

3. Barack Obama, "Remarks by the President to the United Nations General Assembly," The White House, Office of the Press Secretary, September 23, 2009, https://obamawhitehouse.archives.gov/the-press-office/remarks-president-united-nations-general-assembly.

4. Ronald Reagan, "Farewell Address to the Nation," ReaganLibrary.gov, January 11, 1989, https://www.reaganlibrary.gov/research/speeches/011189i.

5. John Winthrop, "City Upon a Hill," Digital History, undated save for notation of 1630 speech, http://www.digitalhistory.uh.edu/disp_textbook .cfm?smtID=3&psid=3918.

6. Barack Obama, "Remarks by President Obama to the United Nations General Assembly," The White House, Office of the Press Secretary, September 28, 2015, https://obamawhitehouse.archives.gov/the-press -office/2015/09/28/remarks-president-obama-united-nations -general-assembly.

7. Barack Obama, "Address by President Obama to the 71st Session of the United Nations General Assembly," The White House, Office of the Press Secretary, September 20, 2016, https://obamawhitehouse.archives.gov/ the-press-office/2016/09/20/address-president-obama-71st-session-united -nations-general-assembly.

8. Stewart M. Patrick, "Can Trump's Successor Save the Liberal International World Order?" World Politics Review, February 10, 2020, https://www.worldpoliticsreview.com/articles/28526/can-trump-s -successor-save-the-liberal-international-order.

9. Ibid.

10. John Gerard Ruggie, Amazon.com Editorial Reviews, "The Best Laid Plans: The Origins of Multilateralism and the Dawn of the Cold War," published December 12, 2008, https://www.amazon.com/Best-Laid-Plans -American-Multilateralism/dp/0742562980.

11. Colum Lynch and Amy MacKinnon, "Greed and Graft at U.N. Climate Program," Foreign Policy, August 14, 2019, https://foreignpolicy.com/ 2019/08/14/greed-and-graft-at-un-climate-program-united-nations -undp-corruption/.

12. Sam Sachdeva, "NZ's Involvement in UN's Corruption Claims," Newsroom, September 3, 2019, Updated September 6, 2019, https:// www.newsroom.co.nz/2019/09/03/786982/nzs-involvement-in-un -corruption-claims.

13. Colum Lynch and Amy MacKinnon, "Greed and Graft at U.N. Climate Program," Foreign Policy, August 14, 2019, https://foreignpolicy.com/ 2019/08/14/greed-and-graft-at-un-climate-program-united-nations -undp-corruption/.

14. Ibid.

15. Ibid.

16. Sam Sachdeva, "NZ's Involvement in UN's Corruption Claims," Newsroom, September 3, 2019, Updated September 6, 2019, https:// www.newsroom.co.nz/2019/09/03/786982/nzs-involvement-in-un -corruption-claims.

17. Colum Lynch and Amy MacKinnon, "Greed and Graft at U.N. Climate Program," Foreign Policy, August 14, 2019, https://foreignpolicy.com/ 2019/08/14/greed-and-graft-at-un-climate-program-united-nations -undp-corruption/.

18. Sam Sachdeva, "NZ's Involvement in UN's Corruption Claims," Newsroom, September 3, 2019, Updated September 6, 2019, https://

www.newsroom.co.nz/2019/09/03/786982/nzs-involvement-in-un
-corruption-claims.

19. United Nations System Chief Executives Board for Coordination, "Directory of United Nations System Organizations," https://www .unsystem.org/members.

20. United Nations System Chief Executives Board for Coordination, "Directory of United Nations System Organizations: Specialized Agencies," https://www.unsystem.org/members/specialized-agencies.

21. United Nations System Chief Executives Board for Coordination, "Directory of United Nations System Organizations: Funds and Programmes," https://www.unsystem.org/members/funds-and -programmes.

22. United Nations System Chief Executives Board for Coordination, "Directory of United Nations System Organizations: Other UN System Organizations and Entities," https://www.unsystem.org/more-entities.

23. United Nations System Chief Executives Board for Coordination, "Directory of United Nations System Organizations: Regional Commissions," https://www.unsystem.org/agencies/regional -commissions.

24. United Nations System Chief Executives Board for Coordination, "Directory of United Nations System Organizations: UN Research and Training Institutes, https://www.unsystem.org/agencies/united-nations -research-and-training-institutes.

25. Fred Lucas, "Socialist, Refugee Advocate to Run UN for Next 5 Years," The Daily Signal, October 23, 2016, https://www.dailysignal.com/2016/10/23/ socialist-refugee-advocate-to-run-un-for-next-five-years/.

26. United Nations, "United Nations Secretary-General: Biography," https:// www.un.org/sg/en/content/sg/biography.

27. United Nations, "United Nations Secretary-General: Former Secretary-General Ban Ki-moon," https://www.un.org/sg/en/formersg/ban.shtml.

28. United Nations New Economic Paradigm Program, "United Nations NEP Calls on All People and All Nations to Adopt 'HAPPYTALISM' over Capitalism/Socialism on Occasion of July 4 US Independence Day 2019," PR Newswire, July 4, 2019, https://www.prnewswire.com/news-releases/ united-nations-nep-calls-on-all-people-and-all-nations-to-adopt-happy talism-over-capitalismsocialism-on-occasion-of-july-4-us-independence -day-2019-300880251.html.

29. Ibid.

30. Laura Hillard and Amanda Shendruck, "Funding the United Nations: What Impact Do U.S. Contributions Have on U.N. Agencies and Programs?" Council on Foreign Relations, April 2, 2019, https://www .cfr.org/article/funding-united-nations-what-impact-do-us-contributions -have-un-agencies-and-programs.

31. Ibid.

32. UNDP, "The United States and UNDP: A Partnership That Advances US Interests," undated, https://www.undp.org/content/dam/undp/library/corporate/PG_Brochures/UNDP_PG_US_Brochure.pdf.

33. United Nations Development Programme Evaluation Office, "Evaluation of UNDP Partnership with Global Funds and Philanthropic Foundations," UNDP, August 2012, link to downloadable report: http://web.undp.org/evaluation/evaluations/thematic/gfpf.shtml, p. 33.

34. Ibid.

35. Ibid.

36. Bill and Melinda Gates Foundation, "How We Work: Grant: Common Core Inc.," Bill and Melinda Gates Foundation, December 2009, https://www.gatesfoundation.org/How-We-Work/Quick-Links/Grants-Database/Grants/2009/12/OPP1011748.

37. Ford Foundation, "The Ford Foundation Center for Social Justice," https://www.fordfoundation.org/about/the-ford-foundation-center-for-social-justice/.

38. The Rockefeller Foundation, "Grants: Virginia Organizing," https://www.rockefellerfoundation.org/our-work/grants/.

39. Natalie Huet and Carmen Paun, "Meet the World's Most Powerful Doctor: Bill Gates," Politico, May 4, 2017, updated May 8, 2017, https://www.politico.eu/article/bill-gates-who-most-powerful-doctor/.

40. David Axe, "Bill Gates Might Save the World. Or Waste Billions on Vaccine Hunt," The Daily Beast, April 11, 2020, https://www.thedailybeast.com/bill-gates-might-save-the-world-or-waste-billions-on-vaccine-hunt?ref=scrollm.

41. Tom Huddleston Jr., "Bill Gates Is the Top Target for Coronavirus Conspiracy Theories," CNBC, April 17, 2020, https://www.cnbc.com/2020/04/17/bill-gates-is-top-target-for-coronavirus-conspiracy-theories-report.html.

42. United Nations Development Programme, "Procurement Notices," posted October 16, 2019, https://procurement-notices.undp.org/view_notice.cfm?notice_id=60267.

43. United Nations Development Programme, "Procurement Notices," posted July 1, 2019, https://procurement-notices.undp.org/view_notice.cfm?notice_id=57067.

44. United Nations Development Programme, "Procurement Notices," posted January 30, 2020, https://procurement-notices.undp.org/view_awards.cfm.

45. United Nations Development Programme, "Procurement Notices," posted January 29, 2020, https://procurement-notices.undp.org/view_awards.cfm.

46. United Nations Development Programme, "Procurement Notices," posted January 24, 2020, https://procurement-notices.undp.org/view_awards.cfm.

47. United Nations Development Programme, "Procurement Notices," posted July 10, 2019, https://procurement-notices.undp.org/view_notice.cfm?notice_id=57307.

48. USAID, "Moldova: History," https://www.usaid.gov/moldova/history.

49. Kaunain Rahman, "Moldova: Overview of Corruption and Anti-Corruption with a Focus on the Healthcare and Procurement Centers," Transparency International, U4 Anti-Corruption Resource Center, December 2017, https://www.u4.no/publications/moldova-overview-of-corruption-and-anti-corruption.

50. Alexander Tanas, "With Moldova in Crisis, Two Rival Governments Hold Meetings," Reuters, June 10, 2019, https://www.reuters.com/article/us-moldova-politics/with-moldova-in-crisis-two-rival-governments-hold-meetings-idUSKCN1TB1GQ.

51. Democratic Party of Moldova, "Statute: DPM, a Social Party," http://www.pdm.md/en/statute/.

52. Kenneth Rapoza, "Billion Dollar Theft: In Moldova, One Rich Banker's 'Crime' Has a Nation Doing Time," Forbes, August 1, 2016, https://www.forbes.com/sites/kenrapoza/2016/08/01/billion-dollar-theft-in-moldova-one-rich-bankers-crime-has-a-nation-doing-time/#7272bac64f7e.

53. Joe Biden, "Remarks by Vice President Joe Biden in Chisinau, Moldova," The White House, Office of the Vice President, March 11, 2011, https://obamawhitehouse.archives.gov/the-press-office/2011/03/11/remarks-vice-president-joe-biden-chisinau-moldova.

54. Ibid.

55. Ibid.

56. The White House, Office of the Vice President, "Fact Sheet: U.S. Assistance to Moldova," The White House, Office of the Vice President, June 7, 2014, https://obamawhitehouse.archives.gov/the-press-office/2014/06/07/fact-sheet-us-assistance-moldova.

57. U.S. Embassy in Moldova, "The U.S. Government and the Government of Moldova signed Agreements to Support Democratic and Economic Development of Moldova," U.S. Embassy in Moldova webpage, September 2016, https://md.usembassy.gov/u-s-government-government-moldova-signed-agreements-support-democratic-economic-development-moldova/.

58. Darren Spinck, "Washington's Strong Message to Moldova's Criminal Oligarch," *Washington Times*, January 23, 2020, https://www.washingtontimes.com/news/2020/jan/23/washingtons-strong-message-moldovas-criminal-oliga/.

59. RFE/RL's Moldovan Service, "U.S. Bans Fugitive Moldovan Tycoon from Entry for 'Significant Corruption,'" Radio Free Europe/Radio Liberty, January 13, 2020, https://www.rferl.org/a/fugitive-moldovan-tycoon-plahotniuc-u-s-entry-ban-corruption/30375065.html.

60. Hollie McKay, "What Is Burisma Holdings? The story Behind the Scandal-Tied Ukraine Firm That Hired Hunter Biden," Fox News, November 18, 2019, https://www.foxnews.com/politics/burisma-holdings-ukraine-hunter-biden.

CHAPTER 8

1. Scott Bland, "George Soros' Quiet Overhaul of the U.S. Justice System," *Politico*, August 30, 2016, https://www.politico.com/story/2016/08/george-soros-criminal-justice-reform-227519.

2. Luke Rosiak, "Backed by Soros Cash, Radical District Attorneys Take Control in DC Suburbs," *The Daily Signal*, November 14, 2019, https://www.dailysignal.com/2019/11/14/backed-by-soros-cash-radical-district-attorneys-take-control-in-dc-suburbs/.

3. Christine M. Flowers, "George Soros Wading into the Delco District Attorney Race Shows Problematic Influence," *Philadelphia Inquirer*, November 1, 2019, https://www.inquirer.com/opinion/george-soros-delaware-county-district-attorney-stollsteimer-krasner-20191101.html.

4. Shane Devine, "Soros Aims to Transform the Justice System by Funding DA Races," Capital Research Center, December 17, 2019, https://capitalresearch.org/article/soros-aims-to-transform-the-justice-system-by-funding-da-races/.

5. Tim Storey, "GOP Makes Historic State Legislative Gains in 2010," Rasmussen Reports, December 10, 2010, https://www.rasmussenreports.com/public_content/political_commentary/commentary_by_tim_storey/gop_makes_historic_state_legislative_gains_in_2010.

6. Ibid.

7. Louis Jacobson, "2010 State Legislatures: GOP Chalks up Historic Gains," *Governing*, November 3, 2010, https://www.governing.com/topics/politics/2010-state-legislatures-republicans-historic-gains.html.

8. Tim Storey, "GOP Makes Historic State Legislative Gains in 2010," Rasmussen Reports, December 10, 2010, https://www.rasmussenreports.com/public_content/political_commentary/commentary_by_tim_storey/gop_makes_historic_state_legislative_gains_in_2010.

9. Illinois Sunshine, "Illinois Justice & Public Safety PAC," November 24, 2019, quarterly report, https://www.illinoissunshine.org/committees/illinois-justice-public-safety-pac-35859/.

10. New York State Board of Elections, "Candidate/Committee A22968—New York Justice and Public Safety PAC," October 2019, https://cfapp.elections.ny.gov/ords/plsql_browser/ind_exp_report_test?filerID_in=A22968&type_in=L&e_year_in=2019.

11. Justin Jouvenal and Rachel Weiner, "Money from PAC Funded by George Soros Shakes up Prosecutor Races in Northern Virginia," *Washington Post*, April 24, 2019, https://www.washingtonpost.com/local/public-safety/money-from-pac-funded-by-george-soros-shakes-up-prosecutors-races-in-northern-virginia/2019/04/23/5c754d14-6513-11e9-a1b6-b29b90efa879_story.html.

12. Ryan Brooks, "The Campaign to Change Policing in the US Has Found a New Way to Win," BuzzFeed News, March 7, 2018, https://www.buzzfeednews.com/article/ryancbrooks/the-campaign-to-change-policing-in-america-has-found-a-new.

13. Ballotpedia, "George Soros Political Activity," 2015–2017 election cycles, https://ballotpedia.org/George_Soros/Political_activity.
14. Federal Election Commission of the United States of America, Disbursements, Justice and Public Safety PAC, June 17, 2019, and May 7, 2019, https://www.fec.gov/data/disbursements/?data_type=processed &committee_id=C00651505&recipient_name=new+virginia +majority&two_year_transaction_period=2020.
15. Federal Election Commission, "Report of Receipts and Disbursements: Justice & Public Safety PAC," FEC documents online, July 31, 2019, https://docquery.fec.gov/pdf/008/201907319161278008/2019073191612 78008.pdf#navpanes=0, p. 36.
16. Working Families, "Announcing Our First Wave of NY Progressive Champions!" New York Working Families Party, June 18, 2019, https://workingfamilies.org/2019/06/announcing-our-first-wave-of-ny-progressive-champions/.
17. David Brand, "Urgency Inspires Big Donations in Final Days of Queens DA Race," *Queens Daily Eagle*, June 16, 2019, https://queenseagle.com/all/11-day-report-queens-da-final-donations.
18. Sally Goldenberg, "Cabán's Success Marks a Win for Working Families Party—Without Union Support," Politico, July 2, 2019, https://www.politico.com/states/new-york/albany/story/2019/07/02/cabans-success-marks-a-win-for-working-families-party-without-union-support-1084512.
19. Israel Salas-Rodriguez and Carl Campanile, "Melinda Katz Easily Wins Queens District Attorney Race," *New York Post*, November 5, 2019, https://nypost.com/2019/11/05/melinda-katz-easily-wins-queens-district-attorney-race/.
20. New Virginia Majority, "Our Ten Year Vision for Democracy, Justice and Progress," New Virginia Majority website, https://www.newvirginiamajority.org/tenyearvision.
21. Communications New Virginia Majority, "Fueled by People of Color, Women, Younger Voters, Virginia Flips House and Senate," New Virginia Majority, November 5, 2019, https://www.newvirginiamajority.org/weflippedvirginia.
22. Christine M. Flowers, "George Soros Wading into the Delco District Attorney Race Shows Problematic Influence," *Philadelphia Inquirer*, November 1, 2019, https://www.inquirer.com/opinion/george-soros-delaware-county-district-attorney-stollsteimer-krasner-20191101.html.
23. VPAP.org, "Justice and Public Safety PAC 2019: Donations Reported by Biberaj for Loudoun County Commonwealth Attorney," Virginia Public Access Project, https://www.vpap.org/donors/337496/recipient/325342/?start_year=2019&end_year=2019&recip_type=all.
24. Ibid.
25. Ibid.
26. VPAP.org, "Justice and Public Safety PAC 2019: Donations Reported by Hingeley for Albemarle Commonwealth Attorney," Virginia

Public Access Project, https://www.vpap.org/donors/337496/recipient/326469/?start_year=2019&end_year=2019&recip_type=all.

27. CJ Paschall, "Albemarle County Commonwealth's Attorney Jim Hingeley Takes Oath of Office," NBC29.com, December 17, 2019, https://www.nbc29.com/2019/12/17/albemarle-county-commonwealths-attorney-jim-hingeley-takes-oath-office/.

28. Jill Castellano, "Billionaire Soros Pumps $400K into DA's Race to Get Jones-Wright Elected," INewsSource.org, May 7, 2018, https://inewsource.org/2018/05/07/billionaire-soros-pumps-400k-into-das-race-to-get-jones-wright-elected/.

29. Scott Bland, "George Soros' Quiet Overhaul of the U.S. Justice System," Politico, August 30, 2016, https://www.politico.com/story/2016/08/george-soros-criminal-justice-reform-227519.

30. Monivette Cordeiro, "Orange-Osceola State Attorney Aramis Ayala to Leave Office When Term Ends But Says, 'I'm Not Out of the fight,'" Orlando Sentinel, October 31, 2019, https://www.orlandosentinel.com/news/crime/os-ne-aramis-ayala-leaves-state-attorney-20191031-uz25n7oiv5bhpn7cvcmmojafaa-story.html.

31. Ibid.

32. Emilee Speck, "What We Know About Fallen Orlando Police Master Sgt. Debra Clayton," ClickOrlando.com, October4 8, 2019, https://www.click-orlando.com/news/2017/01/11/what-we-know-about-fallen-orlando-police-master-sgt-debra-clayton/.

33. WKMG (WTSP), "Gov. Rick Scott Wins Legal Battle Against State Attorney Aramis Ayala," WTSP10 News, Sugust 31, 2017, https://www.wtsp.com/article/news/local/gov-rick-scott-wins-legal-battle-against-state-attorney-aramis-ayala/469841835.

34. Ibid.

35. Open Society Institute, "Ideas for an Open Society: The Death Penalty Debate," OSI, Volume 1, Number 3, July/August 2001, https://www.opensocietyfoundations.org/uploads/081483b8-f9d8-4c34-b765-8d0d1dd3b82a/ideas_death_penalty.pdf, p. 8.

36. Ibid.

37. Erika D. Smith, "George Soros Wants to Fix America's Justice System. Sacramento's DA Race Is a Good Place to Start," *Sacramento Bee*, May 18, 2018, https://www.sacbee.com/opinion/opn-columns-blogs/erika-d-smith/article211351439.html.

38. Tony Pugh, "Progressive Groups Investing in District Attorney Races as Path to Criminal Justice Reform," McClatchy DC, May 6, 2018, https://www.mcclatchydc.com/news/politics-government/article203622774.html.

39. Scott Bland, "George Soros' Quiet Overhaul of the U.S. justice system," Politico, August 30, 2016, https://www.politico.com/story/2016/08/george-soros-criminal-justice-reform-227519.

40. Elyssa Cherney, "Aramis Ayala Upsets Jeff Ashton for State Attorney," Orlando Sentinel, August 31, 2016, https://www.orlandosentinel.com/ politics/os-primary-state-attorney-judges-20160829-story.html.
41. Christine M. Flowers, "George Soros Wading into the Delco District Attorney Race Shows Problematic Influence," *Philadelphia Inquirer*, November 1, 2019, https://www.inquirer.com/opinion/george-soros -delaware-county-district-attorney-stollsteimer-krasner-20191101.html.
42. Marcellus Drilling News, "NYU Buying Frivolous Enviro Lawsuits by Hiring Lawyers for State AGs," Marcellus Drilling News, December 14, 2017, https://marcellusdrilling.com/2017/12/ nyu-buying-frivolous-enviro-lawsuits-by-hiring-lawyers-for-state-ags/.
43. Jim Willis, "Michael Bloomberg Buying AG Offices Through the NYU Law School?" NaturalGasNow.org, via Marcellus Drilling News (MDN), March 9, 2018, https://naturalgasnow.org/michael-bloomberg-buying-ag -offices-nyu-law-school/.
44. PND by Candid, "Bloomberg Helps Launch NYU Center for Environmental Litigation," Philanthropy News Digest, August 21, 2017, https://philanthropynewsdigest.org/news/bloomberg-helps-launch-nyu -center-for-environmental-litigation.
45. Ibid.
46. Ibid.
47. Ibid.
48. Jim Willis, "Michael Bloomberg Buying AG Offices Through the NYU Law School?" NaturalGasNow.org, via Marcellus Drilling News (MDN), March 9, 2018, https://naturalgasnow.org/michael-bloomberg-buying-ag -offices-nyu-law-school/.
49. Tom Shepstone, "Michael Bloomberg Is Buying Power from Political Corrupt Attorneys General," Natural News Now, September 2, 2018, https://naturalgasnow.org/michael-bloomberg-buying-power-corrupt -attorneys-general/.
50. Chris Horner, "Law Enforcement for Rent: Appendices of Report," Competitive Enterprise Institute, September 15, 2017, https:// secureservercdn.net/166.62.112.193/o91.197.myftpupload.com/wp -content/uploads/2018/08/Appendix-Law-Enforcement-for-Rent.pdf, pp. 3–4.
51. Tom Shepstone, "Michael Bloomberg Is Buying Power from Political Corrupt Attorneys General," Natural News Now, September 2, 2018, https://naturalgasnow.org/michael-bloomberg-buying-power-corrupt -attorneys-general/.
52. Ibid.
53. Chris Horner and Victoria Toensing, "How Bloomberg Pays to Prosecute the Trump EPA," *Wall Street Journal*, July 5, 2019, https://www.wsj.com/ articles/how-bloomberg-pays-to-prosecute-the-trump-epa-11562360993.
54. William Allison, "Massachusetts Attorney General Sued over Use of Bloomberg-Funded Attorneys," June 5, 2019, https://eidclimate.org/

massachusetts-attorney-general-sued-over-use-of-bloomberg-funded
-attorneys/.

55. Valerie Richardson, "Virginia Blocks Mike Bloomberg's Climate Lawyers,"
Associated Press, April 18, 2019, https://apnews.com/38938e39f23c6b8f
3a900b221797143e.

56. Ibid.

57. Courtney Gross, "Bloomberg Takes Centrist Message to Virginia in First
2020 Campaign Stop," Spectrum News NY1, November 25, 2019,
https://www.ny1.com/nyc/all-boroughs/politics/2019/11/26/michael
-bloomberg-president-run-2020-presidential-election-virginia-first
-campaign-stop.

58. Gabriel Debenedetti, "Ranking the Most Influential Democratic Donors
in the 2020 Race," New York Intelligencer, August 22, 2019, https://
nymag.com/intelligencer/2019/08/most-influential-democratic-donors
-2020-elections.html.

59. Ibid.

60. Calvin Baylock and Andrew McIndoe, "The Unsung Hero Who
Financed the American Revolution, and His Lesson for Today," Heritage
Foundation, August 6, 2018, https://www.heritage.org/american-found-
ers/commentary/the-unsung-hero-who-financed-the-american-revolution
-and-his-lesson.

61. NPR Morning Edition, "Robert Morris: America's Founding Capitalist,"
NPR, December 20, 2010, https://www.npr.org/2010/12/20/132051519/
-robert-morris-america-s-foundin-capitalist.

62. OpenSecrets.org, "Adelson, Sheldon G.: Donor Detail," Center for
Responsive Politics, June 10, 2019, https://www.opensecrets.org/
outsidespending/donor_detail.php?cycle=2018&id=U0000000310&
type=I&super=N&name=Adelson,+Sheldon+G.+&+Miriam+O.

CHAPTER 9

1. TheNewspaper.com, "Florida Lawsuit Against License Plate Readers
Advances," TheNewspaper.com, October 15, 2019, https://www
.thenewspaper.com/news/68/6823.asp.

2. Ty Russell, "Coral Gables Resident Can Move Forward with Suing City
over Use of Automated License Plate Readers," CBS Miami, October 28,
2019, https://miami.cbslocal.com/2019/10/28/coral-gables-resident
-can-move-forward-with-suing-city-over-use-of-automated-license-plate
-readers/.

3. Stitcher, "Big Brother Grows Bigger," Bold and Blunt podcast,
Washington Times, February 27, 2020, https://www.stitcher.com/podcast/
the-washington-times/bold-and-blunt/e/67654421.

4. Ty Russell, "Coral Gables Resident Can Move Forward with Suing City
over Use of Automated License Plate Readers," CBS Miami, October 28,
2019, https://miami.cbslocal.com/2019/10/28/coral-gables-resident-can
-move-forward-with-suing-city-over-use-of-automated-license-plate-readers/.

5. Ibid.
6. Legal Information Institute, "Bill of Rights," https://www.law.cornell.edu/constitution/billofrights.
7. Emily Rittman, "License Plate Reader, Cameras Help Police Arrest Murder Suspect in 8 Hours," KCTV News 5, May 7, 2019, https://www.kctv5.com/news/license-plate-reader-cameras-help-police-arrest-murder-suspect-in/article_c9183296-701d-11e9-9ff0-9fbcce4451ca.html.
8. PoliceOne Staff, "7 Cases Solved Thanks to ALPR Data," PoliceOne.com, June 12, 2018, https://www.policeone.com/police-products/traffic-enforcement/license-plate-readers/articles/7-cases-solved-thanks-to-alpr-data-doayALt3VGwqCIN5/.
9. Tanvi Misra, "Who's Tracking Your License Plate?" CityLab, December 6, 2018, https://www.citylab.com/equity/2018/12/automated-license-plate-readers-privacy-data-security-police/576904/.
10. Electronic Frontier Foundation, "Data Driven: What We Learned," Electronic Frontier Foundation, https://www.eff.org/pages/what-we-learned.
11. Matthew Feeney, "Facial Recognition Technology Is Getting out of Control," Business Insider, March 8, 2020, https://www.businessinsider.com/facial-recognition-technology-getting-out-of-control-needs-regulation-2020-3.
12. Patrick Grother, Mei Ngan, and Kayee Hanaoka, "Ongoing Face Recognition Vendor Test (FRVT) Part 2: Identification," National Institute of Standards and Technology, U.S. Department of Commerce, November 2018, https://nvlpubs.nist.gov/nistpubs/ir/2018/NIST.IR.8238.pdf, pp. 2–3.
13. Gemalto, "Facial Recognition: Top 7 Trends (Tech, Vendors, Markets, Use Cases and Latest News)," Gemalto, a Thales Company, February 16, 2020, https://www.gemalto.com/govt/biometrics/facial-recognition.
14. Erik Lorenzsonn, "Wisconsin Company That Microchipped Its Workers Envisions an 'Internet Of People,'" Cap Times, January 24, 2018, https://madison.com/ct/business/technology/wisconsin-company-that-microchipped-its-workers-envisions-an-internet-of/article_f621ba3a-3e51-50be-8aef-d306cb7fa083.html.
15. Andrew Keshner, "States Are Cracking Down on Companies Microchipping Their Employees—How Common Is It?" MarketWatch, February 4, 2020, https://www.marketwatch.com/story/states-are-cracking-down-on-companies-microchipping-their-employees-how-common-is-it-and-why-does-it-happen-2020-02-03.
16. Kelvin Chan, "With Painted Faces, Artists Fight Facial Recognition Tech," Associated Press via West Virginia's News, March 8, 2020, https://www.wvnews.com/newsfeed/politics/with-painted-faces-artists-fight-facial-recognition-tech/article_3f66e229-686f-5e20-9b6b-8ba409afb641.html.
17. Katharine Schwab, "You're Already Being Watched by Facial Recognition Tech. This Map Shows Where," Fast Company, July 23, 2019, https://

www.fastcompany.com/90379969/youre-already-being-watched-by-facial
-recognition-tech-this-map-shows-where.

18. Mordor Intelligence, "Iris Recognition Market—Growth, Trends, and
Forecast (2020–2025)," Mordor Intelligence, study period 2019–2025,
https://www.mordorintelligence.com/industry-reports/iris
-recognition-market.

19. Heidi Ledford, "Google Health-Data Scandal Spooks Researchers,"
Nature, November 19, 2019, https://www.nature.com/articles/d41586
-019-03574-5.

20. Ibid.

21. Louise Matsakis, "How the Government Hides Secret Surveillance
Programs," Wired, January 9, 2018, https://www.wired.com/story/stingray
-secret-surveillance-programs/.

22. Julia Angwin, Jeff Larson, Surya Mattu, and Lauren Kirchner, "Machine
Bias," Pro Publica, May 23, 2016, https://www.propublica.org/article/
machine-bias-risk-assessments-in-criminal-sentencing.

23. Mark Puente, "LAPD Pioneered Predicting Crime with Data. Many Police
Don't Think It Works," *Los Angeles Times*, July 3, 2019, https://www.
latimes.com/local/lanow/la-me-lapd-precision-policing-data-20190703
-story.html.

24. Luke Wachob, "Regulating the Internet: A Dangerous Trend for Free
Speech," Institute for Free Speech, August 9, 2018, https://www.ifs.org/
research/regulating-the-internet-a-dangerous-trend-for-free-speech/.

25. Ibid.

26. Ameer Rosic, "What Is Bitcoin? [The Most Comprehensive Step-by-Step
Guide]," BlockGeeks, 2017, https://blockgeeks.com/guides/what-is
-bitcoin/.

27. Andrew Hecht, "What Is Bitcoin? Basic Facts You Should Know About
Bitcoin," The Balance, June 25, 2019, https://www.thebalance.com/
is-bitcoin-a-commodity-4126544.

28. Bitcoin.org, "How Does Bitcoin Work?" Bitcoin.org, https://bitcoin.org/
en/how-it-works.

29. Paxful Team, "100 Things You Can Buy with Bitcoin," Paxful, October 22,
2019, https://paxful.com/blog/what-can-you-buy-with-bitcoin/.

30. Andrew Hecht, "What Is Bitcoin? Basic Facts You Should Know About
Bitcoin," The Balance, June 25, 2019, https://www.thebalance.com/
is-bitcoin-a-commodity-4126544.

31. StackExchange, "How Is Bitcoin Infinitely Divisible?" StackExchange,
question posed in 2014, https://bitcoin.stackexchange.com/questions/
19661/how-is-bitcoin-infinitely-divisible.

32. Ari Levy, "Twitter CEO Jack Dorsey Says Bitcoin Will Be the Single Global
Currency," CNBC, March 25, 2018, https://www.cnbc.com/2018/03/25/
bitcoin-will-eventually-be-the-single-global-currency-twitters-jack-dorsey
.html.

33. Catherine Clifford, "This Is Why a Single Global Currency (Like Bitcoin)
Won't Happen, Says Online Payments Company CEO," CNBC, December

28, 2018, https://www.cnbc.com/2018/12/24/payoneer-ceo-why-single -global-currency-like-bitcoin-is-not-realistic.html.

34. Daniel Phillips, "Bitcoin: Designed for Liberals, Most Utilized by Conservatives," Be In Crypto, June 8, 2019, https://beincrypto.com/ bitcoin-designed-for-liberals-most-utilized-by-conservatives/.

35. Anthony Cuthbertson, "Bitcoin Self-Proclaimed Cryptocurrency Creator Craig Wright Ordered to Pay Billions," The Independent, October 29, 2019, https://www.independent.co.uk/life-style/gadgets-and-tech/news/ bitcoin-inventor-satoshi-nakamoto-craig-wright-court-lawsuit-a9084146 .html.

36. Zoe Bernard, "Everything You Need to Know About Bitcoin, Its Mysterious Origins, and the Many Alleged Identities of Its Creator," Business Insider, November 10, 2018, https://www.businessinsider.com/ bitcoin-history-cryptocurrency-satoshi-nakamoto-2017-12.

37. Avi Mizrahi, "Who Is Satoshi Nakamoto? An Introduction to Bitcoin's Mysterious Founder," Bitcoin.com News, March 8, 2020, https:// news.bitcoin.com/satoshi-nakamoto-founder-of-bitcoin/.

38. Feng Xiang, "AI Will Spell the End of Capitalism," *Washington Post*, May 3, 2018, https://www.washingtonpost.com/news/theworldpost/ wp/2018/05/03/end-of-capitalism/?outputType=amp&__twitter _impression=true&noredirect=on.

39. Ibid.

40. Mike Brown, "Universal Basic Income: The U.K. May Host One of the Biggest Trials Yet," Inverse, March 5, 2020, https://www.inverse.com/ article/55791-universal-basic-income-the-uk-may-host-one-of-the-biggest -trials-yet.

41. Eric Morath, "Coronavirus Relief Often Pays Workers More Than Work," the *Wall Street Journal*, April 28, 2020, https://www.wsj.com/articles/ coronavirus-relief-often-pays-workers-more-than-work-11588066200.

42. Cheyenne Haslett, Lauren Lantry, and Benjamin Siegel, "Employers Struggle to Compete with $600 Coronavirus Unemployment Payments," ABC News, May 21, 2020, https://abcnews.go.com/Business/employers -struggle-compete-600-unemployment-payments/story?id=70800696.

43. Andre Damon, "Capitalism and the Artificial Intelligence Revolution," World Socialist Web Site, April 6, 2018, https://www.wsws.org/en/ articles/2018/04/06/pers-a06.html.

44. Robin Clapp, "The Growth of Artificial Intelligence Technology," Socialist Party, formerly Militant, from the *Socialist Newspaper*, December 5, 2018, https://www.socialistparty.org.uk/articles/28384/05-12-2018/ the-growth-of-artificial-intelligence-technology.

CHAPTER 10

1. Jack Ross, "Mapping American Social Movements Project: Socialist Party Elected Officials 1901–1960," University of Washington, https:// depts.washington.edu/moves/SP_map-elected.shtml.

2. US History, "Eugene V. Debs and American Socialism," USHistory.org, https://www.ushistory.org/us/37e.asp.

3. National Archives, "1912 Electoral Vote Tally, February 12, 1913," The Center for Legislative Archives, https://www.archives.gov/legislative/features/1912-election.

4. Erick Trickey, "When America's Most Prominent Socialist Was Jailed for Speaking out Against World War I," Smithsonian Magazine, June 15, 2018, https://www.smithsonianmag.com/history/fiery-socialist -challenged-nations-role-wwi-180969386/.

5. Maurice Isserman, "Socialists in the House: A 100-Year History from Victor Berger to Alexandria Ocasio-Cortez," In These Times, November 8, 2018, https://inthesetimes.com/article/21570/socialists-house-midterms -victor-berger-ocasio-cortez-tlaib.

6. US House of Representatives History, Art & Archives, "BERGER, Victor Luitpold, Biography," https://history.house.gov/People/Detail/9304.

7. US House of Representatives History, Art & Archives, "Oath of Office," https://history.house.gov/Institution/Origins-Development/Oath-of-Office/.

8. Eric Blanc, "From Meyer London to Alexandria Ocasio-Cortez," Jacobin, March, 2019, https://www.jacobinmag.com/2019/03/meyer-london -alexandria-ocasio-cortez-congress.

9. Ibid.

10. Anne Speckhard and Ardian Shajkovci, "ISIS Fighter Claims Attack Plot Via Mexico, Underscoring Border Vulnerability," HomelandSecurityToday.us, June 3, 2019, https://www.hstoday.us/ subject-matter-areas/terrorism-study/perspective-isis-fighter-claims -attack-plot-via-mexico-underscoring-border-vulnerability/.

11. Ryan Saavedra, "328 Chinese Nationals Caught Trying to Illegally Enter U.S. at Southern Border," The Daily Wire, March 4, 2020, https:// www.dailywire.com/news/328-chinese-nationals-caught-trying-to -illegally-enter-u-s-at-southern-border.

12. Library of Congress, "Progressive Era to New Era, 1900–1929: Immigrants in the Progressive Era," Library of Congress, http://www.loc.gov/teachers/ classroommaterials/presentationsandactivities/presentations/timeline/ progress/immigrnt/.

13. Ibid.

14. Steve Holland and Todd Eastham, "Obama complains About 'Fat-Cat Bankers,'" Reuters, December 11, 2009, https://www.reuters.com/article/ us-financial-regulation-obama/obama-complains-about-fat-cat-bankers -idUSTRE5BA4IF20091211.

15. Elizabeth McKillen, "The Socialist Party of America, 1900–1929," Published at Oxford Research Encyclopedias' American History page by Department of History, University of Maine, June 2017, https://oxfordre .com/americanhistory/view/10.1093/acrefore/9780199329175.001.0001/ acrefore-9780199329175-e-413.

16. James Gregory and Rebecca Flores, "Socialist Party Membership by States 1904–1940," University of Washington Mapping American Social

Movements Project, https://depts.washington.edu/moves/SP_map
-members.shtml.

17. Ibid.
18. Michael Savage, "Savage Exposes Bernie the Bolshevik," The Michael
    Savage Podcast, Stitcher, February 12, 2020, https://www.stitcher.com/
    podcast/westwood-one/the-savage-nation-with-michael-savage/e/
    67300563.
19. Jack Ross, "Mapping American Social Movements Project: Membership
    by State, 1904–1940," University of Washington, 2015, https://depts
    .washington.edu/moves/SP_map-elected.shtml.
20. John Simkin, "Socialism in the United States," Spartacus Educational,
    September 1997, updated January 2020, https://spartacus-educational
    .com/USAsocialist.htm.
21. James Gregory and Rebecca Flores, "Mapping American Social
    Movements Project: Socialist Party Membership by States, 1904–1940,"
    University of Washington, 2015, https://depts.washington.edu/moves/
    SP_map-members.shtml.
22. Ibid.
23. Ibid.
24. Ibid.
25. Ohio History Central, "First Red Scare," https://ohiohistorycentral.org/w/
    First_Red_Scare.
26. History, "This Day in History: Bolsheviks Revolt in Russia," History.com,
    Published February 9, 2010, Updated November 4, 2019, https://www
    .history.com/this-day-in-history/bolsheviks-revolt-in-russia.
27. Ibid.
28. GMU, "Lenin and the First Communist Revolutions V: The First
    Communist Dictatorship," https://econfaculty.gmu.edu/bcaplan/
    museum/his1e.htm.
29. Jack Ross, "Mapping American Social Movements Project: Membership
    by State, 1904–1940," University of Washington, 2015, https://depts
    .washington.edu/moves/SP_map-elected.shtml.
30. Melvyn Dubofsky, "When Socialism Was Popular in the United States,"
    Viewpoint Magazine, March 29, 2016, https://www.viewpointmag.com/
    2016/03/29/when-socialism-was-popular-in-the-united-states/.
31. New York Times Archives, "Ex-Mayor Freese of Norwalk Dies, Socialist
    Served Five Terms Between 1947 and 1959," New York Times, September
    13, 1964, https://www.nytimes.com/1964/09/13/archives/exmayor-freese
    -of-norwalk-dies-socialist-served-five-terms-between.html.
32. John Mihelic, "The Socialist Party of America in Connecticut's Past:
    Jasper McLevy," Western Connecticut State University Archives' Digital
    Collection, http://archives.library.wcsu.edu/omeka/exhibits/show/
    socialist/danbury-politics/jaspermclevy.
33. WordDisk, "List of Mayors of Norwalk, Connecticut," https://worddisk
    .com/wiki/Mayor_of_Norwalk,_Connecticut/.

34. John Haltiwanger, "Here's the Difference Between a 'Socialist' and a 'Democratic Socialist,'" Business Insider, February 11, 2020, https://www.businessinsider.com/difference-between-socialist-and-democratic-socialist-2018-6.

35. John Nichols, "When Socialists Was Tried in America—and Was a Smashing Success," *The Nation*, April 2, 2019, https://www.thenation.com/article/archive/socialism-milwaukee-democrats-2020/.

36. The San Bernardino County Sun, "SOCIALISTS ELECTED," published April 4, 1920, clipped from *San Bernardino County Sun*, San Bernardino, California, on July 22, 2015, Newspapers.com, https://www.newspapers.com/clip/2864964/socialist-cl-barewald-elected-mayor/.

37. Robert E. Weir, "Solid Men in the Granite City: Municipal Socialism in Barre, Vermont, 1916–1931," Vermont Historical Society, Winter/Spring 2015, https://vermonthistory.org/journal/83/VHS8301SolidMen.pdf.

38. Jack Ross, "The Socialist Party of America," University of Nebraska Press, April 15, 2015, p. xcviii.

39. "Arkansas Socialist Mayor: First One Ever Chosen in the State Is Elected at Hartford," *New York Times*, April 4, 1912, https://www.nytimes.com/1912/04/04/archives/arkansas-socialist-mayor-first-one-ever-chosen-in-the-state-is.html.

40. Jack Ross, "The Socialist Party of America," University of Nebraska Press, April 15, 2015, , p. xcviii.

41. Ibid.

42. Ethylwyn Mills, "Legislative Program of the Socialist Party," published at the Socialist Party, National Office, Chicago, 1914, copy via Florida Atlantic University Library, http://fau.digital.flvc.org/islandora/object/fau%3A5198/datastream/OBJ/view, pp. 5-6.

43. Ibid.

44. Ibid.

45. Robert E. Weir, "Solid Men in the Granite City: Municipal Socialism in Barre, Vermont, 1916–1931," Vermont Historical Society, Winter/Spring 2015, https://vermonthistory.org/journal/83/VHS8301SolidMen.pdf, p. 45.

46. Ethylwyn Mills, "Legislative Program of the Socialist Party," published at the Socialist Party, National Office, Chicago, 1914, copy via Florida Atlantic University Library, http://fau.digital.flvc.org/islandora/object/fau%3A5198/datastream/OBJ/view, pp. 22-39.

47. Ethylwyn Mills, "Legislative Program of the Socialist Party," published at the Socialist Party, National Office, Chicago, 1914, copy via Florida Atlantic University Library, http://fau.digital.flvc.org/islandora/object/fau%3A5198/datastream/OBJ/view, pp. 39-40.

48. John Nichols, "When Socialists Was Tried in America—and Was a Smashing Success," *The Nation*, April 2, 2019, https://www.thenation.com/article/archive/socialism-milwaukee-democrats-2020/.

49. NCC Staff, "FDR's Third-Term Election and the 22nd Amendment," National Constitution Center blog, November 5, 2019, https://

constitutioncenter.org/interactive-constitution/blog/fdrs-third-term
-decision-and-the-22nd-amendment.

50. Federal Judicial Center, "FDR's 'Court-Packing' Plan," Federal Judicial
    Center history page, https://www.fjc.gov/history/timeline/fdrs-court
    -packing-plan.

51. Ethylwyn Mills, "Legislative Program of the Socialist Party," published
    at the Socialist Party, National Office, Chicago, 1914, copy via Florida
    Atlantic University Library, http://fau.digital.flvc.org/islandora/object/
    fau%3A5198/datastream/OBJ/view.

CHAPTER 11

1. Graham Vyse, "Democratic Socialists Rack up Wins in States," Governing,
   November 9, 2018, https://www.governing.com/topics/politics/gov
   -ocasio-cortez-tlaib-Democratic-Socialists-state-level.html.

2. Daniel Berti, "Marine Vet, Lyft Driver, Socialist: Del Lee Carter Confounds
   His Critics," Prince William Times, January 8, 2020, https://www
   .princewilliamtimes.com/news/marine-vet-lyft-driver-socialist-del-lee
   -carter-confounds-his/article_4ecb5880-323a-11ea-8eb5-5ba353e2dcb3.html.

3. Admin K, "Press Release: Southern Maine DSA Endorses Mike Sylvester
   for Maine State Representative, District 39," Southern Maine DSA, March
   22, 2018, http://southernmainedsa.org/tag/mike-sylvester/.

4. Katherine Mangu-Ward, "The New Socialists Didn't Win," Reason magazine, January 2019 issue, https://reason.com/2018/12/10/the-new
   -socialists-didnt-win/.

5. Ballotpedia, "Kristin Seale: Elections 2018," Ballotpedia, November 2018,
   https://ballotpedia.org/Kristin_Seale,

6. Alexi McCammond, "Democratic Socialist Victories in the 2018
   Midterms," Axios, September 14, 2018, https://www.axios.com/
   democratic-socialist-candidates-who-have-won-in-2018-midterms
   -6bf604a3-ee98-4ab3-9e63-349aec324c43.html.

7. Edited by Richard Winger, "New Registration Data for the United States,"
   Ballot Access News, July 27, 2017, http://ballot-access.org/2017/07/27/
   new-registration-data-for-the-united-states/.

8. Alan Greenblatt, "Socialism Goes Local: DSA Candidates Are Winning in
   Big Cities," Governing, July 24, 2019, https://www.governing.com/topics/
   politics/gov-socialist-cities-elected.html.

9. Ibid.

10. Eric Lutz, "'A Leftward Shift': Communist Party USA Sees Chance as
    Progressives Surge," Guardian, June 23, 2019, https://www.theguardian
    .com/world/2019/jun/23/communist-party-usa-chicago-cpusa
    -convention.

11. Elizabeth McKillen, "The Socialist Party of America, 1900–1929,"
    Department of History, University of Maine, published online at Oxford
    Research Encyclopedias: American History, June 2017, https://oxfordre

.com/americanhistory/view/10.1093/acrefore/9780199329175.001.0001/
acrefore-9780199329175-e-413.

12. Will Witt, "Can You Define Socialism?" PragerU, March 17, 2020, https://
www.prageru.com/video/can-you-define-socialism/?fbclid=IwAR3nwp
NFZv9xlDu011bmBH8lPgSXl5aX3Q_BvJe-Ybd3OVLqK2MCPFlvV7U.

13. Frank Newport, "The Meaning of 'Socialism' to Americans Today,"
Gallup, October 4, 2018, https://news.gallup.com/opinion/polling
-matters/243362/meaning-socialism-americans-today.aspx.

14. Karl Marx, transcribed by Sally Ryan, "Reflections of a Young Man on the
Choice of a Profession," MECW Volume I, written between August 10 and
August 16, 1835, https://marxists.catbull.com/archive/marx/works/1837
-pre/marx/1835-ref.htm.

15. Andrew Prokop, "Read Bernie Sanders' Speech on Democratic Socialism
in the United States," Vox, November 19, 2015, https://www.vox.com/
2015/11/19/9762028/bernie-sanders-democratic-socialism.

16. Bridget Read, "28-Year-Old Alexandria Ocasio-Cortez Might Just Be the
Future of the Democratic Party," *Vogue*, June 25, 2018, https://www.vogue
.com/article/alexandria-ocasio-cortez-interview-primary-election.

17. Cathy Lynn Grossman, "Christ, Marx and Che: Fidel Castro Offers Pope
His Religious Views," *Washington Post*, September 21, 2015, https://
www.washingtonpost.com/national/religion/christ-marx-and-che-fidel
-castro-offers-pope-his-religious-views/2015/09/21/a916aad6-6095-11e5
-8475-781cc9851652_story.html.

18. Noam Chomsky, "Notes on Anarchism," excerpted from "For Reasons of
State," 1973, https://chomsky.info/state01/.

19. Denise Quan, "U.S. Racism 'Everywhere,' says Dave Matthews," CNN
Entertainment, September 21, 2009, https://www.cnn.com/2009/
SHOWBIZ/Music/09/21/qa.dave.matthews/index.html?iref=mpstoryview.

20. Kim Jong II, "On Preserving the Juche Character and National Character
of the Revolution and Construction," KoreaDPR.com, June 19, 1997,
http://korea-dpr.com/lib/111.pdf.

21. DealBook, "DealBook's Interview with Michael Moore," *New York
Times*, September 23, 2009, https://dealbook.nytimes.com/2009/09/23/
dealbooks-interview-with-michael-moore/.

22. Stephen Sackur, "Hugo Chavez Grants Rare Interview to Western Media,"
Guardian, June 13, 2010, https://www.theguardian.com/world/2010/jun/
13/hugo-chavez-bbc-hardtalk-interview.

23. Pablo Gilabert and Martin O'Neill, "'Socialism,'" *The Stanford Encyclopedia of
Philosophy*, Fall 2019 Edition, edited by Edward N. Zalta, published online July
15, 2019, https://plato.stanford.edu/archives/fall2019/entries/socialism.

24. Nancy Pelosi, "Women's Economic Agenda," Congresswoman Nancy
Pelosi, California's 12th District, Home/Issues webpage, undated, https://
pelosi.house.gov/issues/womens-economic-agenda.

25. Chuck Schumer, "Schumer Announces, After His Push, Just-Unveiled Tax
Package Would Make College Tuition Tax Credit Permanent," Charles E.
Schumer, US Senator for New York, congressional webpage, December 16,

2015, https://www.schumer.senate.gov/newsroom/press-releases/_schumer-announces-after-his-push-just-unveiled-tax-package-would-make-college-tuition-tax-credit-permanent-schumer-authored-tax-credit-provides-much-needed-relief-to-middle-class-families-now-paying-sky-high-college-tuition-costs.

26. Jacob Passy, "Elizabeth Warren Wants to Force Companies to Give Employees Predictable Schedules," Market Watch, December 4, 2019, https://www.marketwatch.com/story/elizabeth-warren-wants-to-force-companies-to-give-employees-predictable-schedules-2019-12-03.

27. Susan Jones, "'Spread the Wealth Around' Comment Comes Back to Haunt Barack Obama," CNS News, October 15, 2008, https://www.cnsnews.com/news/article/spread-wealth-around-comment-comes-back-haunt-obama.

28. Barack Obama, "Obama to Wall St.: 'I Do Think at Some Point You've Made Enough Money,'" YouTube, April 28, 2010, https://www.youtube.com/watch?time_continue=24&v=X0-YJ1zCJAU&feature=emb_logo.

29. George W. Bush, "President Bush Signs American Dream Downpayment Act of 2003: Remarks by the President at Signing," The White House, Office of the Press Secretary, December 16, 2003, https://georgewbush-whitehouse.archives.gov/news/releases/2003/12/20031216-9.html.

30. Associated Press, "President Bush Signs Massive Housing Bill," NBCNews.com, July 30, 2008, http://www.nbcnews.com/id/25928299/ns/business-real_estate/t/president-bush-signs-massive-housing-bill/#.XnZox-pKiM8.

31. Adam Harris, "The College-Affordability Crisis Is Uniting the 2020 Democratic Candidates," *Atlantic*, February 26, 2019, https://www.theatlantic.com/education/archive/2019/02/2020-democrats-free-college/583585/.

32. Trevor Hunnicutt and Sharon Bernstein, "Democrat Biden Tacks Left, Backs Warren Bankruptcy Plan with Student Loan Relief," Reuters, March 14, 2020, https://www.reuters.com/article/us-usa-election-bankruptcy/democrat-biden-tacks-left-backs-warren-bankruptcy-plan-with-student-loan-relief-idUSKBN21115J.

33. Vladimir Lenin, "Where to Begin: 1901," Seventeen Moments in Soviet History, An Online Archive of Primary Sources, from Origins of the Press, 1917, http://soviethistory.msu.edu/1917-2/organs-of-the-press/organs-of-the-press-texts/where-to-begin/.

34. Rebecca Flores, "Socialist Newspapers and Periodicals 1900–1920," University of Washington, Mapping American Social Movements Project, https://depts.washington.edu/moves/SP_map-newspapers.shtml.

35. Margaret H. Blanchard, "History of the Mass Media in the United States: An Encyclopedia," Routledge, December 19, 2013, posted https://books.google.com/books?id=vupkAgAAQBAJ&dq=the+advocate+new+york+socialist+newspaper&source=gbs_navlinks_s, pp. 307–308.

36. Ibid.

37. Richard Samuel West, "Radical Magazines of the Twentieth Century Series: The Masses Index, 1911–1917," by Theodore F. Watts, foreword by Richard Samuel West, Periodyssy Press, copyright 2000, http://dlib.nyu.edu/themasses/the_masses_index.pdf.

38. State Historical Society of North Dakota, "North Dakota Newspapers on Microfilm: Iconoclast," May 24, 1912– July 21, 1916, https://statemuseum.nd.gov/database/newspapers/index.php?content=newspapers-sort-details&mf_id=1392&rec_id=20821.

39. Steven Boyd and David Smith, "Thomas Hickey, the Rebel, and Civil Liberties in Wartime Texas," East Texas Historical Journal, Volume 5, Issue 1, Article 12, March 2007, https://scholarworks.sfasu.edu/cgi/viewcontent.cgi?article=2500&context=ethj, pp. 44–45.

40. Michael Cooney, "George Lunn and the Socialists of Schenectady," Love and Rage, A News and Views Collective, October 7, 2016, https://loveandragemedia.org/2016/10/07/george-lunn-and-the-socialists-of-schenectady/.

41. Library of Congress, "The American Socialist (Chicago [Ill.]) 1914–1917," https://www.loc.gov/item/sn84046263/.

42. Library of Congress, "About Miami Valley Socialist. [volume] (Dayton, Ohio) 1912–1929," National Endowment for the Humanities, https://chroniclingamerica.loc.gov/lccn/sn88077248/.

43. The Political Graveyard, "Lawyer Politicians in Ohio, S," http://politicalgraveyard.com/geo/OH/lawyer.S.html.

44. Joseph W. Sharts, "Left Wingers Capture the Ohio Socialist Convention: Resolve to Rule or Wreck National Party – 'Communist Party' to Be Formed," Miami Valley Socialist, July 4, 1919, originally unsigned, later attributed to Joseph W. Sharts, posted by MarxistHistory.org, http://www.marxisthistory.org/history/usa/parties/spusa/1919/0704-sharts-lwcapturesoh.pdf.

45. Marty Goodman, "The Liberator," Marxists.org, page last updated December 20, 2014, https://www.marxists.org/history/usa/culture/pubs/liberator/.

46. Jack Schafer and Tucker Doherty, "The Media Bubble Is Worse Than You Think," Politico Magazine, May/June 2017, https://www.politico.com/magazine/story/2017/04/25/media-bubble-real-journalism-jobs-east-coast-215048.

47. Lars Willnat and David Weaker, "The American Journalist in the Digital Age: How Journalists and the Public Think About Journalism in the United States," Indiana University's School of Journalism, October 26, 2017, https://www.researchgate.net/publication/320660897_The_American_Journalist_in_the_Digital_Age_How_journalists_and_the_public_think_about_journalism_in_the_United_States.

48. Mollie Hemingway, "Another Survey Confirms Journalists Are Overwhelmingly Liberal," The Federalist, May 7, 2014, https://thefederalist.com/2014/05/07/another-survey-confirms-journalists-are-overwhelmingly-liberal/.

49. Hadas Gold, "Survey: 7 Percent of Reporters Identify as Republican," Politico, May 6, 2014, https://www.politico.com/blogs/media/2014/05/survey-7-percent-of-reporters-identify-as-republican-188053.

50. Ibid.

51. Michael Fitzgerald, "News Outlets Show Significant Bias in Favor of Same-Sex Marriage," *Pacific Standard*, June 17, 2013, updated June 14, 2017, https://psmag.com/social-justice/news-outlets-show-significant -bias-in-favor-of-same-sex-marriage-60384.

52. Jeryl Bier, "Media Bias at the Border," *Washington Examiner*, July 5, 2019, https://www.washingtonexaminer.com/opinion/media-bias-at-the -border.

53. Ibid.

54. Miles Burton and Lee Harris, "Left-Wing Journalists Discuss Socialism's Future, Goals and Rising Popularity," The Chicago Maroon, March 5, 2019, https://www.chicagomaroon.com/article/2019/3/6/osita-nwanevu -socialism-micah-uetricht/.

55. DSA, "Socialists in the U.S. Media," Democratic Socialists of America, posted clip of C-SPAN "Washington Journal" interview with Maria Svart, October 23, 2015, https://www.dsausa.org/democratic-left/ socialists_in_the_u_s_media/.

56. Ibid.

CHAPTER 12

1. Len Melisurgo and Jessica Remo, "Coronavirus Update: N.J. Curfew, Closure of Schools, Gyms, Bars, Restaurants, Casinos and More. Everything You Need to Know," NJ.com, March 16, 2020, updated March 17, 2020, https://www.nj.com/coronavirus/2020/03/coronavirus-updates -nj-curfew-closure-of-schools-gyms-bars-restaurants-casinos-and-more -everything-you-need-to-know-03162020.html.

2. Alex Rozier, "Churches Use Technology to Stream Services After Coronavirus Shuts Many Down," WFAA, March 22, 2020, https:// www.wfaa.com/article/news/local/churches-use-technology-to-stream -service-after-coronavirus-shuts-many-down/287-8a0f8368-fb16-46ef -90d1-7fac39f15c05.

3. Tucker Carlson, "Police Fine Churchgoers at Drive-in Service Ahead of Easter," Fox News, April 10, 2020, https://www.youtube.com/watch?v =iKIbK3eIkFQ.

4. Michigan.gov, "The Office of Governor Gretchen Whitmer: Executive Orders," Michigan.gov, https://www.michigan.gov/whitmer/0,9309, 7-387-90499_90705---,00.html.

5. Ralph Jennings, "Not Just Coronavirus: Asians Have Worn Face Masks for Decades," VOA News, March 11, 2020, https://www.voanews.com/ science-health/coronavirus-outbreak/not-just-coronavirus-asians-have -worn-face-masks-decades.

6. Ron Lee, "Not Every New Yorker Is on Board with Cuomo's Mask Mandate," NY1.com, April 17, 2020, https://www.ny1.com/nyc/all-boroughs/news/2020/04/17/cuomo-mask-mandate-new-yorkers-.

7. BBC, "Coronavirus: Trump to Defy 'Voluntary' Advice for Americans to Wear Masks," BBC, April 4, 2020, https://www.bbc.com/news/world-us-canada-52161529.

8. Suzanne Merkelson, "Beijing Reintroduces Mandatory Exercises," *Foreign Policy*, April 11, 2020, https://foreignpolicy.com/2010/08/11/beijing-reintroduces-mandatory-exercises/.

9. Hillary Leung, "Why Wearing a Face Mask Is Encouraged in Asia, but Shunned in the U.S.," *Time* magazine, March 12, 2020, https://time.com/5799964/coronavirus-face-mask-asia-us/.

10. Nancy Messonnier, "Transcript for CDC Media Telebriefing: Update on 2019 Novel Coronavirus (2019-nCoV)," Centers for Disease Control and Prevention, January 31, 2020, https://www.cdc.gov/media/releases/2020/t0131-2019-novel-coronavirus.html.

11. U.S. Surgeon General, "Twitter: Seriously People—STOP BUYING MASKS!" Twitter, Feb. 29, 2020, https://twitter.com/Surgeon_General/status/1233725785283932160.

12. Quentin Fottrell, "Trump Administration and Cuomo Finally Agree on One Thing: Americans Should Wear Face Masks—a Timeline of Conflicting Messages and Policy U-Turns," MarketWatch, April 18, 2020, https://www.marketwatch.com/story/cuomo-orders-new-yorkers-to-wear-face-masks-in-public-settings-but-will-they-really-protect-you-from-coronavirus-2020-04-15.

13. Steve Holland and Alexandra Alper, "Trump Advises Voluntary Mask Use Against Coronavirus But Won't Wear One Himself," Reuters, April 3, 2020, https://www.reuters.com/article/us-usa-health-coronavirus-masks/trump-advises-voluntary-mask-use-against-coronavirus-but-wont-wear-one-himself-idUSKBN21L39K.

14. Surgeon General, "How to Make Your Own Face Covering," CDC via YouTube, April 3, 2020, https://www.youtube.com/watch?v=tPx1yqvJgf4.

15. New York Post, "Mask Hole: Virus-Positive Stephanopoulos Steps out With No Covering on His Face," Cover photo: Bigger/Kuntz, *New York Post*, April 21, 2020, via *The East Hampton Star*, https://www.easthamptonstar.com/grind/2020421/after-ny-post-cover-george-stephanopoulos-clears-air.

16. Saul Alinsky, *Rules for Radicals: A Practical Primer for Realistic Radicals*, Random House, copyright 1971, via Archive.org, https://archive.org/stream/RulesForRadicals/RulesForRadicals_djvu.txt.

17. Max Fisher, "Gulag of the Mind: Why North Koreans Cry for Kim Jong Il," *The Atlantic*, December 22, 20011, https://www.theatlantic.com/international/archive/2011/12/gulag-of-the-mind-why-north-koreans-cry-for-kim-jong-il/250419/.

18.   National Center for Constitutional Studies, "Only a Virtuous People Are Capable of Freedom," NCCS, https://nccs.net/blogs/articles/only-a -virtuous-people-are-capable-of-freedom.

19.   Ian Schwartz, "Dr. Birx: Coronavirus Data Doesn't Match The Doomsday Media Predictions," RealClearPolitics.com, March 26, 2020, https:// www.realclearpolitics.com/video/2020/03/26/dr_birx_coronavirus_data _doesnt_match_the_doomsday_media_predictions_or_analysis.html.

20.   John Commins, "Surgeon General Urges Providers to 'Consider Stopping Elective Surgeries.' Hospitals Push Back," Health Leaders Media, March 16, 2020, https://www.healthleadersmedia.com/clinical-care/surgeon -general-urges-providers-consider-stopping-elective-surgeries -hospitals-push.

21.   Centers for Medicare & Medicaid Services, "Non-Emergent, Elective Medical Services and Treatment Recommendations," CMS.gov, April 7, 2020, https://www.cms.gov/files/document/cms-non-emergent -elective-medical-recommendations.pdf.

22.   Ambulatory Surgery Center Association, "State Guidance on Elective Surgeries," ASCA, Updated April 20, 2020, https://www.ascassociation.org/ asca/resourcecenter/latestnewsresourcecenter/covid-19/covid-19-state.

23.   Susannah Luthi and Rachel Roubein, "Congress Gives Hospitals $100 Billion They Demanded in Coronavirus Package," Politico, March 25, 2020, https://www.politico.com/news/2020/03/25/congress-hospitals -coronavirus-funding-148152.

24.   Nathaniel Weixel, "Hospitals Fear Being Shortchanged in Coronavirus Funding," The Hill, April 17, 2020, https://thehill.com/policy/ healthcare/493388-hospitals-fear-being-shortchanged-in-covid-funding.

25.   Charles Creitz, "Minnesota Doctor Blasts 'Ridiculous' CDC Coronavirus Death Count Guidelines," Fox News, April 9, 2020, https://www.foxnews .com/media/physician-blasts-cdc-coronavirus-death-count-guidelines.

26.   Stephen Montemayor, "As Minnesota Senator Casts Doubt on COVID-19 Death Tolls, Conspiracy Theorists Pounced Online," *Star Tribune*, April 20, 2020, https://www.startribune.com/as-minnesota-senator-cast-doubt-on -covid-19-death-tolls-conspiracy-theorists-pounced-online/569785662/.

27.   "The Idea of Restraining the Legislative Authority in Regard to the Common Defense Considered for the Independent Journal: Hamilton," *Federalist Papers*, No. 26, Yale Law School, Lillian Goldman Law Library, "The Avalon Project: Documents in Law, History and Diplomacy," https://avalon.law.yale.edu/18th_century/fed26.asp.

28.   Philip Vander Elst, *The Christian Roots of Freedom and Tolerance*, BeThinking.org, undated, https://www.bethinking.org/worldviews/ christian-roots-freedom-tolerance.

29.   Saul Alinsky, *Rules for Radicals: A Practical Primer for Realistic Radicals*, Random House, 1971, via Archive.org, https://archive.org/stream/ RulesForRadicals/RulesForRadicals_djvu.txt.

30.   2 Timothy 1:7, New King James Version, https://www.biblegateway.com/ passage/?search=2+Timothy+1%3A7&version=NKJV.

EPILOGUE

1. Mairead McArdle, "Facebook Removes Coronavirus Protest Pages at Request of States," *National Review*, April 20, 2020, https://www.nationalreview.com/news/facebook-removes-coronavirus-protest-pages-at-request-of-states/.
2. Craig Shirley, "LinkedIn Targets Conservative Journalist with Infantile Censorship," CNS News, June 11, 2020, https://cnsnews.com/commentary/craig-shirley/linkedin-targets-conservative-journalist-infantile-censorship.)
3. Jenni Fink, "List of Demands in Seattle 'Autonomous Zone' Includes Black Doctors for Black Patients, End to Prisons," Newsweek, June 11, 2020, https://www.newsweek.com/list-demands-seattle-autonomous-zone-includes-black-doctors-black-patients-end-prisons-1510323.
4. Matthew 18:20, King James Version, Bible Gateway, https://www.biblegateway.com/passage/?search=Matthew+18%3A20&version=KJV.

Acknowledgments

I've truly enjoyed working with the skilled staff of Humanix Books to turn this book into something readable and sellable, and I have Mary Glenn and Keith Pfeffer to thank for that, as well as Chris Ruddy, the CEO of Newsmax, and all the other publishing company eyes that went into the making of the final edition.

Of course, *Socialists Don't Sleep* never would have been without the wings of my dear friend and colleague, the bestselling author and Shirley McVicker Public Affairs founder Craig Shirley, whom I've come to know as a kind, generous, and uncommonly trustworthy guy in both business and the personal. Thank you, Craig (and thank you, Zorine), for your encouragement and help and advice and friendship.

Kevin McVicker is owed a huge thank you, as well, for all the hard work of selling, promoting, and marketing my book. Many great books no doubt clutter the dustbins and attics and cellars of stores and homes, unsold and unread. Without Kevin in my camp, *Socialists Don't Sleep* would easily have suffered the same fate.

Great thanks to my esteemed colleagues, both named and unnamed, at the *Washington Times* for all the support both through the years and with this book: Christopher Dolan, Charlie Hurt, Ann Wog, Joe Teipe, Larry Beasley, Ian Bishop, Carol Herman, Christine Reed, and Maria Stainer especially—it's been a pleasure and honor to work with you all.

I want to personally thank several who've attached their names to this book, and who continue on a day-to-day basis to fight for the very principles brought forward within its pages—oftentimes, with little to zero recognition; sometimes, in the face of great adversity: Kevin and Sam Sorbo, Michael Savage, Rep. Jody Hice, Cal Thomas, Mike Huckabee, Phil Robertson, and Will Witt. You all are patriots, examples of true Americans, and it's my wish history remembers you kindly.

There are so many who along the way provided support, encouragement, motivation, inspiration, direction, guidance, and godly influence—but none so steadfastly as my second son, Colvin, and I will miss him greatly in his college years; or so sweetly and unknowingly as my second daughter, Chloe, whose kindness is unrivaled, except maybe by angels.

And finally, firstly and lastly, deeply and devotedly—in loving gratitude to my husband, Doug, who is chalking up, as we speak, piles of crowns in heaven. You make it all meaningful and fun, and your edits are still, after all these years, the ones that matter most. I look forward to our many, many dinner dates, to infinity and eternity.

Index

About the Author

Cheryl Chumley is an author, commentary writer, and the online opinion editor for the *Washington Times*, where she also hosts a podcast, "Bold and Blunt," about politics and culture from a Christian, conservative perspective. Her first book, *Police State USA: How Orwell's Nightmare Is Becoming Our Reality*, hit the bookshelves at a time of great societal unrest, when police faced criticisms for their handling of a black Ferguson, Missouri, 18-year-old named Michael Brown, and rioters took to the streets of St. Louis—much in the vein of the Black Lives Matter and Antifa uprisings of 2020, stemming from outrage over the death of George Floyd at the hands of officers. Her second book, *Devil in DC: Winning Back the Country from the Beast in Washington*, was a solution-oriented look at the political and cultural ills of America, as described in *Police State USA*.

Cheryl is a Robert Novak Journalism Fellow, and spent a year researching and writing about National Heritage Areas and the state of private property rights in the country; she's an award-winning journalist with recognition in state contests for her use of the Freedom of Information Act to root out government corruption and track money in politics; and she's a frequent media guest on national television and radio and an experienced public speaker, passionate about topics related to Christianity and conservativism and the Constitution, and how to keep God-given rights intact in America.

Cheryl, with her husband, Doug, is also a certified private investigator and principal of Chumley Investigations LLC in Virginia, and an ambassador for the Just Ask program, a nonprofit with a mission to educate about sex trafficking. Previously, Cheryl was a Court Appointed Special Advocate, or CASA, volunteer, helping judges make the difficult placement decision for abused and neglected children. She served in the active Army as a 63H (tank-track and wheeled vehicle repairer) and as a diesel mechanic in the civilian sector. She lives in Northern Virginia with her husband, Doug, and with two of their four children—Savanna, Keith, Colvin and Chloe—and enjoys running and T25 in her spare time.

More Titles From Humanix Books You May Be Interested In:

Warren Buffett says:
"My friend, Ben Stein, has written a short book that tells you everything you need to know about investing (and in words you can understand). Follow Ben's advice and you will do far better than almost all investors (and I include pension funds, universities and the super-rich) who pay high fees to advisors."

In his entertaining and informative style that has captivated generations, beloved *New York Times* bestselling author, actor, and financial expert Ben Stein sets the record straight about capitalism in the United States — it is not the "rigged system" young people are led to believe.

Dr. Mehmet Oz says:
"*SNAP!* shows that personalities can be changed from what our genes or early childhood would have ordained. Invest the 30 days."

New York Times bestselling author Dr. Gary Small's breakthrough plan to improve your personality for a better life! As you read *SNAP!* you will gain a better understanding of who you are now, how others see you, and which aspects of yourself you'd like to change. You will acquire the tools you need to change your personality in just one month — it won't take years of psychotherapy, self-exploration, or re-hashing every single bad thing that's ever happened to you.

"*SNAP!* shows that personalities can be changed from what our genes or early childhood would have ordained. Invest the 30 days."
—DR. MEHMET OZ

SNAP!
Change Your Personality in 30 Days
Gary Small, MD
Director, UCLA Longevity Center and Gigi Vorgan